ACKNOWLEDGMENTS

CW01501550

I am very thankful to Karl-Ernst Herrmann for the important contribution of his artwork that appears in this volume. I also express my thanks to the library of the Milan conservatory and in particular to Maria Majno Golub, Elizabeth Giuliani (of the National Library of Paris), and Jacques Tchamkerten (of the Geneva conservatory library) for the precious documents that they made available to me. I am also grateful to Maurice Olender, Stéphanie Cudré-Mauroux, Frédéric Wandelère, and Georges Starobinski for the advice they gave me during the final stages in the preparation of these studies. A reading of my sources reveals how important the invitation from Geneva's Grand-Théâtre and its directors Hugues Gall and Christian Schirm was for a part of the work presented here.

Enchantment

EUROPEAN PERSPECTIVES

EUROPEAN PERSPECTIVES

A Series in Social Thought and Cultural Criticism
Lawrence D. Kritzman, Editor

European Perspectives presents outstanding books by leading European thinkers. With both classic and contemporary works, the series aims to shape the major intellectual controversies of our day and to facilitate the tasks of historical understanding.

For a complete list of books in the series, see pages 263–265

Enchantment

THE SEDUCTRESS IN OPERA

JEAN STAROBINSKI

Translated by C. Jon Delogu

Drawings by Karl-Ernst Herrmann

Foreword by Victor Brombert

Columbia University Press

New York

Columbia University Press
Publishers Since 1893
New York   Chichester, West Sussex
Copyright © 2008 Columbia University Press
Originally published as *Les Enchanteresses* by Éditions du Seuil in 2005

Cet ouvrage, publié dans le cadre d'un programme d'aide à la publication bénéficie du soutien financier du Ministère des Affaires étrangères, du Service Culturel de l'Ambassade de France aux États-Unis, ainsi que l'appui de FACE (France American Cultural Exchange). [This work, published as part of a program providing publication assistance, received financial support from the French Ministry of Foreign Affairs, the Cultural Services of the French Embassy in the United States, and FACE (French American Cultural Exchange).]

The chapters "Singing and Seducing" and "Ombra adorata" appear here for the first time; however, the first Stendhal section of "Ombra adorata" was published previously in the *Opera Quarterly* 21, no. 4 (Autumn 2005): 612–630 (translated by Robert S. Huddleston).

Several texts appeared under different titles in *La Grange*, the journal of Geneva's Grand-Théâtre, on the request of Hugues Gall and Christian Schirm. Studies of individual operas appeared in the journal: *Manon* (no. 1 [September/October 1989]); *The Coronation of Poppea* (no. 2 [November/December 1989]); *Ariane and Bluebeard* (no. 3 [December/January 1990]); *Elektra* (no. 4 [March/April 1990]); *Alcina* (no. 5 [May/June 1990]); *I Capuleti e I Montecchi* (no. 7 [November/December 1990]); *Don Giovanni* (no. 9 [March/April 1991]); *Così fan tutte* (no. 14 [March/April 1992]); *The Marriage of Figaro* (no. 20 [May/June 1993]).

The essay on *Don Giovanni* appeared in another form under the title "Quali eccessi" in *Nouvelle revue de psychanalyse*, no. 43 (Spring 1991): 265–275.

An earlier version of "Lights and Powers: *The Magic Flute*" was published in 1978 in an essay collection entitled *Le Pouvoir* [Power] that gathered together the conference papers presented at the twenty-sixth session of the Rencontres internationales de Genève.

An earlier version of "The Promise of Idomeneo" appeared in the program for *Idomeneo* that was staged in Baden-Baden and Salzburg in 2000 by Karl-Ernst and Ursel Herrmann.

All these essays, originally written in French, have been revised by the author and translated by C. Jon Delogu for the present publication.

Columbia University Press wishes to express its appreciation for assistance given by the government of France through the Ministère de la Culture—Centre national du livre, in preparation of this translation.

Library of Congress Cataloging-in-Publication Data
Starobinski, Jean.
[Enchanteresses. English]
Enchantment : the seductress in opera / Jean Starobinski; translated by C. Jon Delogu.
p. cm. — (European perspectives)
Originally published: Les enchanteresses. Paris : Seuil, c 2005.
Includes bibliographical references (p.   ) and index.
ISBN 978-0-231-14090-4 (alk. paper)
1. Women in opera.   2. Seduction in opera.   3. Operas—Characters.
I. Delogu, Christopher Jon.   II. Title.   III. Series.
ML1700.S79613   2008
782.1—dc22   2007041031

Printed in the United States of America
c 10 9 8 7 6 5 4 3 2 1

CONTENTS

Long after some critics currently in vogue have sunk into oblivion, Jean Starobinski's writings—limpid, thought-provoking, imaginative—will continue to be admired. Erudite without a trace of pedantry, original without stridency, always in sympathy with his subject—whether it be Rousseau, Montaigne, Montesquieu, or a great painter or poet—his aim is to elucidate, stimulate, and share his love. Unerringly, he goes to the heart of the matter when it comes to linking the life of forms to that of ideas. In discussing the enchantment of music, Starobinski is himself something of a magician.

Enchantment (the more enigmatic feminine French title *Les Enchanteresses* conjures up spellbinding characters and their interpreters) concerns itself at the core with the mysterious link between words and music. That is what the incantatory aspect of opera is all about. At a time when the opera world may appear to be subject to the tyranny of stage directors it is good to be reminded that, although we do need inventive and even daring staging, we expect our artistically gifted directors not to be self-indulgent but to enter into the complicity that exists between the librettist and the composer, and remain faithful to the spirit of their work.

The specific enchantment of the lyric stage has much to do with a sense of ritual and celebration. Starobinski speaks meaningfully of operas by Richard Wagner, Jules Massenet, Richard Strauss, and Georges Bizet, whose *Carmen* Friedrich Nietzsche so much admired. He is at his best, however, in discussing Mozart's operas, and especially the composer's collaboration with his brilliant librettist Lorenzo Da Ponte. He stresses their theatrical instinct, their ability to communicate the intonations of desire as well as bursts of laughter, while moving swiftly from the lively recitativo to intense lyric and dramatic moments.

In his discussion of *The Marriage of Figaro* Starobinki is unsurpassed. He makes us relive every moment, every resonance. Rarely have the opera's many charms been discussed with more finesse. The extreme attention to details at no point makes us lose touch with the opera's ambience of mystery, its sense of secret and intimacy, as it moves through the events, the surprises, the plots and counterplots of this extraordinary day, this *folle journée*, toward the nocturnal setting of the last act with its aura of love, acceptance, and forgiveness.

Enchantment also evokes some famous opera lovers, among them E. T. A. Hoffmann, Balzac, and above all that most Mozartian of writers, Stendhal, about whom Starobinski as early as the 1950s wrote some memorable pages. It is hardly surprising to find Stendhal in the company of Mozart. The combination of irony and tenderness in his novels, the contrast between staccato effects and lyrical moments, the taste for lucidity, and the indirections of his style all point to affinities with Mozartian moods. Stendhal loved the human voice, especially in the feminine registers, and its effects on our emotions. He admired divas like Giuditta Pasta, whom he did not tire of hearing, and at whose parties in Paris he was often present.

Starobinski's book in fact concludes with a chapter devoted to interpretations of a single aria that Guiditta Pasta sang with particular expressivity. It is the aria "Ombra adorata" composed by the famous castrato singer Girolamo Crescentini (a favorite artist of Napoleon), which the composer-performer inserted into Nicola Zingarelli's opera *Giulietta e Romeo*. Starobinski's pages on "Ombra adorata" give his book the added dimension of literary history. Even Mallarmé appears briefly in remarks on the relation of "nothingness" to the lyrical impulse. Along the way, we are offered deft digressions on aesthetic questions such as the difference between "expression" and "representation."

But it is the magic of performance that remains in the foreground. A sentence of Baudelaire comes to mind. Upon hearing Wagner's music, the poet dreamt of translating his intense pleasure into knowledge— "*transformer ma volupté en connaissance.*" Starobinski's book provides just such a translation.

Victor Brombert

INTRODUCTION

This book examines some figures of seduction as they have appeared over the course of opera's history. It seems appropriate to add a few additional pages of introduction for this English translation. In this work I present the reasons that led me to recall and decipher the persistently enduring seduction plot. Here and in the following chapters my perspective is that of a reader of the poets of the European tradition. I wish to underscore the importance of some classical or archetypal images as well as the admirable and inspiring expressions of the seductress character within great works of Italian poetry. The material is inexhaustible and I have limited myself to evoking certain emblematic examples.

THE GOLDEN AGE

Gold, silver, bronze, iron. For centuries this was the symbolic scheme used to represent the stages of humanity's progression from an initial happiness to the violence and miseries of our own time. In the preamble to his *Metamorphoses* Ovid served as its principal exponent for the medieval and neo-Latin tradition. It was one of the commonplaces that the literate classes could readily cite in their earliest attempts to collaborate with musicians in reviving classical theater. On the subject of the history of humanity an entire tradition that we could call "primitivist" has spoken of man's happiness as something linked to a bygone age, close to the very beginning, but long since lost.

Back then time is still immobile. There is no work because men are surrounded by a maternal nature that both shelters and nourishes with its abundant wealth. They have no notion of property. There are neither battles nor scheming envy. Everything is theirs. The air is temperate. Plants offer both their flowers and fruits. Death does not exist, only easy sleep. There is boundless leisure. But happiness is not the absence of movement. This time without difference or slope, this eternal today, this world that knows no tomorrow because it has no cares has to be filled up somehow. The poets thus imagined frolicsome play, innocent loves, and banquets. To animate such perfectly free moments, there were songs and dances—music rather than work. In truth, since leisure presupposes leaving nature intact, there are hardly any instruments, at most a few reeds—voices suffice. Human voices and animal voices, since everything is in unison within this universe without separation. Men and beasts understand each other. Among themselves men have no secrets, justice reigns, presence is not perturbed by any shadows. Everything communicates and this universal transparency grows until it becomes melody and rhythm. The eternal present moves out and back on itself in sinuous folds of flowing arcs and circles. Since everything is permitted, there will be solitary singers, couples, and groups that hold hands. Capriciously meandering streams repeat the same shapes. At the center of every paradise is a spring, a limpid pool, pure water—a point from which lovely and lively pulsations flow in all directions and whose freshness is never troubled. In this way human rounds and curving rivers invent the innocent simulacrum of a becoming within this vast and vacant time. However, this becoming or progression goes nowhere; it is a light movement, a fluid élan that is the transport of a happiness without excess or end. Rivers may flow to the sea, but the sea is not to be crossed. The steps of the dancers do not wear a path in the grass, since every path implies servitude, supposes a project and goal, a before and after. The golden age is an enclosed space, like every paradise, like all Arcadias, like all the pleasant places of poetic reverie. When this enclosure disappears, there is a fall into Time. In this primary stage everything is regulated by a principle of plenitude, for there is no plenitude that does not have its contour and boundaries. Spatially, the place of happiness is a finite world. But boredom is unknown because infinity reappears in the variety of its pleasures. True, the ground that the dancers' feet beat rhythmically is always the same, but the dance will change a thousand times, like the threads of a multicolored embroidery all woven into the same fabric. True, the ball will only have soft alternations between shadow and light, and the ballroom will always remain the same, illuminated by the same fixed season—eternal spring—but the scenery of delicate and luxurious vegetation includes all the plants of the world except the poisonous ones, and all the world's animals except poisonous snakes.

A space without obstacles where everything is given over to a freedom that is only free to do good. An immobile time that is not measured but that welcomes the most delicious pastimes. An eternal present, but one that contains moments of felicity distinguished only by the interval necessary to perceive their renewal. These instants are reborn without interruption but also without ever sinking into what would risk becoming the lethargic monotony of a single continuous note. Even though the great time of History does not budge, there is room for a thousand new melodies and for the beating of every rhythm from the languid to the most lively. Only the music of war and mourning are unknown. This essential repose is the stable foundation that allows for spirited dancing and singing. Within this null time palpitates a secret, indestructible beating: the pearly beaded time of the flow of sound waves and songs, the time invented by expressions of happiness. Pastimes are necessary to keep the happy eternity from being a long, undifferentiated sleep. The diverting musical *déduit* (I am intentionally borrowing this term from the *Romance of the Rose*) is entirely the best suited to the principle of plenitude while not in the least altering the integrity of the eternal. For the music of the golden age is not, in its substance, of a time that wears or wastes away. Every note is a pure *now*, and if the beginning of the melody becomes past as the latter progresses and comes to completion, the past inflection remains at one with the present, unthreatened by forgetfulness. When it is called upon, the melody is reborn—both new and identical.

But no one has ever heard the music of the golden age, for the golden age is the retrospective consolation of unhappy humanity. Obliged to work, subject to violence and death, this unhappy humanity takes refuge within a space that predates the evils it must suffer, a reign of Cronos where Chronos does not exist. How does one recover a time where all the riches of novelty abound without the infiltration of the least artifice? Of course the artists of our iron age will have to deploy much artifice to awaken such an image. They will build it from the fragments that remain of their dreams and with the energy that results from privation and impatience. They will display their brief instants of happiness and make of them a long Day before time began. The brief rest periods and ephemeral parties interspersed within man's days of pain will take on the outsized dimensions of a long happiness now disappeared. Their convictions will be so deep that men will not see in their festivities the first model of a mythic golden age, but instead its echo, a weakened imitation, a ritualized commemoration. After casting music and dancing back into the most distant past, they will persuade themselves that their own arts are but a reflection, an inheritance, or souvenir. Their days of happiness will strike them as only the fictional restitution of former perfection. The unhappy time halts briefly, and this halt, brought about through the magic of the masquerade, is something we are supposed to experience as the echo of a lost felicity. Music, especially the duration without loss that it displays, is something we are supposed to hear as a recollection of a fabulous origin. Each instance of enjoyment, each solemn feast will be a simulated return of the presumed insouciance of the earliest times.

Saturnalias reinvented the great equality and the entire freedom of the reign of Saturn. During princely festivals courtesans disguised themselves as shepherds and "savages," and the height of refinement consisted in rediscovering the irresponsible games that preceded civilization. It was a ritualized and intermittent regression whose aim may have been to cast off melancholy and give the illusion of annulling relations of forceful domination. Here, therefore, music and dance *create* the origin for which they take themselves to be the echo. They establish an innocent time, a momentary suspension of the fall into guiltiness. Within a cruel present, how could one not try to reconstitute an image of eternity and an absence of time at the center of which music would be the animating spirit of a happiness that nothing could unseat? The ephemeral artifices of the festival seek to reconstitute an *aura* that is precisely the great *vacancy* of the origin, a space open indefinitely to the celebration of the voice and body.

In this way music acts as the agent of a passage. It leads us out of a time of guiltiness, out of a becoming where everything is soon corrupted and dies, and toward a paradise that excludes all ideas of corruption and death. It establishes a unique space, that of the living. This is how Orpheus, understood by the animals, revives the plenitude of the golden age; this is how he crosses the threshold of the realm of the dead. For a moment, the moment of a performance, he is allowed to witness the abolishment of the mortal consequences of time. But the music that reconquers a parcel of eternity also sees its own duration measured, its moments counted. The musician and the poet have relived the atemporal plenitude of the origin only to relive, in turn, a fall into time and death. They must take hold of a temporal space and build their fable there. But they must also know how to close it after its completion and mark harmoniously a final *cadence*, a lifting of masks, a salute to the public—a fall back into the present where the spectators applaud the enchantment that was, the exploit of art.

SIRENS AND THE DANGER OF PERFECT SINGING

As Calypso's captive, Ulysses prefers the mortal condition, a time of aging and death that is also the time of heroic action and glory. Calypso offers him immortality, a halt to the passing of time within delicious pleasures, and the end of all dangers. Ulysses spends his days tearfully watching the sea and missing the smoke of his own hearth. Work, risk, and a far-off death seem preferable to him. He wants to see again his wife now grown old and his son who will outlive him. He consents, as a man, to the law of time that for him takes the form of a voyage filled with pitfalls. He wants to live this time of guilt, this unhappy time, with courage and experience it by exerting his ingenuity and tasting time's force and his own. He needs something to work at, a succession of adventures with, at the end, that uncertain return and yet more voyages. This is why the garden paradise that surrounds Calypso's cave could not captivate him, nor could the nymph's beautiful body, nor the songs that she sings so beautifully as she weaves with her golden shuttle (*The Odyssey*, Book V). He wrests himself from this promised eternity and from the suave environment that is unable to make him forget his mortal homeland. He refuses the bewitchment that would keep him out of time and stop his destiny half way within a solace hardly befitting a hero. An eighteenth-century philosophical tale by Samuel Johnson (*Rasselas*, 1759) tells us in similar terms about a prince who becomes "disquiet" in a "happy valley" where the plenitude of a paradisiacal life leaves him unsatisfied. He hungers for something else, some good thing he ignores, for unknown satisfactions different from the sensual pleasures that he can partake of at will. This is why he flees the seductions of music. "He often sat before tables covered with luxury, and forgot to taste the dainties placed before him: he rose abruptly in the midst of the song, and hastily retired beyond the sound of musick." (Chapter 2)

But why must Ulysses have himself strapped to the mast of his ship to resist the Sirens' song? What is so dangerous about this song for one who has managed to resist the temptation of immortality? One must remember that the Sirens are companions of Persephone, the goddess of the dead, who have remained on earth.

> And when on land you long had search'd in vain,
> You wish'd for wings to cross the pathless main;
> That Earth and Sea might witness to your care:
> The Gods were easy, and return'd your pray'r;
> With golden wing o'er foamy waves you fled,
> And to the sun your plumy glories spread.
> But, lest the soft enchantment of your songs,
> And the sweet musick of your flat'ring tongues
> Shou'd quite be lost (as courteous fates ordain),
> Your voice and virgin beauty still remain.
>   Ovid's *Metamorphoses*, Book V, 533–571, translated by
>   Sir Samuel Garth, John Dryden et al, 1717

The mythologists add that the oracle had forewarned the Sirens that they would live as long as they could stop every passer-by but that as soon as one passed without stopping, they would perish. "These enchantresses didn't fail to stop with their harmony all those who arrived near them and imprudently listened to their songs." They enchanted them so completely that they no longer thought of their homelands and, as though bewitched, they forgot to eat and drink and died from starvation. "The area where they stayed is bordered by a shore whitened with bones and covered with human debris and rotting flesh." As companions of Persephone, the Sirens sing on the threshold of death. They sing to save their conditional immortality and the price is the death of all those who listen. And what do they say to Ulysses?

"Come here," they sang, "renowned Ulysses, honor to the Achaean name, and listen to our two voices. No one ever sailed past us
without staying to hear the enchanting sweetness of our song—
and he who listens will go on his way not only charmed, but wiser,
for we know all the ills that the gods laid upon the Argives and
Trojans before Troy, and can tell you everything that is going to
happen over the whole world."

Homer's The Odyssey, Book XII, translated by Samuel Butler

This song is nothing but the promise of an unending song, the offer
of a concert, but it already constitutes an extreme peril. Were he not
lashed down, Ulysses would yield:

They sang these words most musically, and as I longed to hear
them further I made by frowning to my men that they should
set me free; but they quickened their stroke, and Eurylochus and
Perimedes bound me with still stronger bonds till we had got out
of hearing of the Sirens' voices.

These clever creatures knew what would attract the hero. Not the
weaver's song that Calypso sang, not the innocent music from before
time began, the rounds of an age prior to the combats of the iron age;
but, on the contrary, the music that follows the action, that celebrates
the battle and the hard-fought work accomplished on the battlefield,
the melodious tale that eternalizes—like that of the epic minstrel—the
memory of those who confronted the pains of time. If he had listened
to the Sirens—a triply perfect epic minstrel—Ulysses would have encountered the image of his own past transfigured by music. He would
have believed his life to be forever saved from oblivion, and he would
have forgotten to live—like all the other travelers whose white bones
litter the Sirens' shore. He would have lost "the day of return" on account of having encountered himself in the melodious perfection of
the tale of his exploits on the Trojan plains.

Here, then, is a fascinating music that develops another relationship
to time than the music of the golden age, a music linked to narrat-
ing speech that can only deploy itself within a succession of temporal
events, a music that elevates to the perfection of song bloody entangle-
ments and heroic patience and suffering, a music profoundly linked to

becoming, to all that the nourishing earth sees pass away. This music lives in time and embraces its joys and torments. In many ways it constitutes the exact opposite of the imaginary music of the golden age. The latter unfolded a simulacrum of time against a background of an eventless eternity and against the threat of monotony. It was a happy *fluidification*. The melodious epos, on the other hand, tears out of time the events that it celebrates and eternalizes; it develops its divine words against the ground of a tumultuous and unstable becoming, and is in fact its glorious *mise en forme*.

Is it not striking that during his homeward journey Ulysses encounters almost everywhere his past already memorialized? The Sirens know of the Trojan exploit. The minstrel Demodocos sings for the Phoenicians of the quarrel of Achilles and Ulysses unaware that Ulysses himself hears his song. It is as though the immortal song were born almost immediately after the mortal exploit—as if the mortal exploit were accomplished only to be used the next moment as a pretext for the song that will transmit it to future generations. In opposition to the immemorial eternity of the golden age stands the eternity to come of human memory. In opposition to the immortality without glory of the time before time stands the glorious immortality of the hero who has gone through the test of time and whose existence is saved by song. For having accepted death, he will live eternally in and through speech. Ulysses cries while listening to the minstrel Demodocos. His tears come from the realization that he is both already famous and still so far from his goal. His immortality acquired during the Trojan exploit is something he can enjoy as though he were seeing himself forever radiant; but this enjoyment is marred by bitterness, since he is now stripped and solitary, just a man still fighting to recover the simple happiness of home. The pleading castaway and the hero in the minstrel's song are one and the same. The glorious song celebrates a *past* action, and the surviving hero, if he is to avoid demeaning himself, must take the place of the minstrel and become the narrator of his own troubles and interminable navigations. Ulysses will thus recount his own miseries and elevate them to the plane of musical immortality, just as the minstrel did for his military victories. The epic song will extend right up to the narration of the return. At the point where it is interrupted, the mortal condition and time the destroyer reassert their dominance. Whether or not it ends in happiness, the end of every epic poem announces to us the end of the age of heroes. This is why many peoples have imagined that the age of heroes, like the golden age, succumbed to the law of fate and subsists forever in our past as sheer memory, a swallowed-up world that was able to find in temporal action and vehement passion a grander life that has been communicated to us through the medium of song.

SONG OF ETERNITY, SONG OF VANITY

During the Middle Ages it was sometimes believed that music could awaken in us a memory of eternity by reviving the obscured image of paradise and the original light. The closer music comes to the perfection it is capable of, the better it carries in itself the trace of the plenitude of the origin, of that "harmony of the spheres" that translates the plenitude and a perfect accord. All music would thus have as a pole of attraction the atemporal eternity, the immobile divine point, the unique note around which adoring circles turn. Moreover, if it is moved by love, the music joins these adoring circles in a time where the borders between present, past, and future tend to melt and all blends into a *nunc stans*, the unchanging Now. According to a very speculative physical theology, since perishable matter is only materialized sound, a fall and imprisonment of music in a shadowy inertia, one must welcome the most humble melody as the beginning of a deliverance of spirit, rendered up to its immaterial sonorous condition. Therefore to sing is a deliverance, an outpouring of the soul beyond mortal time and the universe of corruptible things.

However, there exist songs of guilt—those that I earlier placed in the category of masquerade. The medieval moralists who deplore sensual pleasures and worldly attractions direct their invective against three perfidious "sirens": wine, love, and music. If sacred music reaches heights of atemporal ecstasy, profane music blends with the course of earthly time and comes to embrace a pernicious attraction. It is only a specious suspension wherein the individual, forgetful of his sinful nature, sinks deeper into fault. He allows himself to be spellbound by the earthly music to the point where he turns away from his salvation. Music is therefore the temptress, the secret voice of the demon, the carnal concupiscence taken to its most dangerous level, for it is clothed with the prestige of spirit. Whether it sings of the glory of heroes, of the tenderness of women, or simply of the pleasure of eating and drinking, it chains the soul to its mortal prison and abandons it impenitently to its last hour. Here it is profoundly complicit with terrestrial time, having only displayed the mirage of a false liberty, and having dangerously imitated the joys of paradise so as to retain its victims within the enchanted gardens of springtime. The *Romance of the Rose* establishes a singular homology of relations between the terrestrial garden of Déduit, the Celestial Paradise, and the prairies of the pagan Golden Age. All three resemble each other. Jean de Meung does not care about keeping his hero away from the pleasures of the garden of Déduit, and it is there that he picks the most carnal of roses. But this indulgence toward terrestrial substitutes for paradisiacal happiness does not come without a warning in the form of the superior rights of celestial love. The dances on the earthly prairie are only the imperfect anticipation of celestial choirs. Thus, when the contrast between the temporal and the eternal asserts itself further, we can expect to find music among the most seductive attributes of sin. Among the false powers and divertissements that turn man "from his maker and his end," Pascal ranks music at the very top. "For what does the world think of? Never of that, but of dancing, playing the lute, singing, composing verses, running at the ring, etc." (*Pensées*, 1670, Section II, 146, "The Misery of Man Without God").

In the gardens of the evil enchantress Armide it is no accident that the most dangerous attractions are the nymph musicians of the fountain of laughter who seduce with the beauty of their naked bodies, the gracefulness of their swimming, and the words of their song that falsely proclaims the stoppage of time and the return of the golden age.

> This is the place wherein you may assuage
> Your sorrows past, here is that joy and bliss
> That flourished in the antique golden age,
> Here needs no law, here none doth aught amiss:
> Put off those arms and fear not Mars his rage,
> Your sword, your shield, your helmet needless is;
> Then consecrate them here to endless rest,
> You shall love's champions be, and soldiers blest."
> Torquato Tasso's *Jerusalem Delivered*, 1581, Book XV,
> verse 63, translated by Edward Fairfax, 1600

When one's first duty is to fight in order to conquer Jerusalem, the promised return to the golden age is a demonic trap. The demon's other musical trap, expressed through the plumage of a multicolored bird, is delight in the passing moment, the sharp point of the fleeting day, the ultimate lure:

> With party-colored plumes' and purple bill,
> A wondrous bird among the rest there flew,
> That in plain speech sung love-lays loud and shrill,
> Her leden was like human language true;
> So much she talked, and with such wit and skill,
> That strange it seemed how much good she knew,
> Her feathered fellows all stood hush to hear,
> Dumb was the wind, the waters silent were.
>
> Book XVI, verse 13

The epicurean bird sharpens her song with the evocation of devouring time that grants us only the ephemeral royalty of youth. She recalls the vanity of all living things, but with a view to calling for enjoyment of the melodious minute of the rose's full flowering. And it is true that her song in the magical wood is like a musical flower that blossoms and is soon taken away from us. If we were to listen to it, we would plunge into the most sensual and the most fragile of durations—the vibration of the perishable minute.

To express the attraction of the illusory figures that Armide's magic exerts over Renaud's boat on the Oronte, the poet makes a comparison with the figures that appear on a theater stage. A wave rises up on the river; a feminine figure appears to take shape. The seductive apparition is first compared to an actress on the stage of a modern theater and then to a siren of days gone by—the present of an emerging art form and the past of myth fuse:

> So in the twilight does sometimes appear
> A nymph, a goddess, or a fairy queen,
> And though no siren but a sprite this were
> Yet by her beauty seemed it she had been
> One of those sisters false which haunted near
> The Tyrrhene shores and kept those waters sheen,

Like theirs her face, her voice was, and her sound,
And thus she sung, and pleased both skies and ground.
                                        Book XIV, verse 61

Here Torquato Tasso makes use of the figures of desire that accompanied the birth of opera. This is worth remembering at the beginning of a book that will be concerned often with the descendants of his Armide and the sirens that enchant other gardens and shores where other captivities and deliverances will occur.

CHAPTER I

Singing and Seducing

Here you are again, enchantress.
—Gérard de Nerval, *Pandora*

The voice of the serpent insinuates, "Ye shall be as gods" (Genesis 3:5).[1] The "strange woman" invites, "Come, let us take our fill of love until the morning" (Proverbs 7:18). The Sirens sing, "Come here, renowned Ulysses, honor to the Achaean name, and listen to our two voices. No one ever sailed past us without staying to hear the enchanting sweetness of our song, and he who listens will go on his way not only charmed, but wiser, for we . . . can tell you everything that is going to happen over the whole world" (*The Odyssey*, book 12). The Belle Dame sans Merci leads the knight to her "elfin grot" after singing him a "faery's song." She lulls him to sleep, and he dreams his "last dream . . . On the cold hill side" (Keats). In the moral emblems of the past, seduction marked the point where paths diverged. It promises knowledge and pleasure but leads to death.

Seducers and seductresses are on the lookout from the very beginning. The Bible wisely places the promises of the "more subtil" serpent at the start of time. These figures created by mythic imagination may date from the earliest consciousness of lying. They seem to have been invented as soon as the distinction became established between obedience and disobedience, between the good path and erring, and the alternative between living and perishing.

What is the force that attracts one away from the straight and narrow? Why does one go in the wrong direction? As a first response we may note that in the most ancient tales and legends both a guilty choice and a guilty party who offers that choice are incriminated. The bad path and the deviation are proposed by the Enemy. The origin of bad fortune is thus projected onto an outside: the error is to consent to seduction. To seduce, etymologically, means to lead aside. There emerges a fatal creature of shattering beauty, speaking in a silky voice and offering unknown pleasures. You should not have listened. It would have been better to avoid its glance. One step off the sure road leads to another, and suddenly you find yourself wandering in a state of perdition. In English one may also speak of "leading astray," "diverting," and "disorienting"—in French "fourvoyer," "dérouter," and "désorienter." Indeed there are many such words in many different languages. In the end a kind of dizziness sets in. Kierkegaard defined sin as the vertigo of freedom.

The seductive peril takes on various guises among different people and places. When the hero travels over roads, through forests, or by sea, the enchantress watches for him by the side of the road, reigns over the island where he comes ashore, or haunts the inn where he puts up for the night. The traveler intercepted by Circe needs magical protection to escape from her wickedness and retain his human shape. It would be necessary here to examine closely the spatial structures in the fictional world of The Odyssey. One can see a sort of inverse symmetry establishing itself there. In the maritime world, the king returning from war is set upon by monsters and enchantresses; on land within the palace, his wife who is guarding the symbolic seat of power turns a deaf ear to the insolent suitors.

In more recent myths that for long were declared modern, one finds vulnerable heroines seduced by wicked visitors. The innocent girl who listens to Don Juan's compliments or who accepts Faust's gifts loses the tranquility that protected her. The enchantment reaches into her heart of hearts. The way is then open to psychological interpretations that attempt to understand the experience of strange foreignness. In his analysis of what the German language calls *das Unheimliche*, Freud makes a mistake in confining his investigation to the anxieties of boys.

Modern psychology has made much use of ancient myths. Of course it tends to free itself from old oppositions, but sometimes it borrows their images to construct its theories (Freud was one of the first to do so). But for modern psychologists, enchanted states are hardly believable anymore. If modern psychology accepts shamanistic cures, it does so with the full admission of its own wildly sketchy procedures. At most it makes typical cases or models out of them. It uses them for its own ends, namely by explaining them with causes interior to the psyche: drives, reminiscences, beliefs, and phobias. To believe in enchantments, it would say, is a sign of primitive or regressive thinking that recalls the earliest stages of mental life. Enchantresses therefore are products of desire, and if they appear formidable, it is because the desire is accompanied by the fear of punishment.

Let us attend to the different values that intervene in the lives of words. *"Ravir," "séduire," "charmer," "enchanter"* ("to delight," "seduce," "charm," and "enchant") are terms that had a very concrete primary meaning at an earlier time when a certain faith was linked to these metaphors. This strong meaning could only weaken as the world opened itself to reason and became disenchanted. For a long time now these words have been a part of fallen, everyday conversation in which people speak of being enchanted, charmed, or delighted by this or that. In a civilization that has mastered space and where people are guided by GPS, there is no longer any great risk of getting lost, except perhaps in anxiety dreams. When we are awake, we generally do not lose our way unless we make a game of it such as in blind man's bluff or like many travelers who only discover their own sensations. On the planet today one no longer encounters the edge that separates familiar open fields from the impenetrable forest or any inhabited territory from the backwoods wilderness, that is, those transitional spaces where apparitions used to appear. The word "enchantress" has itself taken on a sort of antiquated ring. It may be grouped with "canoness," "popess," "prophetess," and "poetess"—all terms that signal a refined language of bygone days. This withering began a long time ago. I will give only one example. At the end of the seventeenth century, the libertine poet La Fare sends an "Ode on Laziness" to his friend Chaulieu, and to make the rhyme work out he personifies Laziness as an enchantress:

Laisse-toi gouverner par cette Enchanteresse,
Qui seule peut du cœur calmer l'émotion,
Et préfère, crois-moi, les dons de la Paresse
Aux offres d'une vaine et folle ambition.[2]

Let yourself be ruled by this Enchantress,
Who alone can calm the heart's emotion,
And choose, trust me, the gifts of Laziness
Over those of vain, foolish ambition.

I have looked toward the past as though over my shoulder. I suppose there was a strong, primitive meaning to enchantment, a first magic, and some major figures that represented such things. Who represents them? The question that interests me here requires me to take back my use of the terms "primitive" and "first." Large-scale enchantments are always told from a distant afterward as events of another time. They are stories being retold that conjure up a distant time and place. In these narrated "old days" the space of the unknown world was certainly more vast and profound than it is for us today in the known world. The most ancient examples of enchantment existed already as story and representation. What myths speak of has only existed through myth.

In various contexts and time periods, poetry has taken up the earlier stories, or at least pretended to do so. But has poetry gotten closer to them, or has it instead found a new way to keep its distance? At times it has often tried to revive the image of former enchantments, and at others it has made them into a game thereby to outsmart them. And there have been different literary genres and different arts of representation (especially in the theater) that have relayed the most ancient forms of epic narrative. One of the sources of the powerful attraction exerted by opera is its ability to transform the enchantments of a legendary past into a present enchantment, a risky proposition that comes in crucial instants as one sees the action unfolding and hears the notes being sung. The singularity of opera is to offer bodily presences that are intensely dedicated to the representation of an already fixed destiny. For this reason the now transcends "the old days," "formerly" breaks into the present. In the most beautiful operatic productions, one observes the double energy of a memory that persists and an imagination that invents. The imagination of the director must make us feel as though the music of 1786 is speaking to us from some place that is not our own but without trying to reconstitute that place, which would be to lose it twice over. The truth is in a sort of depth perception that makes the "then" and "now" complicit. One gets the textual evidence of a poem surpassed by the power of the music, and both seized upon again to realize something new. When the curtain rises, and provided the staging has not been a disservice, there occurs the only enchantment to which the belated creatures we are have access. The ingeniousness of some directors today misunderstands this interior historicity (which is not an anecdotal past) and takes pride in its amnesia. They attract attention to their own doings, as though they had been provided with lavish means to put on a one-man show.

THE MARVELOUS

Opera grew out of the ambition to renew the ancient alliance between speech and music. A regret was behind this, and overcoming it meant reestablishing the plenitude of a privileged moment experienced in ancient Greece. To these motives linked to a conjectured past, one must add that the dream of this renewal was energized by the spirit of invention and a bold desire to innovate. Experiments [essais] of all kinds abound at the end of the sixteenth century. Many works announce this in their titles with words such as "experimentum," "tentamen," "cimento," "saggio," and "Versuch." The desire to speak well and correctly was a prominent characteristic of the period that followed the invention of the printing press. For Montaigne writing from his library for his friends, the "essai" was a new way to "recite" himself to himself (3: chap. 4). In a very different way, at the home of Count Giovanni Maria de Bardi in Florence, the reinvention of the "singing recitation" of the ancients was an experiment shared among learned and interested amateurs. The proper way in which ancient theater was performed was the central challenge that attracted these musicians and poets. One can well believe that they wished the painted and sculpted mythical characters that decorated their palaces and gardens to become living bodies and vibrating voices.

The Middle Ages had certainly not forgotten the pagan myths and had visually represented them in their own way. But the taste for images was so domineering during the Renaissance that new varieties of visual production were developed and not without awakening certain iconoclast reactions. Fabulous creatures would be called to appear and re-present themselves and relive their passions with the help of makeup and costumes, and they would be accompanied by instruments perfected by the latest instrument and violin makers. In music, the *stile rappresentativo* was the answer to this ambition. One can easily guess the reason why in the earliest operas there was a preference for figures who were intensely desired or lost—figures of loss or frustrated desire such as Daphne (who escapes from the pursuit of Apollo by turning into a laurel tree) or Eurydice (who returns to the underworld). These operas made visible the unpossessable—the presence of desire deploring the absence of the thing that would satisfy it. The suitors who are shaken off and the fleeing objects of desire would find in recitatives and arias their consubstantial analogs.

Opera found a new pleasure in this concerted mixture of the imaginary and the concrete, of remembered legend and sensorial proximity. The opera represented both a return of a pagan fiction that held literary prestige and a projection of a new musical power onto the consecrated fable. Rivaling sculpture and painting and exploiting all sensory attractions to open horizons for the imagination, opera becomes a place where the élan of passions had the possibility of figuring its excesses under the protective cover of beauty. As though its duty were to shed yet more light on already sacred destinies, this new art demanded of the epic, of grand historical scenes, and of chivalric romances that they furnish it with the materials for a festival illuminated by the sparkle of the new that would fill the stage in three dimensions. To accomplish this, the operatic work would unite the prestigious aspects of all other modes of representation. For their own glory, the princely patrons wanted this feast of representation to suspend the ordinary course of time and add to the real world another world. In an age of absolute rule, the sovereign power loved to celebrate its preeminence through the gift of a party experienced as an event that would inscribe itself on everyone's memory. The privileged public invited to such festivities was placed in front of a space that was both concrete (since the stage is a real volume) and metaphorical (since the stage can represent a palace, Olympus, the underworld, etc.). Often, this fictitious world where the pure pleasure of the prince was made manifest also offered some relation to political affairs, ambitions, or gallantries of the moment. The white magic of the show could also include allusions to less innocent magical arts whose practice remained a subject of fear and foreboding. When Circe and Medea were represented back in the early days of opera, tribunals were still persecuting men and women as witches. Of course, by situating a dramatic action in the classical pagan world, the poets were lacing it with a measure of unreality. The distance from the fiction being shared in common left each spectator free to perceive allusions to the real outside world, and the poets were adept at playing with this distance. In those days when the local power would keep a sharp eye out, poetry was skilled in the art of refraction.

"What's proper to this type of show is keeping the mind, eyes, and ears in an equal state of enchantment." This brief statement by La Bruyère from 1691 is a succinct definition of opera that will be often re-peated.[3] Roughly a century after the earliest experiments, opera was still profiting from its relative novelty. But from the beginning there had already been changes. The marvelous aspects of the fictional story required some mechanical assistance, and in France Lully had some-what reduced the use of "*la machine.*" La Bruyère did not approve of the restrictions introduced by the "Italian Amphion" even though he was hardly in favor of renouncing the mythological extravaganzas with their flights, chariots, and the fanfare of theophanies. La Bruyère found all this good fun. He justified the machinery by claiming that "it expanded and embellished the fictional tale and sustained in the spectators the sweet illusion that is the entire pleasure of theater by throwing a mar-velous quality over everything." The machinery in the theater, like the hydraulic machinery in parks and gardens, marked the public entry of the mechanical into modern societies and occurred at a time that pre-ceded its mobilization in the industrial revolution and its contribution to the gradual disenchantment of the world. In truth, Lully only moder-ated its use. It was also necessary for him to soften the conflict between the violins and the grating noises of the stage machinery.

The word "enchantment" as used at the time by La Bruyère has a very strong meaning. As its primary definition, "enchantment" names an ac-tion resulting from a spell or incantation. According to the Academy, it literally means "the effect of supposed charms." For the lexicographer, the term names a power, but a power weighted by somewhat improper or pre-tentious claims. "To enchant" means "to charm, to bewitch with sounds, words, figures, and supposedly magical operations."[4] For LaBruyère's contemporaries, the literal sense of the term had either vanished or else been blemished by doubt. Enchantment already belonged to the past. The place of enchantment according to these same dictionaries is the epic narrative of the Middle Ages. "Our old romances are filled with enchantments." Therefore, if one takes this term literally, one cannot help associating with it a certain regressive childishness. The same dictionaries, however, also speak of a figural sense of the term that is perfectly acceptable. "Figuratively speaking," they affirm, one may talk about the "enchantments of Love and Poetry," and when speaking of a party [*fête*], one may say "everything was surprising" or that "it was an enchantment, or a succession of enchantments." When the word "enchantment" is transposed into the world of amorous feelings or art, it can be taken positively without the connotations of a false or illegitimate supernatural constraint exerted over the world and individuals. Instead, it designates the natural effect of a feeling (love) or aesthetic success (the party). In the latter cases only the natural resources of the human spirit and man-made arts are thought to be at work, and thereby the illusion remains more or less under control.

AGAINST BOREDOM

At the opera La Bruyère dreaded boredom above all else. "I don't know how the *Opera* with its perfect music and lavishness managed to bore me."[5] This fear is widely shared. How is one to avoid boredom? Don't spare the marvelous, for one thing. Mix together enchantments in both the literal and figurative senses: enchantments in the subject matter being represented—gods, flights, chariots, and so on—but especially the enchantments of the material realization of the show contributed by the poet, the set designers, and the musicians. Play with the marvelous. Every time the audience recognizes, thanks to their traditional attributes, Orpheus, Circe, or Medea, let the recognition come with the added pleasure of surprise. It was often wished that the music be entirely new so as to interest a new public in these illustrious ghosts. To that end, one notices an art claiming its authority from ancient tragedy and favoring an unstable mixture of ritual and novelty. Ritual is the reiteration of an action that already took place far back in the past. By adding the requirement of surprise to this call for re-presentation, the hope was that a trace of a memorable past would be expressed in a way that had never been done before, as though one had never known before then how it was to be presented onstage.

Opera thus sought to reconcile a desire for innovation and the pleasures of recognition by turning to a language that had never before been employed in such an enterprise. Moreover, it shared with theater the trick of being able to allude indirectly to civic affairs of the day by having them brought forth by a set of characters that all derived from the well-known stock of Parnassus. Still, by reusing old myths, opera became an art that was adept at producing its own myth. With one additional but decisive step, opera will not only choose its characters from classical mythology but from the treasure chest of fairy tales and legends out of the heritage of Giambattista Basile, Perrault, and the Arabian Nights. This hybridization of the fairy tale with mythology and sometimes with religious hagiography became very widespread during the age of romanticism. The stories and poems of Nerval set amid nature and the theater offer the best examples. Here is how mystery and the marvelous revive.

In the eighteenth century one finds many reformulations of La Bruyère's idea, and especially the imperative of a double presence of enchantment, both in the subject matter of the opera and in the original production of it that will be elaborated for a new opera season. In 1734 Lefranc de Pompignan affirmed that the marvelous is "the soul of the lyric spectacle" and too often neglected "in most modern operas." Let's open again the *Encyclopédie* of Diderot and d'Alembert at the entry for "Opéra" written by Jaucourt. This author has followed his usual habits and borrowed from many sources. He begins by recalling La Bruyère's short definition and then passes quickly to a declaration of opera's goal: "the representation of a marvelous action." Not only does Jaucourt approve of the use of the marvelous, but he makes it the law of the genre. He summarizes it this way: "It is the divine epic put on stage. Since the actors are gods or demigods, they must announce their presence to mortals through actions, language, and vocal inflections that surpass the laws of ordinary verisimilitude. Their actions are lavishly fantastic. The sky opens, chaos and the elements of nature succeed one another, a luminous cloud carries a celestial being; it's an enchanted palace that disappears in an instant and changes into a desert."

The enchanted palaces are copies of those found in Ariosto and Tasso where one finds the enchantresses Alcina, Armide, and Melissa. Their magical operations are often spectacles within the spectacle that come at moments when the effect of surprise is particularly desired. But at the same time the various feelings, from combat to concord, that constitute the attraction of the opera must not be forgotten. Jaucourt therefore adds this general remark: "But since it has been considered appropriate to join song and music to these marvels, and since the natural material of musical singing is feeling, the artists had to interpret the action to release the passions." One thus sees gods, enchantresses, and magicians appear onstage with the mortals on the receiving end of their domination. But passionate song alone, without leaving the realm of nature and without miraculous events, is able to produce extreme pleasures, and the singers, poets, and composers are thus considered enchanters. One can guess that there is often an imperceptible transition between enchantment in the literal sense—that is, the power exerted by certain characters within the fiction—and enchantment in the figurative sense—that is, "the ecstasy, enthusiasm, and intoxicated feelings" that animate an entire work and are communicated to the spectator. An opera without divine beings or witches but whose passions are noble and grand can still rightly claim to satisfy the expectation for enchantment.

ROUSSEAU THE ENCHANTER

Rousseau, expressing irony with regard to the failures of the marvelous, is the one who defends enchantment linked to feelings alone. He did much reading at Les Charmettes. In the autobiographical poem Le Verger de Madame la baronne de Warens (1739), where Rousseau tells of his reading and studies, La Bruyère is the second author he names: "There, carrying with me Montaigne and La Bruyère, I laugh peacefully over human misery."[6] Rousseau retained a good deal from his frequent perusal of La Bruyère's Characters (1688), including its statements about opera. In the entry "Opera" within his Dictionnaire de la musique, Rousseau repeats the moralist's definition, evoking again the trio of mind, eyes, and ears.[7] But unlike Jaucourt, who distinguishes them, Rousseau places the action as dependent on the passions. Opera, he writes, "strives to reunite all the charms of the visual arts in the representation of a passionate action." He then adds, returning to La Bruyère's definition, "The constitutive parts of an *Opera* are the Poem, the Music, and the Decoration. The Poetry speaks to the mind, the Music to the ears, and Painting to the eyes; the whole must come together to move the heart and make the same impression via different organs." In agreement with his contemporaries but with greater insistence, Rousseau only distinguishes the elements of this art for the sake of claiming for them concordant effects. Passionate action in the opera introduces, on the one hand, recitative to lead the action and the narrative and, on the other, arias to paint "the emotion of the heart." Thus "the attraction of the melody and the effect of declamation" can follow one another.

Rousseau declares his hostility to the mythological marvelous and to the conventions of allegory. And yet he had adapted these practices in his early experiments, notably the opera-ballet *Les Muses galantes*. Rameau, a specialist of the genre, did not give it a favorable welcome. Consequently, Rousseau not only turned against Rameau but against a genre that did not fit his talents. He calls for the renunciation of extraordinary action. Emotion must proceed from the simplest truth. The intervention of a superior power descended from an imaginary heaven ought not to be represented onstage. In his theoretical pages and in the ironic letter of Saint-Preux on the Paris opera, Rousseau condemns laborious artifices. The error of French opera is to have "sought to represent the marvelous" whereas the latter is "only made to be imagined." One would be better off reading. In the theater, Rousseau prefers that the mimetic imperative be linked to human feelings that alone are susceptible to being recognized by the audience. What knowledge do we have, he argues, of the powers possessed by gods? The power of the divine beings on old Mount Olympus is entirely fictional, and therefore we have no basis for judging the imitation of them that art would pretend to give.

Since music's task is to imitate nature as we know it, true music will strive to render feelings as we actually experience them. We are then in a position to judge the accuracy of the imitation and to be moved by it. Music ought to rid itself of the phantom of celestial gods and of demons risen from the depths (these "beings of reason or rather of madness"). Music's job is to deploy its own powers that issue from the soul of the musician and resonate with the feeling soul of the audience. Thus the dilemma between the marvels accomplished by the family of gods and the marvels that are uniquely the product of the composer and the musicians is nullified. The idea of enchantment will be entirely ascribed to the effect of the music, that is, to the stirring of emotion. Of course, Rousseau does not mention what will be called "pure music," especially since instrumental music means nothing to him. The "interest" of which he so often speaks comes via poetic language elevated to musical strength: "As soon as music had learned to paint and speak, the charms of feeling soon turned attention away from the charms of magic; the theater was purged of the jargon of mythology; interest replaced the marvelous; the machinery of poets and carpenters was destroyed; and lyric Drama took on a more noble and less gigantic form."

The terms used by Rousseau are revealing: for him "to paint" is to imitate objects; "to speak" is to express feelings. Painting still implies a distinction—a distance—between the painting and the objects it represents, whereas speaking and singing are the very voices of feeling; they are less the image than the excess, to the extent that music remains linked to speech.

In the myth constructed by Rousseau in his account of the origins of human societies, speech was melodic from the start. Music, he affirms repeatedly, was present in primitive languages, notably in Greek. All the poetry of the Greeks "was musical and all their music was declamatory"; it "was in fact a true recitative." As with the advent of evil, the separation of music and speech came at a point in history distant from their origins. Our task is to search for a remedy or at least a palliative. The different arts operate separately when the speech of the poet becomes purely verbal. The need is felt to reconcile it with melody, and this requires deploying more effects. Art, if it is animated by the enthusiasm of genius, restores a broken alliance. Our stale languages have undergone a loss that must be compensated for by inventing substitutes or "supplements."[8] But one must not err in the choice of means that are turned to. One of our resources could be to call "physical pleasure to the aid of our morals," which in our everyday language possess only "hypothetical and constrained" means. We must "supplement the energy of expression with the attraction of harmony." But some may criticize such means. Yet we know that neither physical pleasure nor harmony occupies the place of *good* within the antinomies favored by

Rousseau. But if they are *bad*, they ought to be used just as one uses poisons that serve as active ingredients within a curative substance. "Modern" music is destined to require artifices that *flatter* the ear. Because this contribution is a type of physical pleasure, one must note a touch of reprobation when Rousseau, in his entry for "Opera," speaks of the "enchanting melody" that tends to impose itself to the detriment of the poem: "Thus, the less one knows how to touch the heart, the more one needs to know how to flatter the ears, and we are required to seek in the sensations the pleasure that the feeling denies us. Herein lies the origin of songs, choruses, the symphony, and that enchanting melody that modern music adorns itself with often to the detriment of poetry but which the man of taste rejects in the theater when he is flattered without being moved."[9]

A nostalgia demanding reparations: failing to reconquer a lost plenitude and unity, music and poetry must remain as close to each other as possible. And as though he were ashamed to accord too much to sensory pleasure detached from speech, Rousseau emphatically underlines the proximity that he believes to be essential. Gluck as well, in his famous preface to *Alceste* (1767), which openly declares its debt to Rousseau, adopts the requirement of intimate proximity among feeling, speech, and music. The musician must "serve the poetry" and pursue a "simple beauty" without trying to shine separately. His *Armide* (1777), paired with the same text of Quinault that Lully had used nearly a century before, proposes a very new musical idiom. Based on that composition, one will strongly argue in favor of a latitude granted by poetry to different musical styles. The more he claimed to be only seeking the truth of feeling, the more Gluck's music most certainly produced an effect of enchantment.

Truth be known, it was not at all displeasing to Rousseau to be the author of enchanting music. When in the fourth book of the *Confessions* he speaks of his misadventure in Lausanne and the "charivari" of his concert at the home of Monsieur de Treytorrens, he ironically consoles himself with a figure of anticipation or prolepsis: "Poor Jean-Jacques: little did you know at this cruel moment that one day your music, performed before the king of France and his entire court, would inspire murmurs of surprise and applause, and that in all the boxes round about you the loveliest women would be whispering to each other 'What a charming sound! What enchanting music! It goes straight to the heart!' "[10]

In *Le Divin du village*, the composer's claim of a rightful power to enchant is evident. The pages of Rousseau's autobiography in which he describes the work's success reveal that through the characters and music the interest of his first audience was focused on the composer himself. In this "intermezzo" the marvelous exists only for young credulous peasants. The village fiction reduces the supernatural to a simulacrum. The prophet consults a "grimoire" and "casts a spell" only to impress the rustic locals. From their superior point of view, the audience does not believe it for a minute: there is nothing occult about the prophet's science; it consists in manipulating the feelings of young lovers by playing on their disappointment, jealousy, and self-love. It is the absence of the marvelous and the apparent naïveté that are operative in *Le Divin du village*. And in the pages of the *Confessions* that I've just mentioned, it is quite clear that by having "the loveliest women" speak in his favor, Rousseau is paying himself a loving compliment: *he* was present in the "enchanting music" that received such high praise. If we are to believe his account, it was women (the only listeners named, in fact) who approved of the feminine qualities of the music. In the account given in the *Confessions*, the beneficent success of *Le Divin du village* redounds on the man, Jean-Jacques. This was no doubt the case in the circumstances described, but the description of them itself redoubles the positive effect.

Amid the very large vocabulary employed in his writings, Rousseau only chooses the adjective "*enchanteresse*" on occasions when he can attach to it an erotic charge. As, for example, when he evokes the first appearance of Madame de Warens: "What I saw was a face radiant with grace, blue eyes full of sweetness, a dazzling complexion, the curve of an enchanting bosom."[11] Another example comes in a famous letter from *Julie ou la Nouvelle Héloïse* when Saint-Preux discovers Italian music: "I've begun to listen to this enchanting music [*musique enchanteresse*]."[12] He takes intense pleasure in it: "Some unknown voluptuous sensation imperceptibly came over me. It was no longer an empty sequence of sounds, as in our récits. At each phrase some image entered my brain or some sentiment my heart; the pleasure did not stop at the ear, but entered the soul."[13]

As though in a reflexive doubling, the epistolary duo of Julie and her lover will celebrate the high powers of music. The still-clandestine love between the two lovers is an operatic situation transferred to "a little town at the foot of the mountains." Under the shock of a sudden revelation, Saint-Preux discovers precious truths about the superiority of Italian music, and he wants Julie to learn to sing this music. She agrees and will very soon be telling him about her progress in the art of singing. Before their physical encounter, they discover in music an object of shared pleasure; they discuss it theoretically as passionate amateurs, and Julie begins her apprenticeship. The appropriate pedagogy (offered by the castrato Regianino, whose patron is Mylord Edouard) soon allows Julie to give her own epistolary lessons.

By inserting the name Héloïse into his title, Rousseau raised the expectation that the work would address the question of ancient interdictions (formerly religious and now social) and the new ("*nouvelle*") form in which they operate in eighteenth-century society. With the requirement of the new, Rousseau introduced into the substance of his novel many aesthetic questions that he was sure would respond to the sensibilities of his time: the beauty of the Alpine landscape, the art of gardens, the portrait, opera, and the music of France and Italy. In these different areas, the beautiful could go as far as enchantment but always under the authority of the natural order. Consider, for example, Julie's great art project, which is to construct an Elysium of plants near the terrace in her garden that reminds Saint-Preux of the end of the world and specifically of the Polynesian islands, Tinian and Juan Fernandez, that he visited on his grand tour. Julie delights in disillusioning her lover: in fact, this luxurious garden was made using the most sober means: "of climbing and parasitical plants" and rerouted streams (that recall the famous episode of the aqueduct in book 1 of the *Confessions*). She declares with irony, "Adieu Tinian, adieu Juan Fernandez, *adieu all enchantment*! In a moment you will have returned from the end of the world."[14] In creating her Elysium story, Julie is an enchantress who reveals her secrets. The marvelous space had been arranged at no great cost. The efficient cause of its beauty was the great simplicity of the work that went into it; the material cause was the choice of the most ordinary species of plants. Mastery of a commonplace horticulture succeeded in creating the illusion of a faraway paradise.

In Rousseau's *Julie*, the extensive passages devoted to music indicate a choice of perspective that signals one of modernity's most important tendencies. The heroes of the novel are budding artists who sometimes, as we've just seen, actually demonstrate their artistic talents. The epistolary duo allows them to present ideas, preferences, and tastes. And the interest of readers, while concerned with what becomes of the characters and with their feelings and affective situations, also focuses on the moral and aesthetic convictions of these people who serve as imaginary delegates of the author. Their passion makes them eloquent, but ultimately of course it is the author who is making them speak that receives the most glory from this eloquence. On this point what counts most from now on is not so much the object represented, the story told, but rather the storyteller, the narrator's genius, the ideas he develops, and the style he invents. There is, one might say, a sort of handing-on of power or perhaps more accurately a recouping of power. The feelings that his heroes express with such beautiful gusto are ones that Rousseau wants to have ascribed to himself. With him this happens frequently.

Even before writing his *Confessions*, Rousseau is almost always taking pains to draw his own silhouette behind the figures and conversations he puts forward. This is why he carefully avoided having any "bad guys" in his novel. One should recall how often Rousseau needs to formulate his convictions, even outside the novel, via some intermediate speaker or double. There is Hésiode in *Les Muses galantes*, the speaker of the preface in the *Discourse on Inequality*, the teacher in *Émile*, the Savoyard priest, Julie or her "lover," Jean-Jacques in the court of judgment, Jean-Jacques under the eye of "Rousseau," and "Rousseau" himself facing "the Frenchman" in the *Dialogues*. These objectified characters are at once his delegates and his alibis. They are a second or third degree of self that the self uses to shine forth and with which it wants to be illustrated. Thus one sees the writer disport high-handedly and make it so that his intellectual or aesthetic invention is testified to through someone else's speech. In this way, Rousseau became the first great representative of the moment that would come to be known as the age of "feeling" and "genius"—a decisive stage toward what will be called "modernity." The work, though of course a product of its creator, calls for open acknowledgment that also redounds with increasing insistence to his person. Thanks to the recognition that he garners for and from his work, he obtains the status of "great man." Of prime importance, one sees, are the categories of the aesthetic (the "interesting" in Kierkegaard's terminology) and the "authenticity" of the artist as a singular person. This occurs to the point that for him, aside from his works, his major responsibility becomes acceding to himself.

PYGMALION'S MONOLOGUE

A very revealing symptom of this evolution can be seen in the way the language and practices of an earlier time take on different values when reused during this age of feeling and "genius." This is especially notice-able in Rousseau's borrowings from Petrarch. He is familiar with the famous verses in sonnet 213 from the *Canzoniere* that enumerate the high "graces" of Laura, each of which acts like a magician and "trans-forms" her adoring admirer ("da questi magi trasformato fui"). Among these graces is "the song that can be heard in one's soul" ("il cantar che nell'anima si sente") that goes along with "the celestial bearing" ("l'andar celeste"), speech, and sighs from the mouth. In Petrarch's poem, "the song that can be heard in one's soul" does not define the powers of music in general but the powers of Laura's voice when she sings. This perfection is linked to the very being of the chosen one. When Rousseau cites this verse, however, the purpose is to praise not Julie but rather a musical style (Italian music) that he is advising her to learn. The challenge of "becoming-an-artist" is central to Rousseau's novel at this moment and will not recede, since the question of edu-cation is a central theme from beginning to end. Saint-Preux assures his friend that her voice "so naturally light and sweet will easily take on this new trait; you will soon find within your sensibility the en-ergy and liveliness of accent that animates Italian music, *Il cantar che nell'anima si sente*." One of Julie's later letters (vol. 1, letter 52) shows us her apprenticeship in action as she receives lessons from the Italian Regianino, whose talent had powerfully revealed the beauty of music to Saint-Preux. In this way Rousseau gives first prize to his own ideal of composition and playing, and Saint-Preux serves as his intermediary in charge of inculcating it in Julie. Whereas Petrarch was celebrating the virtues and voice that Laura possessed in her essence, Rousseau makes his aesthetic choice the basis of a lesson plan. He is of course address-ing all his readers, but here he makes Saint-Preux (with the castrato as assistant) into the Pygmalion of Julie the musician.

In singing Italian music, Julie becomes her lover's work of art. In relation to this episode, one needs to reread the "Lyric Scene" of *Pygmalion* that Rousseau wrote in Môtiers in November 1762.

On August 27, 1748, Rameau had composed a one-act ballet based on this myth entitled *Pygmalion*. It is possible that Rousseau consciously decided to take up the other side. As soon as Rameau agreed to make a ballet out of it, the story of the sculptor in love with his work of art could only disperse into a multitude of figures. The librettist, Ballot de Sauvot, first shows Pygmalion in ecstasy in front of the statue he has made as he implores "fatal Love." He next introduces a certain Céphise, who is dejected about no longer being loved by the sculptor. Thanks to a mechanical device, one sees Love descend from the sky in response to the artist's pleas. A stage direction specifies as follows: "Love flies rapidly across the theater and shakes a torch over the statue... . The statue comes alive." Pygmalion, the statue, and Love exchange words in song, and then enter the Graces, who will teach the statue "the different steps of the dance." A "chorus of people" gathers and celebrates the event with one of Rameau's most beautiful polyphonic compositions: "Love triumphs." The piece ends with a rondo and contra dances. The enchantments in this work are represented in the most conventional manner, and I am inclined to say that therein lies their very real attraction.

For Rousseau, who saw in it only feeling, just two characters occupy the stage, Pygmalion and the statue. The latter only comes alive at the very end, and, as with Condillac's statue, it discovers its existence through the sense of touch and a discrimination of self and nonself. Rousseau therefore chose the form of pathetic monologue interspersed with moments of emotion assigned to the music. For the performance in Lyon in 1772, he turned the music over to an amateur, Horace Coignet, whose music does not shine with any originality. Rousseau was thus the inventor of a new type of spectacle in which declamatory speech and music alternate. It was to be called "*mélodrame*," and its classical examples include the music of Beethoven that borrows scenes from Goethe's *Egmont* and Schumann's *Manfred*, inspired by Byron.

In Rousseau, Pygmalion's monologue begins with a feeling of loss that profoundly affects the sculptor: "I have lost my genius." Nothing has any "charm" for him now, neither friendship nor his "charming models." And yet an "inconceivable charm" keeps him in his studio, which contains a veiled statue underneath a sheltering tent. He addresses his Galatea as though she were a goddess. He clearly sees that this divinity made by his own hands lacks the soul and life of which he feels the excess in himself. It is only a stone, and yet he feels "embraced by its charms." He would like to animate it by giving it his heart and soul and his own life, on condition that he could perpetuate the lack that torments him and "remain always another, so as always to wish to be her, to see her, to love her and to be loved by her." He invokes the gods, specifically Venus, "the soul of the universe," as though they were the metaphorical figure or principal of his own desire, as though they had guided his sculptor's hands: "It is you who formed by my hand these charms and these traits that await only feeling and life." The statue descends from its pedestal. Pygmalion attributes to his "mad love" the "prestige" that he sees coming true (the term "prestige" being used in the strong sense that it formally had when it designated an illusion produced by a spell). It is he, therefore, who is the enchanter at the very moment when he places himself under the dependence of the "charming object" that he has produced. In Pygmalion's last tirade a triple source is evoked when Galatea, now alive, is emphatically declared to be "the worthy masterpiece of my hands, my heart, and the Gods." And the last words are these: "I gave you my whole being, I will no longer live but through you." Pygmalion therefore awaits the return of what he has given. Did the gods collaborate in the sculptor's work? Let's say that they were internalized to the point where they blended within the self of the artist in love. We can formulate this process in another way and say that Galatea is the projection of a subjectivity founded on the "principle of all existence" that mythology, according to Rousseau, personified under the name Venus. The artist gave up his "soul" only to take it back again, thereby reconquering the certainty of the genius that he believed he had lost.

Something of the Narcissus in Rousseau (in love with his portrait in female dress) subsisted in his Pygmalion. But love in *Pygmalion* does not remain an illusion. It manifests itself in the very steps taken by the real statue and in the brief unimaginable syllables born in her from the experience of touching: "Me. . . . It's no longer me. . . . Again me." It is a marvelous aurora. No machinery was necessary for the prodigy to manifest itself and fulfill the expectations of the solitary protagonist. Pygmalion is a fully satisfied Narcissus. And if he is the emblematic figure of the artist, he is all the more so that of the writer, who, by identifying with his characters and with the passions that shoot through them, captivates his readers by attracting to himself their amazed response. Jean-Jacques was such a writer in many of his works. One comes even to neglect what constituted the substance of his thinking as a theoretician. A typical example of this is the concluding declaration by Maurice Barrès in his *Observation Presented to the Chamber of Deputies, 11 June 1912, on the Occasion of Jean-Jacques Rousseau's Bicentenary.* Barrès refused to approve the credits necessary for this commemoration: "For my part, I listen readily and consider him an enchanter in his grand symphonies, but I would not ask for any advice about life from this extravagant Musician."[15]

BEAUTY AS A RELIGION?

Chateaubriand, who wanted to combat and surpass Rousseau, will also be labeled an enchanter. He was the one who gave the clearest signal when it comes to the aestheticization of the religious. One need only recall the subtitle of his *Genius of Christianity* (1802) for a definition of the author's intention: *The Spirit and Beauty of the Christian Religion.* And while Rousseau passes for a very distant precursor, later one sees a metaphysics develop in Germany that situates music at the junction of the most intimate subjectivity and the creative forces of nature. There will be much talk of music as a religion or as a substitute for religion. Within the perspective of a Platonic idealism, music is, according to Jean Paul Richter, "the herald of the celestial home of the soul." In the philosophy of Schopenhauer, whose influence extends through to French symbolism, music is a "secret metaphysical exercise of spirit meditating unconsciously."[16] For E. T. A. Hoffmann, music "allows man to glimpse his supreme principle, and by lifting him out of the absurd activity and agitation of common life, leads him into the temple of Isis where Nature speaks to him an unheard of sacred language that is nevertheless intelligible."[17] Music makes us penetrate into the "realm of spirits." It is "the mysterious Sanskrit of nature that communicates by sounds and fills the heart of man with an infinite aspiration." Hoffmann sees proof of this in the music of Beethoven, which is the subject of a meditation within his *Kreisleriana* (1815).

It should be noted that Hoffmann does not wish this conception of music to be applied only to instrumental music. He wants it to reign in the world of opera thanks to the complicity of librettists. This is the focus of the dialogue "The Poet and the Composer" (1813), later published within the four-volume collection *The Serapion Brothers* (*Die Serapions Brüder*, 1819–1821). This requirement, formulated by the composer Ludwig, makes absolute the "spiritual" ambition such that the territory to be conquered extends to the dimensions of a "world." Imagination and dream must enlarge the sensorial field out to the furthest, secret depths. The result will be a powerful return of the marvelous and enchantments. In order for music to deploy all its powers, the poet who composes the libretto must also be familiar with "the realm of spirits." In such cases, the music will flow from the poem "as its necessary product." The concept of "romantic," employed profusely by Hoffmann to characterize inspirational poetry and the corresponding music, is certainly far too imprecise. But it is nonetheless accommodating enough to be able to include within it the grand heroic and playful narratives of Ariosto and Tasso.

In his dialogue with the poet Ferdinand, the composer Ludwig also quotes enthusiastically from the theatrical fable *The Crow* (*Il Corvo*) by the Venetian writer Carlo Gozzi and holds it up as the model for the kind of dramatic action that could be turned into a libretto for a romantic opera.[18] Typically, this play from the fairy or "*fiabe*" theater of Carlo Gozzi is an elaboration of a story taken from the *Tale of Tales* (or *Pentamerone*) by Giambattista Basile, the seventeenth-century Neapolitan author who collected popular stories that resembled oriental tales. One finds in *The Crow* a whole host of characters: three figures from the commedia dell'arte (Truffaldino, Brighella, and Pantalone), a prince and his brother, two government ministers, a princess of Damascus and her servant, a necromancer, and talking animals. We witness different enchantments and metamorphoses: a man turned into a statue, a woman stabbed but later revived so that the play ends happily, and so on. A steady stream of improbable events creates situations that make the characters undergo extreme tests. The feelings that result cannot be similar to those that would be felt by "individual characters." But Hoffmann is no less opposed to the triumph of a gratuitous fantasy. He sees the action unfolding within the orders of symbol and mystery: "the marvelous appears here as necessary; it is of such poetic truth that one believes in it spontaneously."[19] If we are to believe Hoffmann, the prime example of this sort of marvelous is to be found in *The Magic Flute*. What he admires in that work is the flow of the action and the surprising series of situations. For him, it manifests a type of fantastic that evokes both the law of the world and the great rules of human morality beyond any narrow psychological verisimilitude. Hoffmann is able to see that Mozart and Schikaneder's stage figures are not "individual characters" and have no true interiority. What's so outstanding in their case is that they are interiority become image; they are the delegates of a mythic consciousness vaster than the self of a person. Everything happens as though they were the actors of the universal soul but without having themselves any personal soul. The fable within which they are inscribed onstage is itself the last secret, the allegory that links back up with the primary reality. A fiction among fictions, it has the power to turn us into participants.

Attracted by the desire to stage a symbolic fairy world, Hoffmann composed an opera with his friend Friedrich de La Motte-Fouqué. The latter composed a libretto by taking over the story recounted in his tale *Ondine*. We witness the dramatization of the ambiguous relations between human beings and elementary powers. In the end, the mysterious Ondine, both seductress and victim, returns to the world of water after having experienced the human condition. Taken in by poor fishermen, the only fate she could find among men was to become the betrayed wife of a faithless knight.

But for Hoffmann the marvelous is not simply the result of contact with "the world of spirits." It also appears in opera buffa, where banal reality is subverted by derision. The impossible takes the upper hand, chance happenings accumulate, and there results a liberating weightlessness. Confronted with the unforeseeable, the characters become marionettes, and the restriction of their liberty demonstrates the omnipotence of their creators: the librettist, the composer, the actors, and so on. The irony that denounces the ridiculousness of the finite condition awards itself the prerogatives of infinity. For Hoffmann there blossoms here a type of fantastic that is rather different from that which takes place in the fairy world spectacle.

Here, this time, the fantastic arises in part from the eccentricities of the individual characters and in part from the bizarre play of chance that introduces itself boldly into everyday affairs and turns all things within that daily life upside down. There is no doubt, yes, it is our gentlemanly neighbor in his cinnamon-colored Sunday suit with gold buttons, but what the devil is possessing him to indulge in such odd gesticulations? . . . These strange adventures in which the characters engage, as though fallen into mysterious crises, unless it be chance that draws them in—these adventures must give us the singular impression that we would feel if some absurd witchcraft were turning our own lives upside down and dragging us irresistibly into the circle of its mocking mystifications.

The music, adds Hoffmann, is "capable of expressing all the nuances of comedy."[20] And the model of this, for him, is to be found in Mozart's *Così fan tutte*.

Hoffmann's musical gifts were great, but they had their limits and did not permit him to accomplish entirely the task he assigned to romantic opera. It was literature that imposed its law, in a case of outdistancing that was both narrative and reflexive. Hoffmann realized that by giving free rein to his imagination "absurd witchcraft" can, while evoking music, be achieved perfectly well by means of words alone. To do that Hoffmann needed to invent a mad musician—Kreisler—who would serve as his spokesman and addressee all in one. Hoffmann's "*Lehrbrief*" (1815, "Johannes Kreisler's Indenture," also in the *Kreisleriana*) is sent to him by his double, Johannes Kreisler himself. The master's farewell to the student constitutes the seal of mastery. The self-appointed authority (by specularity) comes with a certain self-sacrifice and self-ridicule: "Farewell, then, my dear Johannes . . . I have the feeling I will see you no more... . If therefore you never find me again, weep for me appropriately, as Hamlet wept for Yorrick, then raise up for me a peaceful *hic jacet*." In the middle of the page the text prints a large funeral cross. The letter adds "Me like You." And Johannes Kreisler signs the letter, adding after his name the title "former music master."[21] Kreisler disappears into death at the same time that he authorizes himself by autoproclamation. This mocking doubling-up (reminiscent of Sterne) between the certifying Kreisler and the certified Kreisler constitutes only one frame. Another character appears, the young Chrysostome. (The name means "mouth of gold," and Hoffmann, who took the name of Amadeus to tag it onto his own, knows that Mozart was born on the day of Saint Chrysostome.) The young man is haunted by the memory of a story that his father told him when he was a child. He in turn retells the story. The narrative voices multiply as though by schizogenesis. The story of the father, retold by the son, would seem to be the founding myth of musical inspiration: the secret, perhaps, of the "mastery" that Kreisler passes on to his double.

The remembered story is the tale of a seduction linked to a supernatural power.[22] A disturbing visitor arrives at a lord's castle. He speaks of faraway lands. "His voice then was lost amid marvelous echoes that without the help of words expressed unknown, mysterious objects. . . . No one could resist the charm of the stranger"—especially the lord's daughter, to whom the demonic visitor teaches "singing and the lyre." He joins her at night "next to an old tree" where she is waiting for him. "Their song and the sounds coming from the lyre could be heard from far away." One fine morning the young woman has disappeared. The lord discovers her lifeless body under the rock where she used to sit with the visitor. This rock covered with multicolored moss is situated in the garden of Chrysostome and his parents. There then begins for him a period of unquenchable thirst for music that his technical abilities acquired in high school are unable to satisfy: "I looked at the rock, its red veins opened like somber carnations whose perfume became visible and shot forth as clear and melodious rays. Mixing with the prolonged fluid accents of the nightingale, the rays took on the form of a marvelous woman, but this form, in turn, was a splendid, divine music." This music (contained in the mineral element and in the forms and colors of vegetation, then turned into a woman) is the dead maid, the victim of the demonic enchanter who has herself become an enchantress.

It hardly matters that Hoffmann uses an epithetic vocabulary to convey amazement and the marvelous. His intuition of correspondences is formulated in a way that is poetic enough to have stuck in the mind of Baudelaire: "The musician, that is one in whose soul music attains clarity, limpidity, and consciousness; such a musician is surrounded everywhere by harmony and melody. It is not for the sake of an empty image or allegory that the musician says that for him colors, lights, and perfumes are sounds, and that in combining them he perceives a marvelous concert."[23]

While not having any model in nature, music is the universal language of nature. With nature, the musician is "in the same relation as the hypnotist with the seer, his energetic will being the question that nature never leaves unanswered." The marvelous is therefore both the intimate side of nature and the foreign all at once. We are invited to accept a coincidence of opposites, whereby the marvelous is at the same time the mysterious exception and the revelation of being in its very truth.

THE GNOSTIC DUALISM OF WAGNER

The advice of Hoffmann was followed. From the romantic period to the modern age Carlo Gozzi became an important source of operatic subjects. His *fiabe* theater gave the stage *Turandot*, *The Love for Three Oranges*, and *The Stag King*, among other works. If there is much Gozzi in Hoffmann, there is also, as Nietzsche remarked, a lot of Hoffmann in Wagner, who stands as the summation of both German and French romanticism.[24] It is in Gozzi that Wagner finds the subject matter for his first opera, *The Fairies*, whose Italian model was called *The Snake Woman* (*La donna serpente*). The libretto tells the story of a fairy who marries a mortal and for whom she breaks the law forbidding the revelation of her identity (just as Lohengrin, urged by Elsa, will also do). She loses her magic power and turns into a stone. Thanks to enchanted weapons and aided as well by the powers of song that attest to his love, the husband will be able to bring her back to life.

From his youth Wagner was attracted by the theme of the betrayal of secrets (as in *Lohengrin*) and the theme of redemption (*Erlösung*), and both will remain very important to him. He was similarly attracted by those aspects of enchantment that result from the confrontation of separate realms: nature, elements, gods, humans, and tribes. Whether imposed by a prediction, a mission, a superior decree, an interdiction, an obligation, or the effect of a magic potion, supernatural constraints are a constant element of Wagnerian fables. His heroes, in their very resistance, must always submit to the law of fate. Nothing happens to them that is not announced under the pressure of a superior necessity that imposes on them the alternatives of destruction or deliverance, both taken as redemptive.

In both "The Poet and the Composer" and the "*Lehrbrief*," Hoffmann wishes opera to place itself within the register of fairy tales. And as Carl Dahlhaus has remarked, *The Flying Dutchman* is "characterized by elements that undeniably place it very close to the fairy tale."[25] Enchantment is triply active in this work that openly names itself a "romantic opera." The marvelous dimensions of the curse, seduction, and salvation are united here. Wagner's merit lies not in the invention of the story (it had already been told by Heine)[26] but in its dramatic and musical elaboration. He gave it the appearance of a "dramatic ballad." The sailor who blasphemes in the storm brings down on himself a divine curse that determines at what price it will be revoked: the absolute love that the demonic captain must win from a woman. The marvelous fact is that the image of the Dutchman (a portrait hanging on the wall at home) had deeply fascinated Senta long before her father, Daland, speaks to her of the rich foreigner whose ship has just docked. The image of the cursed man had conquered her in advance, awakening in her an attraction powerful enough to accept the highest sacrifice.

Nietzsche reproached Wagner for having followed a French model of 1830 in making this somber figure [*ténébreux*] into a seducer.[27] The somber Frenchmen of 1830 were themselves inspired by the marvelous black figure of Faust and by the accursed figures associated with Byron. The "tenebrous" man is certainly a demon figure, but he is still a man, and his damnation is not irrevocable. A gift of love or the sacrifice of a life can bring him salvation. This is the third marvelous facet in this opera.

Consistent with its demonization of pagan gods, the saga of the Christian Middle Ages had transformed Venus into an evil enchantress—Lilith—without taking away any of her radiant beauty. In Germanic lands, her mountain territory was called the Venusberg, and the Minnesinger Tannhäuser considered himself its privileged guest. In folktales, the very ancient theme of loving servitude was thus conjoined with the theme of wild spaces: the forest, the river, the glacier, deep valleys, or marvelous crystalline mountains.[28] The Venusberg motif comes back to life during the romantic period. It is mentioned in various tales including the one in Hoffmann's *The Serpion Brothers* and in certain mocking verses of Heine where the pope, having listened to the confession of Tannhäuser, tells him his sin is incurable and his damnation certain.[29] This becomes for Wagner the subject of a new work also subtitled "A Romantic Opera." Completed in 1845, his *Tannhäuser* opens with a grand ball commanded by Venus to retain her captive. Feeling satiated, however, he tires of the voluptuous offerings of this magic place. His mind turning to much higher things, he invokes the aid of the Virgin Mary. Magic against magic: the festive setting vanishes, but the spell persists within Tannhäuser's soul. After leaving her, he is still unable to forget Venus, and it is to her scandalously that he addresses his hymn at the courtly singing competition. In his libretto, Wagner invents the spiritual love of Elizabeth, whose purity (a superior countermagic) vanquishes the guilty hold of the pagan goddess. By giving the gift of her own life, Elizabeth obtains Tannhäuser's redemption. The latter dies in turn while a miraculous sign reveals the end of the curse. His pilgrim's staff has become covered with flowers, a sign that he has escaped going to hell. Sacred love triumphs, and Venus is the loser.

Enchantment versus enchantment: this opposition, so important in *Tannhäuser*, will never leave Wagner's imagination. He makes this gnostic dualism into the heart of the action in *Parsifal*, his testamentary work. In answer to perverse magic (*Zauber*) comes a chosen savior confirmed and aided by true miracles (*Wunder*). Neither enchanted gardens nor flower maidens nor the loving attentions of Kundry submitting to the will of Klingsor—the self-castrated jealous magician, incapable of loving and only interested in possessing—can stand in the way of the mission of the "pure fool." Parsifal is protected by a simplicity that makes him able to perceive suffering in the world. His folly, that is, his lack of all rational knowledge, is simply miraculous and qualifies him to become the healer and successor of Amfortas, the suffering king. Carrying out the Easter ritual that links the community of knights will thus fall to the predestined officer.

What is striking is the curious relation Wagner establishes between perverse magic, which obstructs the work of redemption, and the saving miracle that makes known the divine will. The latter takes on the appearance of a countermagic that reclaims possession of the very instruments seized by the first magic. Symptoms include the following: Wagner makes the three-quarter time the shared feature of both the aria of the flower maidens and the Good Friday Spell. The seductresses "in flower clothes" in the magic garden of Klingsor are paralleled at a distance by the "enchantress flowers" (*Wunderblumen*) of nature's rebirth celebrating the miracle of Easter. The Holy Spear inflicts pain or relieves it depending on whether it is held by the demonic magician who stole it or by the Lord's chosen one. In the hands of the impure Klingsor and with the complicity of Kundry, the Spear has caused inextinguishable pain to the body of Amfortas.[30] But when Parsifal, after miraculously regaining possession of the spear, touches the point to the wound, the pain no less miraculously disappears. "Only the Spear that opens the wound can heal it."[31] A higher enchantment is performed by the one who has eluded all evil enchantments. In Parsifal's hands the Spear on which Christ's blood flowed recovers its sacred character. Parsifal passes from the state of innocence that ignores all rules and all laws to that of a commander exercising the power to restore both rule and law.

Nietzsche, drawing on the psychiatry of his day, saw in the division of the personality of Kundry the expression of a religious neurotic or hysteric. He adopts the role of the clinical psychologist, whereas Wagner had no intention of creating a case study.[32] It should instead be understood as the indirect result of the composer's will to incarnate a myth by according the enchantress figure a double role related both to the bad magic and to religious miracle. Wagner makes Kundry's being into something similar to the instruments of the Passion—both implicated in the suffering and yet the bearer of curative powers. She was first called Herodias, and like the legendary Ahasverus she offended Christ during his ordeal, laughing in his face as he passed before her. For this she was punished immediately, sentenced to wander forever. Her laughter never stops. And yet this "rose of hell" who becomes Klingsor's tool yearns for deliverance and contributes providentially to Parsifal's sacred coronation. Wagner wanted to have her be Jewish in her rebelliousness and Christian in her desire for peaceful reconciliation. Thus he endows her with a strange language that gives off cries and interjections that cut between insult and complaint. He shows her divided between a desire to harm and a wish to serve. It is her embrace that provoked the wound of Amfortas, the Grail King, but it is also she who tries to find a cure, seeking out medicines that in the end have no effect. These are the abstract threads for which Wagner found musical expression. In the grand scene of the second act when Kundry is given her orders by Klingsor, her language is deployed narratively, melodically, to defeat and ruin Parsifal. She tells him of the sufferings of his mother, Herzeleide, so as to awaken the deepest figure of his desire. She offers herself as though she knew that her greatest chance to seduce would be to adopt the mother's figure. She ardently kisses the young "fool," but in so doing, unable to pull him into impurity, she initiates him into the only worthwhile knowledge, that of pity. As a result of having come so close to it himself, Parsifal understands the defeat of Amfortas and his pain that never subsides. Kundry the wanderer thus places the hero on the path that brings him to his high priestly and military function: his role as the master of order, successor to the king disqualified by his mistake and his wound. Compassion henceforth is at its height and shelters Parsifal's heart from all peril. There will be only one avenue open to Kundry: to be baptized and die. She falters when the Grail shines forth at the approach of the final chord. At the same time, her defeat brings to an end her millenary punishment. Wagner infuses this death with a more profound religious significance than the death of the magician Ortrud at the end of *Lohengrin*, another enchantress who must also pay for her spells with her life.

THE DEFEAT OF THE ENCHANTRESSES

The medieval antecedents of the Wagnerian hero have been much explored. It was illuminating to revisit the texts that the composer meditated over while writing his libretto. But too little attention has been given to a comparative study between his own works and the operas that he directed in his youth, and this seems worth pursuing. A powerful pagan magician, Hidraot, king of Damascus, incites his niece, Armide, also a magician, to charm a Christian knight and hold him captive so as to divert him from battling in the Crusades. This is the plot of Quinault's *Armide*, a story inspired by Tasso's *Jerusalem Delivered* (1580), which served as the libretto for a Lully opera (1686) and later one by Gluck as well (1777). In the Tasso poem, Armida's palace is surrounded by sumptuous gardens where fruits and flowers mingle in an eternal spring.[33] In the Italian epic, Armida's last magic trick (song 18) to block the progress of the Crusaders consists of taking on the form of a tree surrounded by a troop of nymphs. "On stage and on the set we see wood goddesses with naked arms, dresses lifted to show feet in beautiful buskins, and hair worn loose—so appear the fantastic women of the forest. . . . They encircle Renaud who finds himself enclosed within their dances, a point within a circle."[34]

Wagner conducted Gluck's *Armide* in Dresden. He did not find that episode, which was not included in Quinault's opera. He must have noticed, however, the strange docility of the female magician who receives the orders from her uncle, the magician Hidraot, king of Damascus. Armide submits to him just as Kundry will to Klingsor. It is not far-fetched to believe that, like any educated man of his day, Wagner was familiar with *Jerusalem Delivered* and had Tasso's grand tableaux clearly in mind.

To be honest, it is not so much sources that I am seeking as proof of the persistence of a system of images in European culture. The comparison of similarities makes me all the more sensitive to the disparities. These two dangerous women are both adversaries of Christian knighthood. If many analogies can be drawn between these two imaginary figures, there are nonetheless differences that one is led to notice when it comes to the poetic treatment of the mythic material they share. I have already noted the importance of the initiating lesson about pity that Parsifal owes to Kundry. And what about Renaud? When Armide implores him not to leave her, Tasso writes that pity replaces the "fires of love" in the heart of the brave warrior: "His emotion is such that he can hardly hold back his tears; however, he keeps within his heart the feelings that are racing through him and does his best to maintain his composure." Reason and decorum win out. Pity here is only an allegorical element. We are far from the quasi-theological revelation that accompanies Kundry's kiss. Renaud pardons the sorceress and excuses himself courteously. "These are human weaknesses, ordinary mistakes." The major difference is that Tasso's Armida did not seek the eternal perdition of the valiant Renaud. Her loving magic strives only to keep him away from battle to weaken the Crusaders and assure victory for the Muslims. He is just a hostage held by pleasures. He of course fully deserves the reprimands of his liberators for the sins of the flesh into which the handsome warrior has let himself descend, but his situation has nothing in common with the ontological catastrophe undergone by Amfortas. The voluptuous pleasures Renaud tastes in the arms of Armide remain pardonable and do not have the same physical and metaphysical consequences. At the end of this epic tale, Renaud offers a kingdom to the defeated Armide while also inviting her to make a religious conversion. She submits: "Here is your slave." The surrender is accepted and compensated. Wagner, on the other hand, revives the very primitive idea of a "contagious magic" that allows for perdition or cure upon simple contact.

When comparing the concluding moments of *Parsifal* and the *Liberata*, one remains struck by a fundamental analogy: the defeat of the enchantresses is necessarily accompanied by the victory of the Christian knights. In Quinault's version, and later in Gluck, this defeat is only one of the variants of the happy end of the operatic tradition up to that point. The complaint of the abandoned sorceresses losing their powers could be the occasion for beautiful lamentations, but within a free and playful convention. In Quinault's libretto, Renaud pities Armide:

> Too unhappy Armide, alas!
> How your fate is deplorable!

We then see her, lost and desperate, causing her palace to be destroyed by demons and finally leaving the stage "on a flying chariot." Kundry, on the other hand, does not flee. She is first baptized at the end of the first tableau of the last act of *Parsifal*. Then at the end, as the curtain falls, Wagner's stage direction tells us that "she falls slowly to earth, lifeless." Quinault did not leave the fictional framework and made open use of machinery for the enchantress's flight. Wagner, for his part, with less ostentatious effects, seeks to place the spectators within a communion of regenerated faith situated at the imprecise border of Easter ritual and legendary invention. The Wagnerian enterprise mixes religion and the fairy world, miracle and magic, as was done in certain medieval mysteries. The interdiction of any applause at the end of *Parsifal*, now customary in certain places, testifies to the questionable blurring of differences between a product of fiction and the sacred, between aesthetic enjoyment and piety.

NIETZSCHE AGAINST THE "OLD ENCHANTER"

Irritated by Wagner's false piety (*Frömmelei*), his anti-Semitism, and by the triumph of the "ascetic ideal" in *Parsifal*, Nietzsche undertook a dismantling of the *Bühnenweihfestspiel* (literally, "solemn play for the consecration of a theater").[35] The extent of the reversal is revealed by this irreverent question: is not the theme that was so solemnly treated by Wagner—a young man defending his chastity—more suited to comedy or operetta?

Nietzsche was not forgetful, however, of his early enthusiasm for Wagner: "So many things seduce and invite me not to halt. For me, gardens of Armide are everywhere, and it is this fact that provokes new ruptures and new bitterness of heart!" And he continues, "I often look back in anger on the most beautiful things (*das Schönste*) that were unable to keep me back—because they didn't know how to keep me!"[36] The "gardens of Armide," unforgettably celebrated by Tasso, had become an expression for designating the pleasures that fill the senses. This remark from *The Gay Science* strikes me as an allusion to the rupture with Wagner. Wagner's person and his music are to be counted among the "most beautiful things" that did not know how to hold on to Nietzsche. Specifically, the "gardens of Armide" were those of Tribschen. In a letter to his friend Gersdorff dated March 11, 1870, in other words during the initial enchantment shortly after his first visit with Richard and Cosima, Nietzsche declares that "for [him], the names Schopenhauer and Wagner evoke all that is the very best and beautiful [*alles Beste und Schönste*]."[37] By his own admission, the welcome extended by the master and his companion was experienced by the young philologist as an initiation into the great mysteries. It is worth recalling that during one of the first visits to Tribschen at the end of 1869, one pastime with Wagner and Cosima consisted of reading aloud E. T. A. Hoffmann's "The Golden Pot."[38] The love of Anselm and Serpentina is fulfilled at the same moment as the revelation of a cosmic truth where, as Hoffmann puts it, "faith, love, and knowledge" are united. The art and spirit of childhood become guides to life, and in "the life as poem" "the sacred harmony of all beings shows itself to be nature's most profound secret." At the beginning of 1870, Nietzsche writes to his friend Erwin Rohde, "It is absolutely necessary that you also be initiated into this magic."[39] Then in a letter to Wagner from May 1870 Nietzsche writes, "May you remain what you were last year, my mystagogue in the secret teachings of art and life."[40]

At that time Nietzsche was already fond of games of opposition. In siding with the "Dionysiac" genius of Wagner, he had at the same time to condemn the "Socratism" and alexandrinism that he attributed to traditional opera from its earliest Florentine creations in Giovanni de Bardi's *Camarata*. He reproached these first operas for their nostalgia for a "paradisiacal life" and a "theoretic" illusion that consists of wanting to transmit words by having them be understood.[41] But the roles will change after the rupture with Wagner that comes in 1878. Nietzsche will put down on paper all the reasons for his deception. Is it not Wagner who is an ingenious illusionist? In the inventory of Wagner's faults, deceit and enchanting tricks are relentlessly decried. Wagner is an "old enchanter," "the Klingsor of all Klingsors," the "Cagliostro of modernity."[42] Seduced himself, he succumbed to the "enchantment" of Schopenhauer. The seductiveness he exerts leads back (*zurückverführt*) to a religious past. *Parsifal* is above all an "ingenious exercise in seduction." Wagner is nothing but a show-off or, worse, "an ingenious liar."[43] The disenchantment is complete and expresses itself in the language of demystification.

Nietzsche's personal disappointments and wounds and his horror at the crowds that rushed to the inaugural festivals at Bayreuth are not the only causes for these attacks.[44] On an intellectual level, the stakes were philosophical. Nietzsche freed himself from Schopenhauer after having admired him a great deal. While considering him an important "educator," he was unable to follow him toward an aesthetic that led to a "hatred of life" and a renunciation of the will. In contrast, Wagner's fervor for Schopenhauer became ever more pronounced after a reading encounter in 1854. Nietzsche analyzes perfectly the consequences of this encounter. We may recall that Wagner had, early on, wished for music, the servant of drama, to give all its abundance to poetic dramaturgy. By subordinating in this way music to drama, one could think that he was following the same line taken by Gluck (and it was on this basis that he was opposed in France). From the time of the romantic operas, Wagner was not satisfied with giving music the role of expressing the sentiments of the fictive characters; he wanted it to be capable of revealing the profound depths of the world. Music was not supposed to serve merely as a "means or 'medium'" but rise to the status of being the in-itself become manifest. At the same time, the will in which Schopenhauer saw the essence of reality is profoundly destructive. Wagner found in it the lessons of pity and renunciation. Thus his Siegfried goes from being the "revolutionary" in the first phase of the *Ring* project to being the vanquished.

Submerged in his intuition about the "will to power" and wishing to remain faithful to Dionysus, Nietzsche would not accept the "ascetic ideal" and the submission to faith for which Wagner becomes the precentor in *Parsifal*. In protest he drafts a sort of letter of accusation: far from applying his own stated program that intended art to be the inheritor of an exhausted religion, Wagner has become a seducer who returns to the religious attitudes of the past. Far from working on "the art work of the future," Wagner has become a pure reactionary. In Nietzsche's view, Wagner has committed yet another fault: he took liberties that permitted him to transform his musical creation into a vehicle for self-promotion. With his "supposed free thinking of passion" (*Freigeisterei der Leidenschaft*), he falls in with "Rousseau's intention,"[45] for which Nietzsche has no patience whatsoever. Nietzsche's considerations here offer a characteristic example of what later will be called the herme-neutics of suspicion. It consists of denouncing an egocentric interest and hypocrisy:

> He [Wagner] grasped all at once that with the Schopenhauerian theory and innovation *more* could be done *in majorem musicae gloriam*—namely, with the theory of the *sovereignty* of music as Schopenhauer conceived it: music set apart from all the other arts, the independent art as such, *not* offering images of phenom-enality, as the other arts did, but speaking rather the language of the will itself, directly out of the "abyss" as its most authentic, ele-mental, nonderivative revelation. With this extraordinary rise in the value of music that appeared to follow from Schopenhauerian philosophy, the value of *the musician* himself all at once went up in an unheard-of manner, too: from now on he became an oracle, a priest, indeed more than a priest, a kind of mouthpiece of the "in itself" of things, a telephone from the beyond—henceforth he uttered not only music, thus ventriloquist of God—he uttered metaphysics: no wonder he one day finally uttered *ascetic ideals*.[46]

According to Nietzsche, Wagner might well have considered the work of the composer as the manifestation of the profound depths of the world, but that manifestation was supplanted by the artist's self. Tannhäuser, the Dutchman, Lohengrin,[47] and even Tristan—are they not all figures of the artist? The Swedish poet Tomas Tranströmer fixes the image of Wagner in a striking way that Nietzsche would agree with: he is a "King Midas / He who changes into Wagner all that he touches."[48]

After their rupture, Nietzsche becomes more and more convinced that Wagner is an artist who works at building his own heroism. It seems to him that the negating energy that commands the ascetic re-nunciation in *Parsifal* implies, as a counterpart, an expression of self-af-firmation. Authority is transferred from religion to art and from art to the artist and his genius. The result is a glorious consecration to which both the musician and the philosopher lay claim: "What, then, is the meaning of the ascetic ideal in the case of a philosopher? My answer is—you will have guessed it long ago: the philosopher sees in it an optimum condition for the highest and boldest spirituality and smiles—he does *not* deny 'existence,' he rather affirms *his* existence and *only* his existence, and this perhaps to the point at which he is not far from harboring the impious wish: *pereat mundus, fiat philosophia, fiat philosophus, fiam* [let the world perish, let there be philosophy, let there be the philosopher, let there be me]!"[49]

Today, these words would apply perfectly to the "artists without works of art" whose identity is defined by "interventions" and "performances." One needs only to add to the list of Latin imperatives this leitmotif of today: *Pereat ars*—"May art perish." The artist ingeniously maneuvers to arrive alone, next to some pieces of debris, but having carefully established his or her legend and commercial value on the market. This is obviously not the reproach that Nietzsche is leveling at Wagner, he who produced such a sumptuous world, especially in *Tristan*, a work whose magic Nietzsche persists in admiring. The author of a fragmented body of work, he accuses the great musician of carrying over to his person the benefits of the seduction exerted by "the total work of art." With Wagner, the identification of the artist and the work of art as well as the aestheticization of the religious reach their apogee simultaneously.

For Nietzsche, what makes Wagner a show-off and a bigot is above all the victory that he claims to have carried off over carnal enchantments. In certain pages from *The Genealogy of Morals* that are unlikely to have escaped the attention of Freud and the early psychoanalytic circle, Nietzsche comes very close to formulating notions that will later be dubbed "repression," "conversion," and "sublimation." "Sensuality [*Sinnlichkeit*] does not disappear" when "renunciation," "the aesthetic state," or "the ascetic ideal" intervenes: sensuality only "transfigures itself" as soon as it "can no longer penetrate the conscience in the form of sexual excitement."[50] For the verb "transfigured," Nietzsche uses a half-invented borrowing from Latin: "*transfiguriert*," and this word contains and announces all the metamorphoses of the libido that Freud will only need to trace and differentiate into a classification of the various stages of this transfiguration.

The truth defended against the Wagnerian lie is sometimes called the "physiology of the aesthetic"[51] and sometimes "Dionysus." Nietzsche draws concurrently on the language of the biological sciences of his day and on that of myth. Dionysus is the signature he employs in his brief letter to Cosima written in a state of near-breakdown: "Ariadne, I love you." The names Ariadne and Cosima come up in the mad letter from January 6, 1889, addressed to Jacob Burckhardt: "The rest for Madame Cosima . . . Ariadne . . . Now and then there is enchantment."[52] We can entertain this dream: At the last moment, as Nietzsche is losing his intellectual faculties, the names of Cosima, Ariadne, and Dionysus, along with the verb that affirms the magic of enchantment (*zaubern*), constituted a last ensemble of images and intentions.

WHY NIETZSCHE PREFERS *CARMEN*

The acerbic criticism of *Parsifal* and the character Kundry is counterbalanced by the enthusiasm that seizes Nietzsche in November 1881 when he discovers Bizet's *Carmen*.[53] The Carmen character is for him the antidote to Kundry, that hysterical "old maid" pining for the "redemption" delivered by a young man. We now see him won over by the representation of "love as *fatum*, as fatality, cynical, innocent, cruel." He finds in it "nature precisely" and "the mortal hatred of the sexes."[54] Nature only, nothing but naked reality, but saved by the intensity of feelings.

The power of fascination Bizet's opera exerted over Nietzsche resembles an enchantment. It is known that he returned to see *Carmen* (1875) over twenty times between 1881 and 1888. It was the antidote to Wagner that he needed. He became attached to it in a compulsive way. As he says at the beginning of *The Case of Wagner*, Nietzsche discovered in this music a climate where he felt the growth of his own faculties for listening, thinking, and feeling the freedom of his spirit. To explain himself, Nietzsche makes use of a series of comparisons in which he places the accent on how much better he feels in himself and on the change that transforms the outer horizon: "I am becoming a better man. . . . One becomes more of a philosopher. . . . Here in all ways is the climate metamorphosed. Here, another sensuality is expressed, another sensibility, another gaiety." Everywhere a kind of molting occurs expressed by the multiplication of comparatives. Nietzsche sees here the conditions for fulfilling a wonderment that is more intense and all the more overwhelming for being produced soberly: the characters leave the established order, the climate becomes other, and the spectator feels himself becoming *another*. The author of *Zarathustra* finds himself under a southern sky, dry and limpid. He underlines approvingly the "African" characteristics of this opera. Perhaps remembering that Wagner had placed Klingsor and Kundry in a certain relation to the Arab world, Nietzsche perceives a "Moorish" quality in Carmen's dancing and in the two Gypsies whose dancing in the inn of Lillas Pastia opens the second act.

A few geography reminders will allow us to understand many things here. The gardens of Armide were situated in the Fortunate Islands, that is, in the Canaries. Kundry deployed her treachery in the castle of Klingsor, situated by Wagner on a mountainside of "Gothic Spain" turned toward the "Arab" south. The story of Carmen opens on a public square in Seville. There is a certain resemblance when it comes to the locales, all imaginary ones, of the three adventures. Is it possible to pursue the comparison beyond these topographical approximations? Most certainly, for we discover in each case a shared fundamental feature that is plotted in different ways. The common feature is an erotic captivation that turns a soldier away from his duty and in effect makes him desert. Wagner, as we saw, had already presented this turn in the bacchanal in *Tannhäuser*. Then in *Parsifal* he takes it up again in a more perverse way: the role of Venus passes to Kundry, who first wins the battle by wounding and disarming Amfortas but then fails with the "pure innocent one" predestined to become the leader and great pontiff of the Order of the Grail. The attractions of Armide had been entirely successful, but her hostage ended up escaping from her.[55] *Carmen* is yet another story of a lovers' yoke that makes a soldier leave the straight and narrow path prescribed by his duty. And each of these stories finishes badly for the seductress.

There are no enchanted gardens in *Carmen*, only Lillas Pastia's inn. The adventure unfolds within ordinary life; it is represented in a simple, "low" style without sublime pretensions. If there is a distancing effect, it comes from the local color of the Iberian setting. José is not a knight but an uncultivated soldier away from home. Far from being heroic, he must submit to regulations. He carries out orders that require him to enforce orderliness in the street and the workplace—he who will leave order behind him forever. The smugglers he joins up with belong to the picaresque world of rogues. He does not return to the camp when the curfew is sounded, and he is cut off from the voice of his mother who designates for him a fiancée.

Nietzsche's enthusiasm, if my interpretation is correct, pays homage to the elegance with which Bizet renounced all marvelous effects in favor of the advantages derived from a perfectly sober intensity. This would imply that there is a higher level of marvelous to be obtained by renouncing the standard kind. No magical panoplies. No religious stakes. The tragic story takes place under an open sky, without divinities or hell having anything to do with it. No evil instigators such as Hidraot and Klingsor. Carmen is not under hypnotic influence. The strangely uncanny confines itself to the card game from which comes the warning of death. When Nietzsche praises the presence of *fatum*—signaled from the beginning by a haunting musical theme—one must keep in mind that in *Carmen* everything begins with a meeting that should not happen at a place and time that should not be, but out of which, precisely, an irrevocable and relentless passion takes over a man. What Nietzsche calls "inflexible necessity" occurs by chance with the arrival of the cigar makers in the workshop, a world regulated by the work clock and military drills. Carmen, an adventurer and simple laborer, is a free, sovereign woman who accepts the risks of her demands and decisions in love. Her means are those of the body: a look, a dancing movement, and especially her voice and song that give full meaning and force to the central syllable in the word "enchantment." The energy of this song or chant allows the music to inscribe itself within complete orderly structures in accordance with the customary alternation between sequences of speaking and singing in French *opéra comique*—far, in other words, from the "infinite melody" of Wagnerian orchestral discourse. And especially far from the call to religious transcendence that Nietzsche denounces in Wagner as an alibi for his desire to inflate the prestige of the artist's person.

I have been examining some aspects of enchantment as they occur in various texts and musical scores over a two-hundred-year period.
My main concern has been to show how enchantment became the property par excellence of the artist, the power that he takes possession of and the image that he gives of himself. My aim has not been to provide an inventory of seductresses. If my assignment were to display the great female magicians in opera, one would have to say I have failed. Nor have I established an inventory of the rhetorical situations

called for by this type of role: jealousy, frustrated love, declarations of hate, supplication, and commands addressed to demons. The role of Medea has suited great female tragedians and singers. The dramatic works in which she figures have lent themselves to beautiful stage effects. And because wicked illusions are doomed to defeat, one could also put stage-set machinery to work, first to construct magical castles and then to represent their disintegration. The music would then find occasions to pour on the pathos, since the exit aria of vanquished seductresses had typically to be plaintive. The sublime example of Alcina in Handel's opera is a supreme achievement in the art of melody. One hears simultaneously the regret of lost powers and the *lamento* of the abandoned lover. The audience cannot refuse her its pity.

Nietzsche admires in the last scene of *Carmen* the "tragic humor" of José's avowal. He sees in it "the essence of love": "Yes, it is I who killed her, Carmen, my adored Carmen!" In the history of European opera, the moment has arrived when seductresses have no other power than that of their bodies, their voices, and their lives. In symmetry with the rapidity of the love that they cause to be born at first sight, there is the suddenness of their death that is met at the pointed white tip of a brandished weapon or on the order of a tyrant. "Kill this woman," orders Herod at the end of *Salomé* (1905) by Oscar Wilde and Richard Strauss. The knife of Jack the Ripper at the end of *Lulu* seems to have been taken from the hand of José. The jealousy of the poor soldier, which resembles that of Büchner's Woyzeck, gives way to the mad blindness of the serial killer. It was the truth of the moment in Europe in 1935 when Alban Berg died.

Mozart

CHAPTER 2

The Da Ponte Operas

Should we read Da Ponte as a writer? Yes, since he produced work that
Mozart expected of a poet. The librettos he wrote were good guides for
the music. They met with an orchestral and vocal action that exceeds
them but from which they are inseparable. The words of Da Ponte are
always present in the arias they have become. It is forever impossible to
cancel out the music that seized them in flight and illuminated them.
When Da Ponte writes for Martin y Soler or for Salieri, the characteristics of his language are always recognizable. All that's missing is the
complement of musical genius produced by the contact with Mozart.

Mozart's desire to link his musical inventiveness to some theatrical
representation was awakened very early. His consciousness of his gifts
was inseparable from a desire for opera. He had already let this be known
in childhood, and he never missed an occasion to bring his music into
the theater. This desire grew continuously as he became more aware of
his capabilities. In instrumental music, as Charles Rosen has noted, he

excelled at the deployment of the virtual dramatic dimensions of the "classical style."[1] The letter of February 7, 1778, written to his father before leaving Mannheim for Paris, is often cited in this regard: "To write an opera is my obsession: preferably a French opera rather than German, but above all else an Italian opera."[2] He asks to read librettos and examines dozens of them. From the start he becomes aware of the musical genres linked to each language. In the same way that lyric tragedy [tragédie lyrique] is French, the comic opera [opéra bouffe] is Italian. Within the humorous multilingual thread of his letters, Mozart often passes into Italian when he wants to give added bite to some joke or jibe. Comedy attracts him, and it is therefore the Italian language that he needs.

Before meeting Da Ponte in Vienna, Mozart had many occasions to reflect on the relationships between words and music. He knows full well that the poet and the musician must come to an understanding when it comes to the circumstances of the commission, the resources at their disposal, the singers who will be available, and the allusions that the public will be able to find in their work. With Giambattista Varesco, the chaplain of the court of Salzburg, the adjustments to the libretto for Idomeneo (1781), an opera seria, did not come painlessly. Compromises were necessary. But the result allowed Mozart to affirm all his dramatic talent. Later, despite all Mozart's goodwill, the same poet showed himself incapable of injecting life into a subject for a comic opera. His Oca del Cairo became lost in absurdities. With Da Ponte, Mozart finally found a librettist who listened to him, who understood his wishes, and who did not weigh him down with opaque words.

In the beautiful dialogue entitled "The Poet and the Composer" E. T. A. Hoffmann declares that "for his classical operas, Mozart only chose poems perfectly adaptable to music."[3] Hoffmann is probably thinking of Da Ponte and Schikaneder when he affirms metaphorically that the poet can "penetrate to the true essence of the music without having received minor orders at seminary." In fact, Da Ponte, a priest with no parish, had received minor orders and had even taught novices the rules of poetry and rhetoric. Going a bit further, Hoffmann adds, "the linked affinities of the poet and the composer are such that one could say they belong to the same church, because the mystery of language and sound is the same, and it is this which gives both of them access to the supreme initiation." Mozart put it more simply: "The best situation is when a good composer, who understands theater and who is capable of suggesting ideas, meets a poet of sound judgment, a true phoenix."[4] Mozart did not hold back from "suggesting ideas" to Da Ponte who in turn was able to make use of them instantly. In his memoirs, Da Ponte acknowledges that the idea of setting Beaumarchais's *The Marriage of Figaro* to music came to him from the composer. "In conversation with me one day . . . he asked me whether I could easily make an opera from a comedy by Beaumarchais—*Le Mariage de Figaro*."[5] So the initiative came from the musician. In this case, it was not the music adapting to a well-chosen text but the poet who satisfied the request of the musician who had spoken to him of a play that had been a scandalous success in France. It is true that when it comes to literary antecedents, one would have to go back further. When writing his *Barber of Seville* and *Marriage of Figaro*, Beaumarchais had clearly in mind the characters from the commedia dell'arte as well as the theater of fairs and the songs of French vaudeville. Mozart's music, so new, sought a context for itself in this contemporary drama that had recently caused such a scandal in Paris and Vienna but adapted roles from a universe of fictions and character types that had become consecrated by theatrical traditions. It took the supreme skill of Da Ponte for Mozart's music both to tie in with Beaumarchais's sources and to cast in a new language the cascade of events that fill the *mad day* of the French writer.

E. T. A. Hoffmann, as I just mentioned, clearly put forward the responsibility of the librettist. The challenge is to render the action intelligible for the spectators, independently of the clear reception of each of the words being sung. The poet's job is "to arrange the scenes that the subject-matter clearly unfolds before the spectator's eyes." "Almost without understanding one word, the spectator must be able to form an idea of the plot from what he sees taking place. No dramatic medium needs this clarity to a greater degree than opera. Besides the fact that even with clearest singing the words are always harder to understand than elsewhere, the music all to easily transports the listener to distant regions and can be kept under control only by being continually directed to the point at which the dramatic effect is concentrated."[6]

Da Ponte had great instincts when it came to the ordering of scenes. Even before the admixture of music, costumes, sets, and stagecraft, one gets a strong sense of the flow of what takes place simply from listening to the words of the Da Ponte operas. The librettist had a lively knack when it came to editing, the attack of a speech, and apostrophe. His words and sentences stick in the mind and, thanks to Mozart, are propelled by music in such a way that they never leave us: "Se vuol ballare," "Non più andrai," "Madamina, il catalogo è questo," "Batti, batti." The writing of Da Ponte is already pregnant before the music comes to increase its significance further. He manages this by varying the meter of verses, the play of vowels, alliteration, rhymes, and the words pronounced together by two or three performers. The couple Mozart–Da Ponte requires listeners capable of simultaneously perceiving the word, the melody, and its structure, as well as an unexpected modulation, accompaniment, instrumental timbre, or contrapuntal motif. Our senses are subjected to continuous surprises. In response, we need to become more fully awake and in effect change the tempo of our own lives.

As a result, our pleasure multiplies, and we desire to rehear that which has overwhelmed our capacity to hear. One must at the same time focus one's attention and surrender it in order to be able to follow the flux of a life that is faster than life itself. With Da Ponte's complicity, Mozart is the supreme master of cumulative effects. Together, they succeed perfectly at upping the comic ante that drives the opera buffa forward. The principle of this surpassing or outbidding is given in Beaumarchais by the trumping [encore mieux] of Bazile when he is surprised or feigns surprise when the count discovers Chérubin huddled in Suzanne's armchair. Clarity is never lacking when the action that Mozart leads forward has been traced out by Da Ponte. A perfect economy of means contributes to the enchanting flash that comes with a rush of pleasure and not an ounce of confusion.

Opera, a species of theater heightened by the power of music, faces the challenge of its readability. Being linked from its origins to festivals, it needed to be both orderly and prodigious. Voices, spectacles, sets, costumes, and props multiply the sources of excitement and call for a type of attention that allows itself to be overwhelmed. Who is saying what onstage? Who is doing what? What situation, what moment in the action requires an aria? What are the relations of weakness and of power, of love and hate between the characters? In a famous passage from Madame Bovary set at the Rouen opera house, Charles can't make heads or tails of the unfolding action of Lucia di Lammermoor. This is not the case for Emma, whose experience as a reader of romances, writes Flaubert, facilitates for her "the intelligence of the libretto." Who has not felt lost at the opera like poor "charbovari"? The sung words that we have taken in without understanding, perhaps because they've melted into the melody or been covered by the orchestra, escape us and yet capture our imaginations. They are false windows. The accidentally misheard and the phonically equivocal are often charged with a strange poetic quality, like the language of adults misunderstood by children or the language of a foreigner mistaken by the passing traveler. Michel Leiris convinces us of this in the volumes of his *Règle du jeu*: a consciousness that has recovered from its errors recognizes belatedly the charm of the approximations that had led it into illusion. The risk of misunderstanding is far less when the action is traced by a Da Ponte and brought to its fulfillment by Mozart. In the Da Ponte operas the clarity owes much to precise vocabulary, lively syntax, memorable formulations, and especially to a practice of suggestion [*sous-entendu*] that opens the way for a music that makes abundantly clear that which only music has the power to say. The absolute masterpiece in this regard is the recitative and sextet in the third act of *Figaro* (scene 5). Mozart is left all the more free when Da Ponte adroitly restrains the overly loquacious verve of Beaumarchais. Fewer words and more music—that is the secret.

In the programs for the first productions of *Figaro*, *Don Giovanni*, and *Così fan tutte*, the poet and the musician are announced side by side. The poet is even listed before the musician. This was customary, and Mozart had no reason to diverge from it. He knew from experience that a good librettist is something rare. *La Poesia è dell'Ab. Da Ponte [. . .] La musica è del Signor Wolgango Mozzart [sic], Maestro di Cap. Tedesco.* When Da Ponte, whose vanity never sleeps, recounts in his memoirs the success of *Don Giovanni* in Prague, the exclamations through which he says he received the news link the two names in the same order: "*Vive Da Ponte! Vive Mozart!*" Much later, when he stages a production of *Don Giovanni* in New York in 1826, Da Ponte will pay homage in the program to Mozart's genius while at the same time requesting that his modest contribution be acknowledged: "I willingly leave to this immortal genius all the glory that he deserves for his splendid works. But permit me to hope that one ray of this glory will fall on me, since it happens to have been my poetic works that were able to give life to those immortal treasures."

READING, SINGING

Speak the line of poetry before singing it. This is the advice that a singing instructor still gives his students today. Why? Because a singer, and in particular an opera singer, must begin by understanding what it is he or she is singing. This recommendation also applies to the lied.

Read first, and out loud, the operatic text. Do people know just how important this act was in the history of musical theories of the eighteenth century, and notably for Rousseau? In *La Nouvelle Héloïse*, Julie describes her music lessons under the direction of her Italian instructor: "I begin each lesson by reading a few octaves of Tasso or some scene of Metastasio. He then has me pronounce with accompaniment some piece of recitative and I believe I'm continuing to speak or read, something which certainly didn't happen to me with French recitative."[8] The art of singing develops out of the art of speaking so long as it takes place in a language that is naturally musical, such as Italian. Singing is the same as declaiming, but with the substitution of the "voice of song" for the "voice of speech." And composing music is like reading a poem in a way that unleashes its fullest sonority. In the entry "Genius" in his *Dictionnaire de la musique*, here is the advice Rousseau gives the reader: "Take Metastasio and work. His genius will train yours, you will create following his example; that is what makes genius, and other eyes will soon shed for you the tears that the masters made you shed."[9] Such is the weight of the poem in the sequential acts of giving, taking, and rendering. A text of genius chooses its own music and musician, or at least it effortlessly sweeps aside "bad musicians" who possess only "the mechanics of their art." The accents invented by the musician will only amplify the accents of the poetic diction. Melody and its accompaniment must allow their steps to be dictated by the language and by the feeling that animates it. Reaching back to Greece as his distant model, Rousseau wants the accompanied recitative and the opera aria to obey the poem. All is lost, he believes, when music and poetry separate. The evil has already happened, and today it is already too late: "After having tested and felt its strengths, music as soon as it can walk alone begins to disdain the poetry that it is supposed to accompany; it believes it's worth more as it derives from itself the beauties that it used to share with its companion. It still offers, it's true, to render the ideas and feelings of the poet, but it adopts another language in a way; and although the goal is the same, the poet and the musician, being too separate in their work, end up offering two images that are similar but distinct and mutually destructive."[10]

Are these criticisms aimed at Rameau and the French musicians of the Lully tradition? Did Rousseau so poorly recognize their art of phrasing and exacting diction? Is the object of his criticism not rather the vocal virtuosity of the opera seria? This at any rate is the evil that Rousseau's admirer Gluck wants to cure by achieving his famous "reform" that consists of declaring his total submission to the dictates of the text. In the preface to *Alceste* he writes, "I thought of reducing music to its true function, namely to serve poetry and the expression of sentiments and situations within the fable without interrupting the action with ridiculous and superfluous ornaments."[11] One gets the same message, with perfect Rousseauian orthodoxy, in the "Preliminary discourse" that Beaumarchais wrote in 1787 for his dramatic fable *Tarare*. He wants his musician to be no more than a reader-translator: "There is too much music in the music for theater, it is always overloaded; to use the colloquial expression of a deservedly famous man, the celebrated chevalier Gluck, our opera stinks of music: *puzza di musica.* . . . And if my musician possesses a true talent, if he thinks before writing, he will realize that his duty and his success consist only in rendering my thoughts in a more harmonious language, giving them a stronger expression, and not in making an entirely separate work. The imprudent one who wants to shine alone is only a phosphorescence, a will-o'-the-wisp."[12]

What musician would consent to "render the thoughts" of Beaumarchais and not "shine alone"? Beaumarchais had hoped that in Paris it would be Gluck himself. In fact, it turned out to be Salieri who was recommended by Gluck, and Beaumarchais has no end of praise for the composer's docility. But when it came to putting on *Tarare* in Vienna, Salieri realized that for the brilliant Italian artists who worked there, the music that he had composed for the French, who are "more actors than singers," was too "short on song." In Paris acerbic critics had said that Beaumarchais required music that wasn't music. For the Viennese productions it was not enough simply to translate Beaumarchais. A new libretto had to be composed and the music considerably altered. The musical element needed to be given a more ample role, be allowed to overcome its subordinate position, and let a few sparks fly. Lorenzo Da

Ponte was put in charge of the Italian adaptation of the libretto for this allegorical tale. He saw no objection to the musician exercising greater liberty. It was moreover a flattering commission for a princely wedding. From the French *Tarare* was born the Italian *Axur*, and it was well received, even though the preparations that recalled Da Ponte to Vienna made him miss the final rehearsals in Prague of his *Don Giovanni*.

Mozart, for his part, wanted to keep a free hand. He denied himself nothing. That is why he needed a librettist who would also refuse him nothing—and especially one who could accept that from the opening bars of the overture the music would lead the way with the words seeming to rise up out of the music. For the dramatic spirit to take wing, at no moment could the music appear captive to the written page that only served as its support. To satisfy Mozart's wish, the important thing was that a mixture of music and words occupy every instant in the constant flow of a dramatized adventure. Music, henceforward, is not the redundant fulfillment of poetic language but its unpredictable relay. With a Da Ponte text this strategy was possible. I am not saying simply that in their concision and lightness, with their deft little tricks, the libretti of Da Ponte allowed Mozart sufficient room to work. His texts had themselves such an energetic charge and such drive that the music, bouncing off the words and with the words, could chart a path within a space that submitted to its law. For this reason Da Ponte was the perfect answer to Mozart's wishes. "In an opera, it is absolutely necessary that poetry be the obedient daughter of the music."[13] Alfred Einstein remarked that this famous declaration of Mozart in a letter to his father dated October 13, 1781, is "the exact opposite of the theory of Gluck who with his 'reform' of opera seemed to have forgotten that he was a musician."[14] Let's recall again Mozart's insistent affirmations in this same letter: "Yes, an opera will be all the more pleasing when the outline of the drama is well established and the words have been written expressly for the music instead of being chosen to allow for this or that supposedly agreeable rhyme. . . . The latter that sometimes go on for verse after verse can ruin the composer's whole idea." It is easy to conjecture that this is precisely the contract that was tacitly agreed upon by Mozart and Da Ponte. And other composers who collaborated with Da Ponte, though not Mozart's equals, were nevertheless able to give the best of themselves.

Da Ponte's memoirs are not noted for their modesty, and yet he does not actually attribute any merit to himself other than being an excellent purveyor of "dramas for music." He claims for his texts the honor of having paved the way for a large number of theatrical successes. Too happy to have received his commissions, he didn't concern himself with defending the theoretical preeminence of poetry. He wanted only to beat out rival librettists, principally Giambattista Casti, whom he depicts as a rogue but who did hold a dominant position in Vienna thanks to a clique of supporters. It is certainly not Lorenzo that Clemens Krauss and Richard Strauss were seeking to represent with their creation of the poet Olivier in *Capriccio*.

But let's let him describe his work habits in his own words. We can reread the famous passage in which he recounts how he managed to take on the job of writing simultaneously *Don Giovanni*, *The Tree of Diana*, and *Axur re d'Ormus*. He relates or reinvents the report he gave to the emperor: "I shall write evenings for Mozart, imagining I am reading the *Inferno*; mornings I shall work for Martini [Martin y Soler] and pretend I am studying Petrarch; my afternoons will be for Salieri. He is my Tasso!"[15] He makes use of inspirational reminiscences. The poet who has put himself in the service of three different musicians positions himself as a reader of the founding geniuses of Italian literature. He has no fear of presenting his own writing as an imagined reading; he depicts himself as going back and forth between models from the past and theatrical productions yet to come. He asks the assistance of those models while at the same time making the most of his turn to write and yet doing so under the express wishes of the musicians who will be reading him very soon. He establishes his work as a relay between the written word of earlier masters of poetry and the new music that a contemporary maestro will distribute to voices and an orchestra. He accepts being a link within a grand tradition.

Isn't it remarkable that the same reference to important predecessors applies both to *The Tree of Diana*, an erotic fable invented by Da Ponte himself (who borrowed from the myth of Endymion and from the dramatic style of Gozzi), and to the libretti where he relied directly on recent texts of Giovanni Bertati (for *Don Giovanni*) and Beaumarchais (for *Axur*)? Da Ponte could no longer say openly that he considered himself an epigone following the example of his rivals. Justly proud of his promptness and unstoppable ardor, he made hardly any distinction among creating, imitating, and rewriting. The truth is that he did not conceive of his role as a poet as requiring the manifestation of an original personality. It was enough for him as a librettist to make hit shows. His declarations in this regard need to be taken literally: he writes to please Joseph II, for his mistress and protégée la Ferrarese, to answer the demands of the composers, and so on. These objective goals are very different from the subjective ones that romanticism will assign to the act of writing. When it's Mozart who seizes on the words and who sees the subjective depth as being music's prerogative, one can be thankful that Da Ponte was content with his artisan's conception of the poem.

Happily, he never suspected—to my knowledge—that his genius was linked to an intuition of the rhythms of speech. The very complicated art of weighing syllables came automatically for him. He did not turn it into a subject for theoretical speculations; he had a feel for it that was simply a natural gift. But Da Ponte's tact with language did not cross over into his relations with people. In his personal life he was rather ill-behaved. His whims would turn into failures, his good fortune into misfortune. Many times, by his own fault, he was required to flee. He would not compose his memoirs in a castle in Bohemia like his friend Casanova but instead scribbled them in New York while juggling book-selling, teaching literature, importing and selling various articles, and show managing—always needy and always tied to expedients.

His memoirs give an inside view of everything that went into his work as a librettist. One learns that it was established practice for him to be in charge of directing the actors and supervising the staging. Moreover, we know that in Prague demands for last-minute changes in *Don Giovanni* were submitted to Da Ponte (who received advice from Casanova). Directing the actors was included in the job description of the "poet" hired by a given theater. For the duration of his tenure as poet of the King's Theater in London, Da Ponte tells us that his responsibilities included producing adaptations but also various editing jobs and the stage production for all plays.[16]

Nevertheless, it should be recalled that the works that have survived thanks to their beauty and etched themselves into our memory were made to change hands and to be sung by new voices and reach new audiences. The creators do not remain masters of the game for long. The specialists recruited from the very beginning for opera—theater directors or troupe directors, composers or first violinists turned conductors, set designers, stage directors—become the trustees of that which the culture has not wanted to erase from its memory. Da Ponte had the extraordinary privilege of being doubly present for three of Mozart's greatest works: both at the moment of their conception and later for their world premieres. He has left a written record of his initial contribution, but there remains no such trace of the second important moment.

Listening to Da Ponte's answers to what was asked of him, it would seem Mozart did indeed find the élan for his music that he needed. Today it is up to the director to add to the creative élan of the musician a new reading offered to the senses of the audience. The direction that comes late into the picture has taken on the status of an autonomous art associated with the work of the set designer. The staging is also a creation with the privilege of being the work of a living person intended for the eyes of other living people. It is a choreography that extends over the whole spectacle, and it is haunted by the temptation to steal the show. The recent fashion of creative stagings has brought attention to directors for whom the masterpieces of the repertoire are pretexts for the free expression of their personalities and in some cases have been turned into the soundtrack of their phantasms. It would seem that they seek the public's admiring endorsement of the audacity of their own personal dance. I breathe more easily when a contemporary musician teams up with a poet, and the two try to cooperate, despite the risks, with a set designer and stage director. Berio and Calvino were able to do this for *Un Re in Ascolto*.

True, when a work is created nowadays there is some chance of there being an inspired direction of the actors thanks to the leadership of the writer and composer, as was the case with Da Ponte and Mozart in Prague. When it comes to breathing life into the masterpieces of the past, the job of today's performers is to reinvent a relationship of complicity. One can judge from the results the link between Mozart and Da Ponte at the moment of creation. It is impossible to reconstitute it in all its freshness. This is why directors must absolutely connect with it via their imaginations and play the game that was executed so successfully by the originators.

CHAPTER 3

The Marriage of Figaro

VERY EARLY IN THE MORNING, LATE AT NIGHT

The opera of Da Ponte and Mozart was, for the time, unusually long. Some spectators in Vienna complained about this.

Da Ponte justifies himself in his preface: the librettist may have tried to condense Beaumarchais's text to the point of reducing it to an "extract," and yet "the opera would not be among the shortest works that have been staged." The great length, he insists, could not be avoided in a "drama" of such "amplitude and grandeur." For the public, what comes out of the collaboration between poet and musician is a "genre of spectacle almost never seen before."

Even though their dimensions are exceptional, *The Marriage of Figaro* (1778, 1784) and *Le nozze di Figaro* (1786) nevertheless remain, in keeping with classical convention, within "a single passage of the sun": the rule of the unity of time is perfectly respected. There is just one day, but it is filled to the very brim.

Beaumarchais entitled his play *La Folle Journée* (*The Mad Day*). Madness is in everyone and everything. It is in the agitation that gives free rein to the unpredictable and to emotions that are constantly interrupted and transformed into their opposites. Everyone rises early in the castle of Aguas Frescas . . . and everyone goes to bed very late on a wedding night. During the day people run from surprise to surprise, from desires to disappointments to new desires.

The plot includes so many twists, its machinery introduces so many characters, so many plans are traversed, and so many misunderstandings, tricks, and revelations occur that need to be taken into account. The social obstacles are everywhere, but they exist only for our pleasure in seeing them fall. When it comes to the energy of life, the more it is opposed, the more it is joyously victorious: it shoots the gulf and invents oblique passageways that attain the desired goal better than the direct route would have. The duration of the work is necessarily long since the thicket of events grows rapidly. The speed with which things change extends the apparent length of the day. Chance is prodigal and the cup overflows. At every moment, instead of something that we expect happening, something else occurs—a catastrophe or an ephemeral success. In this way comes a torrent of provocations and expedients, with projects being supplanted by other projects, travesties leading to more travesties, marriages leading to other marriages or arrangements.

Figaro was a stolen child. He rediscovers his parents in the odd couple—the *dottor* Bartolo and Marcellina—that wants to hinder his marriage. Along the way many objects and people will get lost, substituted, and found. Those rediscovered are not the ones that were being sought. Capricious fortune delights in having one pop up in the place of another. "Non la trovo," sings Barbarina at the beginning of the fourth act, when a needle has fallen from her hands. "Non la trovo, e girai tutto il bosco"—"I cannot find her and I looked through the whole wood"—sings shortly afterward the count, who is pursuing Susanna. Not knowing what objects are being looked for, it is hardly surprising that the spectator gets frequently lost as well!

A DRIFT AWAY AND A RETURN

The initiative in the first two acts belongs to Figaro. As soon as the count's designs on Susanna are known, Figaro undertakes to dupe him, to "divide" his mind, by rendering him jealous of the countess and putting him on the track of a false Susanna, Cherubino, dressed in Susanna's clothes. "Così potrem più presto imbarazzarlo, confonderlo, imbrogliarlo, rovesciargli i progetti"—"thus I will all the quicker be able to bother, confuse, and entrap him and upset his projects" (act 2, scene 2). But the one who wanted to overturn finds himself overturned: in the second act; Figaro's plan goes awry. From this moment the ingenious servant loses the upper hand. This entire act, so full of effervescent emotions, is one immense ado about nothing.

In what follows, Figaro will be tricked almost as much as the count, but in ways that will redound in his favor. He thinks he is betrayed by Susanna, but he's not. The count believes he has been lucky in love, but he has only been lured in. The second plot, hatched by the women, gives them command over events. This new stratagem will succeed; it drives the last two acts forward and leads to the happy dénouement. Let's recall the gears and springs assembled by the clockmaker Beaumarchais. Chérubin must slip away, now being too suspect. In his place, the countess will put on Susanna's dress for the evening party, and it is therefore the spouse who will capture the wandering desire of the unfaithful count. This second substitution has the effect of turning the libertine drifting-away of the count into a return that was not at all what he had wished for. So near to his amorous goal and believing he's about to take hold of new prey, it turns out he's being faithful despite himself.

The return and the recognition. We rediscover here a time-honored law of dramaturgy, but which holds as well in the area of the other chronometric art that is music. According to Diderot, musical composition is to be regulated by laws of successive departure and return, out and back.[1] And this is what Mozart does with the tonalities of the different acts and throughout the entire opera. The lure of a new love throws the count at the feet of his rightful spouse. Tripped up by his own infidelity, l'uccellatore (the bird catcher) gets caught in a cage of his own making, and extreme disorder will finally have served to restore order. It turns out that the count is abused neither by his valet nor by his handsome page but by the object of his desire. D major is both the shore of departure and of return.

Hours pass by in this way at a leisurely pace, and a profusion of whims and domino effects precipitates an endless stream of catastrophes. Amid the tight succession of instants that erase each other, amid the rush toward an uncertain future whose restored order is only accidental, there is also a place for some suspended moments. The sublime arias of the countess have no precedent in Beaumarchais. They are innovations of Mozart and Da Ponte that give the opera a profound quality that the French text lacks. These lyrical moments made up of superficial ricochets insert into the action a dimension of regret and a backward glance toward the past. Yet these "meditative pauses" (the expression comes from Jean Rousset) of the melancholy wife have an accent and a consequence that do not at all interrupt the chain of events. We know better to whose heart the final request for pardon will be addressed and who will be granting that request. The moving-about only slows down at the beginning of the fourth act with the arias of Marcellina and Basilio. These are only self-portraits or commentaries conferred to secondary characters, but they occur sufficiently late not to compromise the general dynamic of the work.

GIVING PRIORITY TO MUSIC

In Da Ponte's memoirs, the account of the composition of *Figaro* says more than it seems at first: "I set to work, accordingly, and as fast as I wrote the words, Mozart set them to music. In six weeks everything was in order."[2] It is impossible to imagine the poet and the musician not being together every step of the way, impossible to think of them not conferring about the division into acts or that Mozart did not have in mind the distribution of solo arias, duos, ensembles, and the movement that would be accorded to the finales. From the table where the poet was writing, the newly minted text would pass directly for inspection to the composer, its first and unique addressee, before the theater public became the general recipient of the joint efforts of the poet and the musician.

And since it seems to me his will would be very great, I can only imagine that Mozart made his librettist adhere to what he alone could decide would be the direction to advance in. He could not receive a part of Da Ponte's libretto without understanding with his ears what would come next in the dramatic action and choosing the voice, the character, or group of actors who would then have to receive their cue in order to enter into the musical development. He would also know what events, what keys, and what tempi were musically necessary for the work to progress. Therefore he probably gave Da Ponte appropriate guidelines so that the following sections of his work as poet would correspond to what the internal dynamic of the opera-in-progress called for (with all concessions of course being made to the contingencies at hand: the talent of the singers, vocal ranges, whims, and vanities to be satisfied). Mozart had too much to say to leave it up to the poet to say whatever he liked. The text he needed would have to lend itself to being worked on and surpassed by the music. If this were not so, how is one to explain the fact that when writing for Mozart Da Ponte composed so many ensembles—indeed far more than one finds in his libretti written for other musicians? Nowhere in the poems he wrote for Salieri or Martin y Soler does one find a succession of duos, trios, and so on comparable to that which constitutes the weave of the admirable second act of *Figaro*.

The sovereignty of motion, so noticeable in Beaumarchais's play, probably determined Mozart's choice. It was not simply that the comedy by the French author was surrounded in scandal or that it poked holes in the prerogatives of the nobility. Mozart no doubt appreciated anything that could activate musical expression—and that offered a story that was not likely to put one to sleep! Mozart was exasperated by all the attention given to rhyme, by the running in place, and prolixity that characterized the work of most librettists. He needed very lively action that would rapidly transform the situations on stage and the feelings of the characters.

The work of Beaumarchais possessed this kinetic élan. It only needed to be made a bit less long-winded, to be slimmed down when it came to the liberal circulation of bons mots in the recitatives and the bursts of dry and short exchanges, and to be nourished with true lyricism. In Mozart's way of thinking, the music asked only to run with the action. The music would surely find in Beaumarchais all that would give occasion for solos in a given situation and beautiful parting arias. But with the help of Da Ponte the music would also find everything that was missing from the usual libretti: the occasion to construct ensembles through which situations would metamorphose and where the plot would take on further ramifications thanks to the polyphonic confrontation between characters.

Before Da Ponte set to writing his text, one has to imagine that

Mozart let him know what he desired when it came to musical requirements; in other words, what would belong to the recitative, what to soloists eager for the limelight, and what to ensembles that would allow his musical verve to run free. There is no doubt that in the libretto for *Figaro*, the contribution of Da Ponte's genius consisted not only in the speed and precision of each gesture but also in his attentiveness to Mozart's intentions. It seems difficult to believe that Da Ponte would have taken on his own authority the initiative of planning out and editing the sequence of accompanied recitatives and arias—the idea, for example, of the terzetto of the first act, of the immense and superb finale of the second act, of the prodigious sextet of recognition in the third act, and so forth. And one can imagine that upon receiving the written composition of his poet, Mozart would specify the layout and arrangements that he envisioned for the next part of the project. Da Ponte was talented enough to bring to the composer a highly polished libretto that would outline sufficiently the shape of the action while allowing the musical discourse to develop from surprise to surprise. In other words, the language left open the considerable room for maneuver demanded by the music. The latter could proceed unhindered beyond the text and take feelings to their extreme limits, namely, to mad intoxication and extreme happiness.

The "room" I am talking about could also be called *il resto*, "the rest." The emblem of the music surpassing the libretto is offered in the words of Figaro in the grand aria of the fourth act (scene 8): "Il resto nol dico"—"The rest, I don't say." This rest, so troubled, so voluptuous, so painful sometimes, is not something verbal discourse has the power to express. The heavy laugh of the chorus in the orchestral accompaniment articulates this rest with sufficient acuity and irony. Of course, in the first scene, when Figaro makes his demand, "udir bramo il resto"—"I want to hear the rest"—Susanna gives her answer. But even when the text lets us know the scandalous rest, the words of the poet alone are not able and neither do they wish to say everything. Because the irreducible "rest" belongs to music, and it alone can deliver its fleeting plenitude. The message is given again in the exquisite duettino of the letter in the third act (scene 10), a letter whose promise and gentle caress so lightly insinuated in its Sicilian rhythm are also a lesson for the listener: "Ei già il resto capirà"—"The rest he will understand already."

THE RANGE OF CHARACTERS

Even by reducing the sixteen characters in the French play to eleven, Da Ponte and Mozart had plenty to work with when it came to mobilizing this world of social conditions and vast catalog of diverse passions.

They retained the space that Beaumarchais chose for his little people to circulate in. From the gardener to the count, from the doctor (Bartolo) to the legal expert (Curzio), from Figaro to the singing master Basilio with his "low black hat, short soutane, and long coat" (treated by Beaumarchais as an organist with some clerical experience)—the different rungs on the social ladder are remarkably well represented. The count is the only nobleman, and the people (the chorus) let their voices be heard, from bass to soprano. Third estate, clergy, and nobility: the actors of the Estates General of 1789 were rehearsing with joyful unconsciousness the roles they would take up again seriously once the curtain went up on the Revolution, but then for very different stakes.

Furthermore, no one stays in his place. People go up and down the stairs of the castle for pleasure and personal gain. Cherubino even knows how to jump. The count and Cherubino are rival prowlers in the quarters of the gardener's daughter and meet up in the quarters of Susanna, the gardener's niece. The gardener will burst in with his crushed carnations in the upper floors of the castle. Basilio, the count's messenger, has an eye on everything. Well schooled in observing the affairs of the world, he considers he has sufficient experience to say, as will Don Alfonso, the "philosopher," "Così fan tutte le belle." As for Cherubino, the little "serpent," the "devilish page," the *demonietto*, he worms his way into everything with the complicity of chance. He was chased away long before the first scene, but he remains secretly present, appearing here and there in various disguises, disturbing the action, upsetting everyone, and leaving a singular irritation in his wake. A figure of an unanchored eros who spans the entire universe for want of attaching to any definite object, he is a catalyst of disorder and also one whose kisses are lost in the confusion of nighttime. With an imaginary helmet and turban, he is a future soldier whose military prowess glorified by Figaro in his famous aria inspires no more confidence than the religious virtue of Basilio. In fact, there is a general disrespect. Nothing is out of bounds in this castle. And there is no character who is not capable, when necessary, of passing from one role to another and, in the case of Cherubino, from one sex to another or, in the case of Marcellina, from the role of marriage material to mother.

THE AGES OF LOVE

The ages of love are not less well represented than the stages of life. We witness a sort of pilgrim's progress of love at all ages:

- The as-yet-diffuse eroticism of Barbarina and Cherubino, who have barely emerged from childhood and who only know the confused awakening of love.
- The clear certitude of love in the case of Figaro and Susanna, young adults who have the will to give themselves to one another without restrictions and who thus expose themselves to intense wells of disappointment.
- Hardly any older, the count and countess have arrived at the stage of lassitude and chagrin and the experience of divisiveness and interior contradictions. The count, though unfaithful, is jealous, as though he were still in love. The countess, though faithful, is not insensitive to the devotion of Cherubino.
- In maturity, represented by Marcellina, there is the risk of a singular confusion of feelings. She is a ridiculous Jocasta, and Figaro has no trouble escaping from the fate of Oedipus.

Everyone's love is burning in its own way, and every type of love has its own music assigned to it. It's open season for polymorphic intonations of desire and every accent of the passions. Once love in all its forms is on the scene, there is ample room for gaiety, melancholy, cupidity, fear, malice, vanity, repentance, pardon, and so on.

We see and hear a microcosm of human feeling in circulation, a microcosm that miraculously finds its rhythm, its timbres, and tonal colors. The noble indignation of the count comes across in an affective register entirely different from the revolted anger of Figaro with its rancor and bitterness. Mozart was just waiting for this occasion to employ all the expressive faculties that he knew he possessed. Da Ponte praises the composer (and, along the way, himself) when in an attempt to justify the excessive length of the work, he observes, "the variety of threads woven together that make up the action of this drama" and "the multiplicity of musical pieces that needed to be composed . . . in order to express trait for trait, and with different colors, the diverse passions displayed in it."[3]

The passions themselves wear the changing colors of the hours of the day. It is morning during the light duettino that occurs as the curtain first goes up; we hear that night has fallen in the cavatine of Barbarina at the beginning of the last act. But for impatient desire, time passes too slowly. From the first act (scene 6), set during the morning, the count lets Susanna know that he will wait for her that evening "in giardin, sull'imbrunir del giorno"—"in the garden, at dusk." And we know from Basilio (scene 7) that Cherubino was roving about already in the early morning: "sul far del giorno, passegiava qui intorno"—"he was walking in the area at the break of day." Temporal markers are clearly indicated. The characters who meet or are talked about in the morning in "the unfurnished room" of the fiancés will all be reunited at nightfall "under the pines" of the large garden. In the meantime, around the middle of the day, the count will have had time to go hunting, to receive a note, and to come back hastily to try and surprise his wife.

THE INCREASE IN NUMBERS

The motion never stops and the inventive genius never comes up short. The promise was perfectly spelled out to us by the first seven measures of the overture with the suavely skittish eighth notes in the violins, joyously yet mysteriously oscillating from the tonic to the dominant and back. Seven measures instead of the customary eight, as though it were necessary to represent the haste for pleasure. The initial shiver of the first five notes is then immediately included in the melodic flow. One recognizes the ascending motifs of the overture in the last measures of the opera at the moment when the joys of reunion are expressed in the exclamation "Corriam tutti." The final allegro based on the triad of the perfect D major of the overture celebrates the sentimental order that has provisionally been reestablished but launches again the race for happiness as though its pursuit could not stop with the last measure. Yet, once the curtain goes up, the élan of the overture is already communicated in the first notes sung by Figaro: "Cinque . . . dieci . . . venti . . . trenta . . . trentasei . . . quarantatre. . . ." One notices in Mozart and Da Ponte, swept along by an admirable rhythm, the heightened vitality and euphoria of the series of increasing numbers. The ascending notes capture it well: it is an arithmetical desire, a masculine desire symbolized by numbers. Everything begins in calculations carried out less in submission to a measurable reality than as an anticipation of the pleasure of love and its expansion. And notice the added dynamism of Mozart and how different it is from the dry opening sentence of Beaumarchais's *Figaro*: "Nineteen feet by twenty-six." That is static. Nothing is fermenting. Beaumarchais's lead character is only establishing a relationship between length and width, while Mozart and Da Ponte, still faithful to their model, manage to surpass it with a smooth elegance and especially with a greater symbolic charge. Here a conquering energy is at work. It implies, while admittedly taking its cue from Beaumarchais, a will toward enlargement and enrichment on all fronts. It is an unprecedented energy born at that instant. It is capable of eliminating the hereditary prerogatives of a noble master.

Why? Because within the order of desire, all are equals. The aria "Se vuol ballare, signor contino" expresses the jealous resentment that turns into intellectual superiority and puts it to work right away. This new enlarged stature of Figaro effects a symmetrical diminishment of the count, now reduced to being no more than a *contino* or "little count" obeying the dance steps imposed by the guitar of his valet. The count lacks neither dignity nor pride, but he has only taken the trouble to be born—"la peine de naître." Beaumarchais's phrase could not be used in the opera. Figaro's aria substituted by Da Ponte lets it be known clearly enough that the valet, either gaily or bitterly, possesses the means for reversing the relations of high and low birth. The musician, the dance master of the moment, is clever enough to dictate the steps and dominate the fate of the predator who believes that his birth and riches can assure him only good fortune.

SUSANNA IN THE CENTER

Morning, noon, afternoon, night: each of the four acts takes place during one of these "moments of the day" that painters and poets in classical times enjoyed allegorizing. In each of these acts, and in a way that is clearer than in Beaumarchais's plot, Susanna occupies a central position. Her role was preciously bestowed by Mozart on a woman he was infatuated with, Nancy Storace. It is around her that Figaro, the count, Cherubino, and even Basilio, the count's matchmaker, all gravitate. It has been observed that there is no duo in the opera in which she is not involved. She is the one the abandoned countess is waiting for at the beginning of the second act, and the last great aria of the opera belongs to her: "Deh vieni, non tardar"—"O, come! Do not delay" (act 4, scene 10). And as an effect of her irresistible attractiveness, it is to her that purses, rings, and more all come.

And if, for purposes of the plot, Susanna finally puts on the countess's clothes, it is more than travesty: one sees in it an augmentation of stature equal to Figaro's. In it there is, albeit fictively, a well-merited promotion, an elevation of social status. Wise, tricky, clairvoyant, quick to act, she is the desired prize, but she functions as a liberator. She rescues those who are threatened by the count's anger or jealousy, namely, the countess, Cherubino, and Figaro himself. By saving others, she herself avoids all traps. She plays with fire, since she feigns to yield to the libertine's plans—but it is thanks to her that all the compromising situations are righted. True, she is only a maidservant (as Despina will be): she runs when she hears the countess's bell ring, and she tends carefully to the dress and personal needs of her mistress. As with Figaro, however, her subaltern status is a false appearance. The constancy of the fiancés, their courage and gaiety, make them latent masters. And this makes the agitation, the worries, and errant running-about of the other characters all the more noticeable.

At the end of the Beaumarchais play, Figaro, a calculator from his very first words, has not lost sight of his interests, and he makes careful count of his gains of the day, which are substantial ("triple dot, femme superbe"—"triple dowry, a superb wife"). Da Ponte and Mozart spare us this financial recapitulation, since at the end of so much buffoonery (*quante buffonerie!*) that rises into musical sublimity no one any longer has a cool head. The race through love's labyrinth and the ultimate sacrament of forgiveness have confounded and transported every soul. It is not a moment for calculating and evaluating capital gains. It's time to spend: "Corriam tutti a festiggiar."

THE CIRCULATION OF OBJECTS

Objects are in active circulation within the Beaumarchais play and the Da Ponte–Mozart opera. (Stage managers and the props department must pay attention to this!) Judging from what happens, it would seem as though the movement of the passions required some material representation, some conducting bodies.

Like in a dream, a whole host of woman's objects (the *mundus muliebris*, to use Baudelaire's expression) become displaced in the general commotion. The "little bouquet of orange blossoms" (Beaumarchais) or the tall white hat (Mozart and Da Ponte) that Susanna designed for her wedding day and that she displays proudly in the first duettino will be placed on her head by the count during the afternoon ceremony (act 3, scene 14). They will adorn the countess in the shadowy evening. Cherubino will be clumsy, and the count as well, like two butterflies attracted by a flower (act 4, scene 11). It is the clear center of the spectacle.

Another feminine fetish is the ribbon that belongs to the countess and that Cherubino rips from Susanna's hands. The page will wear it around his arm, stained with the blood from a cut. The countess understands this precious contact very well and hopes it will be repeated. If not, why would she bother, in the second act, to retake possession of this ribbon by exchanging it for another? Cherubino desired the indirect contact with the body of the countess, and the countess wishes to wear on her person the drop of blood spilled by her godson. It is a telling sign, the tacit accomplishment of erotic ritual and contagious magic. With formal reserve, things go no further in the opera. The countess will not wear it since in Da Ponte's libretto, contrary to the stage directions in Beaumarchais, the ribbon does not reappear. We will not see it fall from the countess's corsage at the moment when she is looking for the pin intended to seal the letter dictated to Susanna.

I invite directors to find in the libretto some other signs: the handkerchief at the beginning of the second act that the countess uses to wipe Cherubino's tears is the same one she brings to her mouth when she attempts to "hide the disorder of her feelings." This gesture takes place at the most intensely emotional moment, when, instead of the page, the countess sees Susanna appear in the door to the room the count has just opened. The slightly moist handkerchief is another mediator, even more sensual than the ribbon.

As for the pin motif, so rich in tactile and symbolic value, it wanders throughout the opera just as dictated by the Beaumarchais play. The pin is the female counterpart to the sword used by the count to threaten Cherubino, who is locked in a closet. Point, counterpoint. A pinprick, as is known, causes a very finely localized "exquisite pain." There is something very similar in the heat of a slap, another epidermal sensation though slightly more diffused that Susanna is versed in distributing frequently *a tempo*, with a lightning hand and timing.

In Cherubino's recitative in the first act (scene 5), he envies Susanna's privilege to supervise the clothes and hair of the countess: "Felice te . . . che la vesti il mattino, che la sera la spogli, che le metti gli spilloni, i merletti—"The happiness you have . . . you who dress her in the morning and undress her in the evening, who place her hairpins and lace." Beaumarchais had imagined Susanna in the second act dressing Cherubino as a woman and singing "with pins in her mouth." This staging was impossible in the opera and had to be abandoned, but not much was lost because the decisive gesture comes after the duettino with the letter, when the countess's pin pricks the missive that she has dictated to Susanna. The pin pricks the unfaithful husband at the supreme moment of the nuptial party. Let's recall the details. The count, adjusting the virginal hat on the head of the fiancée, encounters the hand of Susanna, who slips him the secret rendezvous letter. The count pricks his finger and quickly understands that he is expected: "Le donne ficcan gli aghi in ogni loco . . . Ah! Ah! capisco il gioco"—"Women are always poking their needles . . . Ah! Ah! I understand the game." In the following act—O irony!—this same pin, returned to Susanna by the hand of Barbarina, will be lost and replaced by another that Figaro takes from the coiffure of his mother. As though all women were the same. Figaro's pin play prefigures the bitter deception that pours out of his grand aria against the entire female sex: "Guardate queste femmine, guardate cosa son." All the female characters of the libretto will, one after another, have touched the original pin or the one that replaces it, and the count and Figaro participate in this singular round.

The pin is the dart of perfidy that accompanies an inauthentic love letter. It is a seal with no guarantee. Other letters and legal papers whose validity is no better assured also circulate. From Figaro to Marcellina, the recognition of debt and the promise of marriage are null and void in advance. The seal (*il sigillo*) of Cherubino's military commission is missing. Given to Cherubino, lost during the flight out the window, found by the gardener Antonio, the commission is the permit to go on a lover's hunt (*delle belle turbante il riposo*). The only true inscription is the scar of earliest infancy, the forceps mark on the right arm of Figaro that is equal to a birth certificate. The objects and signs that pass from hand to hand are vehicles of deception. They are a currency with no certain value beyond the mental agility of those who know how to make it circulate. In all these exchanges, it is only worth something because each person indulges in illusions and stays on the surface.

BARBARINA'S LAMENT

The encyclopedists, opposed as they were to counterpoint and ornamental songs, wanted music to be the melodious expansion of poetry, its most elaborate accentuation, its excess. They stood by the musical aesthetic that had been proposed during the Renaissance by theoreticians who sought to revive the music of classical antiquity. According to this aesthetic program, as I said in an earlier chapter, the invention of the word, under the dictates of feeling, in turn dictated in advance a certain music. The latter was only a mode expressing the primacy and perseverance of speech. The desire to assure the complete presence of the feeling in the music, to have them flow from the same source, was indeed considerable, but there remained a persistent distance between the meaning of the word and the melodic inflection. One could call it a sort of freedom ransom that was granted to the composer: the melody was not able to be fully contemporary with the words; it was the prolongation, the imitation, the re-presentation, sometimes the commentary. This slight discrepancy, this minor hiatus within the psychic temporality, casts a melancholic shadow over the melody. The latter did not live completely in the present; it was lined with memory. Also, beginning with Monteverdi, it excelled at deploring loss. "I've lost my servant" (Rousseau in *Le Divin du village*). "I've lost my Eurydice" (Gluck in *Orpheus and Eurydice*). And Mozart, too, knows how to sing in this melodic style.

He uses it for the lament of Barbarina in the fourth act of *Figaro*, when she is searching at night by the light of her lantern for the lost pin: "L'ho perduta. . . . Me meschina!"—"I've lost it. . . . Woe is me!" Here the pin I spoke of earlier returns. An additional remark comes to mind: in Beaumarchais, the pin is never lost! The loss of this pin and Barbarina's lament were imagined by Da Ponte and Mozart to join together two scenes in acts four and five and to give an aria to this small female role. And yet one might find it suspicious: why does such a frivolous object provoke such a moving expression of desperation? It was the agreed-upon sign, therefore the symbol, of the tryst arranged by the count. I understand it to be a soft parody of the melodious lamentations so loved by the public. Mozart and Da Ponte, being capable of any piece of trickery, make us hear and understand that they can get the job done at the drop of a . . . pin, any pin. Figaro finds a pin in the clothes of Marcellina, his mother, that can stand in for the lost object. One need only announce their equivalency to make it work.

THE MUSICIAN CHARACTERS

The hypocrite Basilio is Susanna's singing teacher. He uses his position to transmit the count's proposals to her as we learn in one of the first recitatives. In the Beaumarchais play, as in his *Barber of Seville*, Basile is the one who "introduces the harpsichord to Madame"; he is also the one who teaches "the mandolin to the pages." He was therefore able to teach Chérubin the art of romance. This master-student relationship disappears in Da Ponte and Mozart, who well understood that, in their particular dramaturgy, a Basilio who functions as source and dispenser of music would have had dissonant consequences.

Instead the role was redistributed. The musical interventions in the opera are done by several characters: by Figaro, who imagines himself playing the guitar when he sings the threatening cavatine; by the countess, who knows tunes to which she can pair new words for a false gallant letter (*canzonetta sull'aria* . . .); and by Susanna, who vigorously takes up her mistress's guitar when a moment to play the accompanist presents itself. In addition, the ambient male and female peasants perform the role of chorus.

THE TWO SONGS OF CHERUBINO

The principal composer and singer in *Figaro* is of course Cherubino. He appears carrying a *canzonetta* in his pocket that he wrote himself. This *canzonetta* belongs to the system of circulating objects and reveals its full complexity. The ribbon does not circulate by itself. It is paired from the start with the paper on which the song is jotted down.

During his early morning intrusion into the room of the future couple and after taking possession of the ribbon, Cherubino offers as payment the manuscript that he takes from his pocket. It is literally his pocket money, and he attempts to buy in this way the ribbon that had passed over the body of the troubling godmother.

In a bold gesture in the first act, where he asks that his song be read to the countess, Susanna, and all the women of the palace, Cherubino finds himself transported to a troubling precipice. The idea of this auditory contact makes his heart miss a beat. The hope of the future song brings about an excess of love and gives way to *agitato*: "Non so più cosa son, cosa faccio"—"I no longer know what I am or what I am doing." As though it were improvised, the song makes us hear the miraculous store of expended and resurgent energy that cannot be limited to bodies and objects. The desire for love that carries over to far-off spaces finally turns back on itself because of the overriding need to attain a goal amid everything that is slipping away. Mozart and Da Ponte, who followed Beaumarchais's text closely, ingeniously add the hesitant, triumphal reflection of speech turning back on its own source: "E, se non ho chi m'oda, parlo d'amor con me"—"And if I have no one to listen to me, I speak of love with myself."

At the beginning of the second act, in the bedroom, the love letter delivered by Susanna is in the hands of the countess: the caress has been achieved by intermediary of this object. Cherubino, who has had himself preintroduced in this way, can now approach his beautiful godmother. He has thus invented a melody ("Voi che sapete"). He blushes: yes, he is the author; he asks only to sing it. Here we are far, far away from Beaumarchais, who was content to have Chérubin pay a compliment to his godmother to the tune of the popular and frequently used "Malbrough s'en va-t-en guerre." With Mozart, when Cherubino sings his romance (or hers, since the role is assigned to a cross-dressed female singer) he (she) is accompanied by Susanna, with the countess as audience. The hand of the servant girl appears to play the melody and pizzicato accompaniment of the song sung by the handsome page and addressed to her as well as to the countess. The two women are the joint addressees of this call: "Ricerco un bene fuori di me"—"I seek a good outside of myself. I don't know who possesses it, I don't know what it is." What a package! Added to this, and no less enveloping, are the woodwinds coming from deep within the orchestra. One hears the most intense voice of love in the avowal of the ignorance of what love is. Cherubino's romantic address proves that he already grasps the essence of what he asks to learn, that essence being the very worrying over its existence.

The romance, this roll of paper covered with musical notations, thus caresses in return, first by the delivery of the paper, and second via the insistent melody. There is a singular resemblance of form—the image of an unfolding—that links the ribbon and the staffs on which the music is jotted down. They are however perfectly dissimilar in this respect: the one is only a visual accessory of the show, whereas the others carry inside themselves, virtually, everything communicated through singing and the orchestra. Cherubino's paper is all of opera in miniature; it is the "*mise en abyme*" of the work that we are seeing and hearing. For this reason, at the beginning of the second act, his message is not only addressed to the two women on stage: it is offered to all women—known and unknown—that is, to an infinitely large audience. The romance addresses itself to a plural, indeterminate "you": "Voi che sapete"— "You who know what love is." The romance is sung to travel to the ends of the earth.

AIR AND ARIA

The singing of the countess, Susanna, and Cherubino takes wing from the impulse of amorous desire, its movement continued by the circulation of the multiple voices from the orchestra: the vibrations of the string instruments as well as the variety of breaths from the wind instruments.

The feeling we get from this circulation is further enhanced on almost every page of the libretto by the ambiguity of the word "aria," which is susceptible to being used in many ways. It designates the body and its seduction ("quell'aria brillante"), it extends to the atmosphere, to the "aura" that envelops a garden ("finché l'aria è encor bruna"), and it transports our attention to the marvelous melody of the duettino ("canzonetta sull'aria"). At the same time, the words of this song make one long for the winds and breezes of the evening ("che soave zeffiretto questa sera spirerà").

The equivocation surrounding the [French] word "*air*" is apparently banal, and one finds it in a large number of European languages besides Italian, French, and English. It took a musical genius to translate it, amplify it, and render it literally sensible in language that would be infinitely more efficient. When night falls, the circulation of objects is over since they can no longer be distinguished. The pin has been lost and replaced haphazardly. No one is recognizable anymore. Everything is drifting and tenebrous. Some insignificant figures move about and displace some of the shadowy zones. Only the garden and the music are breathing. The last symbolic objects, it might be pointed out, are the retreats into which the characters disappear: the pavilions where, one after another, all the women and Cherubino hide to escape from danger (all the while sharing the fruit and brioche that Barbarina has brought along). The pavilions, which one can imagine on the edge of the stage set up like the little "follies" of European gardens, are the equivalent of the small room where Cherubino and Susanna are enclosed in the second act or the armchair of the first act where Cherubino takes refuge as though within a cave, hidden under a dress providentially placed there by Susanna. These are all receptacles of life, chrysalises of the *farfallone amoroso*, the "loving butterfly."

In the fourth act, the objects having vanished in the night, the way is left open to voices. A wonderful illusion is constructed out of the counterfeit voices—put on and off like clothes—of Susanna and the countess. Beaumarchais had imagined this vocal complement of disguise, this feint of an instant with the recognition that follows. Going from the theater to the Mozart opera, this stratagem's first purpose is not to serve within a comedy of imitation but to heighten the listening experience. Figaro recognizes Susanna by her voice: "Io conobbi la voce che adoro"—"I recognized the voice I love." The voice, issuing from the most intimate level of being, is the truth finally revealed at the end of this mad day—a day that has also been an apprenticeship and a trial of initiation. It requires the most attentive listening. Susanna, Figaro, the countess, and the count—they all beg to be listened to so that the misunderstandings and the lack of love will cease.

The last lesson, shared among several voices, is surely this one where all the action is in service to the ear: Listen! Listen to the one you doubted and whom you have found again. Listen to the one who loves you and who never stopped loving you. Listen to the one who forgot you and who is asking for your forgiveness now that he recognizes you.

CHAPTER 4

Registers of Excess

Don Giovanni

The opening scene of *Don Giovanni* (1787) is one of the most beautiful examples of theatrical positing of all time. The work begins literally in full swing. Spectators quickly understand that the comic monologue of the servant who stands guard is the cover for the scene of violence that cannot be shown.

Taking off from his predecessors—Tirso de Molina, Molière, Goldoni, Giovanni Bertati—Da Ponte developed a series of events whose verbal trace leaves the way entirely open for the music. This free rein allows Mozart to take the buffoonery and the pathos to their utmost extremes and mix them in masterful combinations. The poem allows for everything that a *dramma giocoso* could carry out in terms of musical excess. To understand it through the medium of language, all we need hearken to are the few occurrences of the word "*eccesso*," the Italian equivalent of the English "excess" or the French "*excès*."

The first time the word comes up is in the trio that concludes the first scene. Wounded by Don Giovanni, the commendatore is lying on the ground, close to death; he calls for help: "Ah, socorso! . . . son tradito . . ."—"Help! . . . I'm betrayed. . . ." In counterpoint, in a melodic line used early by Donna Anna to express desperate furor, Don Giovanni sings: "Ah! gia cadde il sciagurato"—"Ah, already the unlucky one succumbs." Leporello, the character that the psychoanalyst Otto Rank and the poet Pierre Jean Jouve see as Don Giovanni's shadow,[1] brings forth his judgment with eight more syllables: "Qual misfatto! qual eccesso!"—"What a misdeed! What excess!" These four repeated syllables are heard underneath the complaint of the dying commendatore, "l'assassino m'ha ferito"—"the assassin has wounded me"—and underneath the words "affannosa e agonizzante"—"tormented and agonizing"—that Don Giovanni utters while watching the life leak out of his victim. The word "eccesso" thus comes from the mouth of the witness who is fully aware of what has transpired, an event that he summarizes immediately afterward in a dialogue of recitativo secco: "Sforzar la figlia, ed ammazzar il padre"—"Accost the daughter and skewer the father." Moral sentiment has thus had its say thanks to the verbal quip of the comic character. Except for the invitation to the statue in the cemetery scene of the second act, all the events that will be answered for by the supernatural punishment take place in the first scene. The sovereign art of Mozart teaches us everything with the concert of voices that surround the death of the father.

BESIDE ONESELF, OUTSIDE THE LAW

Let's leave the stage for a moment and inquire further in the company of philosophers and theologians. The word "excess," as soon as one's thinking and linguistic memory pause over it, raises a singular diversity of meanings.

In the Latin of the Bible, *excessus vitae* is the exit from life, the access to "another life." It is a name for death. But this word also names moments of trance during which the soul leaves its anchorage to visit a superior place. The *excessus mentis* is therefore the equivalent of *extasis* in the Greek text. Thus in the Acts of the Apostles (10:10 and 11:5), Peter recounts, "While I was praying, I fell into ecstasy and I had a vision" (*vidi in excessu mentis*). Excess is therefore a going-beyond. It is obedience to an authority that uproots us from ourselves. According to the Platonic tradition, it can be understood as the privilege of the soul spurred on by enthusiasm, freed from its corporal chains by "fury," that then regains its true home. This religious image occurs frequently in the pages Montaigne devotes to a consideration of poetry. Excess affirms a superiority; it defines the distance between the judgment of ordinary minds and a particular poetic beauty that they cannot grasp. That type of poetry is "the good, the *excessive*, the divine." In the minds of those that listen to it, excess spreads, the trance is contagious. When it escapes beyond the limits of the body—tomb or prison—excess is deliverance. It is a dazzling light that cannot be looked at with "a firm and steady gaze . . . any more than one can take in the splendor of a bolt of lightning."[2] This ecstatic, mystical sense, however, is hardly what we think Leporello has in mind when he criticizes the excess of his master.

Although an entire intellectual tradition sees the flight of the soul out of its material bonds to be a positive good, another learned tradition that also goes back to ancient sources appeals to a different sense of the word "excess" to designate that which goes beyond the correct proportions in the material order itself. In other words, anything that compromises the natural balance of the humors or the network of tensions inside any body. Here excess is disproportion, sickness, or the cause of sickness. Rational thinking, from earliest antiquity, inscribes human passions within this quantitative and medical register. It views the passions as intimately related to the life springs and temperaments of the body. Therefore it would seek to understand human behavior as an effect of natural causes. Human passions were thus excused while at the same time one wanted to find remedies for them. For that type of psychology, there can be no statues coming to life to avenge the victims of the impious. It prefers instead to take up an analysis of the relevant material forces and their combinations as an explanation of our well-being or our suffering. If we consider the portrait of the character as given to us by Molière, Dom Juan is clearly a man of calculation ("I believe that two and two make four, Sganarelle, and four plus four makes eight" [act 3, scene 1]), as were also the "libertine" philosophers of his time and the materialists of the eighteenth century. Ridicule falls on the Sganarelles and Leporellos when for the sake of defending moral principles they sermonize to their masters while continuing to serve them. The staging of these comic situations by Molière and Da Ponte has us laugh at the awkward servants and appreciate the cause of the elegant libertine.

If the ridiculousness of the valet and the incoherence of his reproaches, coming from below, serve as a foil to the success of the master, it is so that in the end a judging edict from above will prevail. In what sense, under what authority are the excesses of Don Giovanni criminal? They transgress a certain *measure* that is not simply respected communally by popular opinion but prescribed by divine will. Here again the meaning of the word "excess" derives from a notion of exit, this time, however, as designating not an ecstatic transport but instead the movement by which the individual excepts himself by excluding himself from communal law and religious duty. In other words, excess here names delinquency and sin. The myth of Don Juan came about at a moment in European history when the subject of the inconstancy of the human heart and the related subject of its various drives—feeling, knowing, dominating (*libido sentiendi, libido sciendi, libido dominandi*)—were intensely debated by moralists of the day. What would man be without grace? The theological answer was that he would remain subject to his appetites and self-love, indifferent to all authority that went contrary to his free, pleasure-seeking will. In Tirso de Molina's *El Burlador de Sevilla* (1630, *The Playboy of Seville*) and Da Ponte's *Don Giovanni*, authority is clearly symbolized by the commendatore. While alive, sword in hand, he is nothing but an old man easily beaten by one stronger than he; however, he returns as the *uom di sasso*—the "man of stone"—to impose a supernatural commandment. When in the second act Don Giovanni, followed by Leporello, leaps over the cemetery wall and when he invites the statue, he is committing the supreme transgression: he leaves the world of the living to insult with laughter the other world. It is the inverse movement from that of "ecstasy," in which the word "excess" comes to us in its first meaning, its first face so to speak. Excess can take the direction of good as well as evil.

THE CONTRIBUTION OF MUSIC

The myth of Don Juan, as Jean Rousset has aptly remarked, was made to encounter music.[3] "Don Juan's nature is music," said Kierkegaard.[4] And this is not merely a romantic reading of Don Juan.

Mozart knew instinctively the truths that Friedrich Melchior Grimm (his host in Paris during part of his stay in 1778) put forward in reasoned arguments in the entry "Poème lyrique" within the *Encyclopédie*.[5] One sees to what extent opera, for any experienced spectator, was linked to the idea of excess. Music is not simply, like mime or other gestural arts, a universal language capable of expressing the fine nuances of feeling. Music has the power to render the expression of passions more intense and confers on them a heightened energy. Musical art has the privilege of carrying the emotions to their highest degree—something the most sublime poetry is unable to do. Music is superlative with respect to words. Let's listen to Grimm: "The expressions of music . . . , going right to the heart, so to speak, and not passing through the mind, necessarily produce effects unknown to all other idioms, and this direct wave that prevents it from giving its accents the precision of discourse, by conferring the act of interpretation to our imagination, makes the latter experience an empire that no other language could exert over it."

Music produces an emotional amplification. In a spoken tragedy, the situation will of course be moving and perhaps even bring tears. But the same situation expressed by a great musician will be exacerbated. It will become a "pain" and a "madness" that "tears" and "rips out" the heart of the audience. "The musician who manages to make me shed a tear or two during an ephemeral tender moment would certainly not be exercising his art to the full." A similar gap exists between a spoken comedy that "enchants" and a "comedy set to music." While the spoken comedy "represents men as they are . . . the comedy set to music gives them a touch more liveliness and genius—they are bordering on madness." This is the attraction of the opera buffa. The same idea will be repeated by others. When the musical arts are associated with comedy, asserts Quatremère de Quincey in 1789, "violent contrasts are necessary; the least little affections become passions, and the passions become madness."

Within this conception of opera, the expressive overflow finds its musical resource in the passage from recitative to aria. Rousseau, who loved simple and touching melodies, had already spoken of musical "impressions" in similar terms. And he had recourse to the notion of excess: "They are excessive or nil, never weak or mediocre; one must remain insensible or allow oneself to be moved beyond measure; either it is the empty noise of a language you do not understand, or it is an impetuosity of sentiment that pulls you along, and that is impossible for the soul

to resist."[6] Of course, "the charm of the music is not active in the recitative." And yet the obligatory recitative merits our highest attention.
The alternation between segments of recitative and "symphonic traits"
and "the melody delivered with the full orchestral impact are what is
most touching, ravishing, and energetic in all of modern music." And
need one be reminded that it is precisely in the required recitative that
Mozart demonstrated his most extraordinary mastery by packing enormous significance into these moments that Rousseau called "passages
alternatifs." The composer gave countless examples of the emotion that
results from the transition between the sung declaration and the aria,
where the music's sovereignty far exceeds the words.

   In the work of Da Ponte and Mozart the misdeeds (*misfatti*) of Don
Giovanni, the excesses he commits, propel the action, but this happens within a general system of excess and overflow that pursues its
own energy in the musical thought process itself. A dead man grows
into a statue: the entire adventure is an overwhelming of the real by
the supernatural. Mozart senses the necessity of showing this through
the tonalities, timbres, and rhythms of the music. Moreover, the genre
of the *dramma giocoso* authorizes exaggeration at all levels, from the
geometrical increase of the passions to the accentuation of clownish
features. As one already finds with farce and *commedia*, the figure of
the thinking servant shocked by his master's behavior includes a large
dose of cowardice and furtive playfulness. Voices diversify and multiply. The "feminine group," to use Jean Rousset's expression, expresses
itself in an unusual number of arias and ensembles. As with Molière,
Da Ponte brings together opposed social stations: noble women with
female peasants or servants. The group onstage includes both objects of
past conquests and figures who are the current objects of the seducer's
attentions, the latest successes that he promises himself. Thanks to
the sublime arias, the pain of the women who have been seduced and
thrown aside takes on a more moving accent than in the theater. An
already very full orchestra is joined onstage by musicians for the finale
of the first act, and three little musical groups create the confusion that
Don Giovanni can exploit to sweep Zerlina off her feet. Since Don
Giovanni never keeps his word, a blankness builds around him into
which new desirable figures never cease to appear, not to take on new
roles but to people his discourse: the chambermaid of Elvira or the girl
in the street who mistook him for Leporello because he was wearing

his clothes, for example. The last finale is again a scene of expenditure, and Don Giovanni is emphatic about proclaiming the link between his expenditure and his enjoyment:

> Giacchè spendo i miei danari
> Io mi voglio divertir

> From the moment I spend my money
> I want to enjoy myself.
>
> (act I, scene 15)

The pleasures of the music are once again redoubled onstage. And even tripled. An orchestra plays three recent songs from Martin y Soler, Sarti, and Le nozze di Figaro while Don Giovanni, the only one eating, ingests with a barbarous appetite (barbaro appetito) "gigantic mouthfuls" (bocconi da gigante). Don Giovanni (and indeed the public) probably knows the words to the aria from Figaro that the orchestra is playing. If he was able to pick up on the double meaning, the libertine would hear the presage of some bad news: "Non più andrai"—"You will no longer, gallant butterfly, trouble the repose of the beautiful." Da Ponte amplifies all the sensual appetites of his hero before the apparition of the statue. And the last moments of the action are filled with echoes and changes from a comic to a marvelous register even as the dreadfulness mounts. When Don Giovanni opens the door, Leporello is hiding under the banquet table; of course this clownish movement below the table will be taken up and amplified by the tragic movement that pulls Don Giovanni below into Hell. In the brief exchanges near the end, the word "tempo" is to be taken both in the sense of eternity, when the commendatore declares that time is counted and that he is exhausted ("più tempo non ho, tempo più non v'è"), and in the sense of the bustle of human affairs, when Leporello declares that his master is too busy to reply to the commendatore's invitation ("tempo non ha"). It is an oddly fitting word for this dissolute man who accords no future-oriented duration to his promises. In Molière's play a ghost—first a veiled woman, then a figure of Time—crossed the stage to signal that the end was near. Before the final cry of Don Giovanni as he's swallowed up by the earth (and its echo by Leporello who remains unharmed), the last word of the text sung by the "invisible choir" tells of the increase of evil: "Vieni: c'è un mal peggior!"—"Come! There is a worse evil." The comparative "*peggior*," "worse," signals a crescendo of punishment.

WHAT THE POETS HEAR

The famous aria "Fin ch'an dal vino / Calda la testa" ("So long as the wine / Warms the head," act 1, scene 15, no. 11) is one of the moments when, before the action comes, Don Giovanni presents a project. It is the only time that an entire aria is used in this way. The dissolute man depicts himself. He orders Leporello to prepare the party. The aria concludes with the announcement of the result: the erotic victories will increase by another ten. The libido needs more prey, which only exists in the abstract mode of pure number. The recipe is to invite the young women who were met in the public square and to let the wine flow freely. The ball will be without order (*senza ordine*), and many different kinds of dances will be danced. Don Giovanni counts on taking advantage of the disorder to serve his desires. These new pleasures, as soon as they've been consumed, will leave no trace in his memory and simply be added to the list, a kind of treasury of shadows. Mozart's music is carried by a vital energy that speaks more than the words pronounced and the actions announced.

According to the arguments of religious morality, the individual who seals himself within the finite word of carnal pleasures forgets the preference that is owed to God. Such an individual is a licentious, violent liar and a captive of sin. His punishment demonstrates that divine justice can sometimes arrive a bit late but ultimately never fails to strike. Since the romantic age, however, many interpreters have not been satisfied with the mere charges of misconduct. For them, Don Giovanni is not only the impious figure that Heaven has allowed far too long to go unpunished. He wants to enter Heaven, but by illicit means. His passion for women is an absolute desire but one aimed precisely at the wrong target. His heart is not only forgetful of his duties but foments a revolt that knowingly defies divine authority. That is why the great figure Death awaits him in the cemetery. Moreover, if Don Giovanni is not only a man to be judged but an adversary, the whole character takes on a satanic dimension. His vagabond ways would then link him to rebellious angels and those great figures exiled from Paradise or the Golden Age. Not only would he be looking for the lost homeland along errant pathways, but he would be conducting a war against the imposed order of a great rival.

Baudelaire celebrated these character traits in the Wagner operas with which he was familiar. It was precisely excess that he liked. In the essay that Baudelaire devoted to Wagner, the composer of *Tannhäuser* is praised for making one feel "the overflow of an energetic nature that directs toward evil all the forces that are owed to the culture of the good."[7] He knew how "to depict the excess of desires and of energy and the immoderate, untamable ambition of a sensitive soul that has gone astray." Moreover, Baudelaire, who had made a written outline for a drama of his own to be called *La Fin de Don Juan*, does not resist the temptation of comparing the object of desire in *Tannhäuser*, Venus, with the very real women loved by the Don Giovanni of Mozart: "In the stage representation of the idea, he freed himself luckily from the insipid crowd of victims, the countless Elviras. The pure idea, incarnated in the singular Venus, speaks more highly and with much more eloquence. We do not see here an ordinary libertine, vaulting from beauty to beauty, but man in general, universal, living morganatically with the absolute ideal of voluptuousness." Listening to *Tannhäuser*, Baudelaire salutes the "immense, unbounded love that is raised to the level of a counter-religion or satanic religion."

In his beautiful volume devoted to Mozart's *Don Juan*, Pierre Jean Jouve analyzes the impression produced by the aria "Fin ch'an dal vino" (act 1, scene 15, no. 11). He finds in Mozart the type of excess that, as we've seen, Baudelaire seems to have believed was the exclusive merit of Wagner. For Jouve, there is nowadays a new way to stage Mozart, another way to listen to him, that dissipates the false image of frivolity associated with this aria in Baudelaire's day. A religious dimension is detected within it, but a religious dimension within the order of evil. "This aria appears light and frothy; that is, it wears the terrible mask of frivolity. But the agreeable mask lets one imagine all the better the demon's grimace. . . . From the way it is sung (and must be sung) nowadays, this aria becomes in a few bars a formidable mechanism of desire characterized by the unbounded play of repetition. Yes, it could be repeated for all eternity—an eternity that knows no satisfaction."[8]

It is well demonstrated that the frenzy of Don Giovanni knows no direction, no moving on, and only culminates in the inert fetish of the list, "his true object of love."⁹ And yet Jouve detects some happiness in this aria, a happiness that is "probably the reflection of another state that the weak gaze of the man ignores." This happiness "constitutes the duty, the task of living—and it encompasses death itself, latent within this happiness—a death nesting within life that confers on it the hastiness for pleasure with each barely sufficient ration."¹⁰ Jouve makes what he hears arrive at the listener's self-awareness: "We understand from listening to it what we are within the order of fatality: a diabolical unconscious."¹¹

We can see that in his approach to the opera, Jouve refers constantly to a religious metaphysics and symbolic system. He evokes "another state" and a "diabolical" part of our being. It is clear that the Da Ponte libretto speaks very little of such things, but Mozart's music does not prohibit these ideas. Jouve associates this religious metaphysics closely with perspectives based on the psychological profundities of the human condition. The assurance with which this Freudian-influenced poet develops an entire psychotheology of *Don Giovanni* is disconcerting and yet also undeniably important to us for the way it renews and modernizes the interpretation of fablelike material that would seem to belong to a bygone era of moral theology. He risks deciphering the unspoken motives of the libertine. Why must the conquests be tabulated in a list? Jouve has a ready answer that derives from his understanding of the hero's intimate life story: "Tending always toward a past Form, namely, an inaccessible mother whom he wants to possess and who would be the only one able to give him calm and rest, and having introjected her into his innermost soul to the point of resembling her, he can only possess women by violence. And as soon as he does so, he trips again over his own femininity such that he must reaffirm his virility by attacking a new object. The power accorded to him via aggression devours itself. He has no contact with it except by setting it aside, by consigning it within an endless series. Hence the list. The list is a guarantee of reality. What the demonic [*la démonie*] needs most is reality."¹²

As one can see, Jouve is unwavering in his interpretation of *Don Giovanni* via the Oedipus myth. He relies on an explanatory model that is frequently invoked by psychoanalytical discourse and that applies to the frenzied chase or, as here, to the supposed bisexuality of the hero. He assigns the hero a mother who exists nowhere in the text.

The same holds when Jouve's reading seeks to append to the actual ending another more ultimate denouement. It is the commentator who, by means of his personal experience of reviewing the opera, arbitrates over the salvation or the perdition of the impenitent sinner. On the last page of his book Jouve writes, "In the true light of death . . . God and Don Giovanni are reconciled."[13] As with many figures of romanticism and modernism, Jouve gives to art and beauty the role of reconciling the excess as fault with the excess considered as an exit outside the constraints of the mortal condition.

Having inaugurated a legend adorned with excess, romanticism's continuators, including those operating on the shores of surrealism, could only side with Don Giovanni. With the bravura of his defiance—the repeated obstinate "No" with which he answers the invitations to repent—does he not force God to appear? Justice is done. It is as though the obstinacy of the sinner had served God's cause: here is the libertine thrust back into the theological order that he never cared about and sanctified to boot without even having repented. Such an interpretation oddly extends his credit after all his expenditures. Thus Georges Bataille can write, "Don Juan is nothing but . . . a personal incarnation of the party, of the happy orgy that negates and divinely overturns obstacles."[14] Why is it that the adverb "divinely" [*divinement*] has to be introduced here? Would it be because what predominates in this reading is the temptation to confuse the mystical and the criminal senses of the word "excess"? Is a divine value being attributed to human energies turned against the human?

WHO SPEAKS OF EXCESS?

When Da Ponte introduces the word "excess" into his libretto, he is fully aware that it's a word of a reflective mind that measures and judges. This word is not suited to the heat of action or to moments of deep, overwhelming emotion. It implies a distance; it describes recent actions that already belong to the past. As we've seen, this is how Leporello uses it in the terzetto of the commendatore's death. The place for such a word is in the recitative, and that is where it will reappear three times over the course of the second act: twice spoken by Ottavio and once by Elvira.

It is probably Da Ponte's deliberate intention to put these nearly clichéd formulas into the mouth of Ottavio: "After such enormous excesses, we can no longer doubt that Don Giovanni is the wicked murderer of Donna Anna's father" (act 2, scene 10); "This bawdy fellow's grave excesses will soon be punished" (act 2, scene 12). But Da Ponte's ease in this regard is itself revealing. His courageous and gentle Ottavio remains within the human order. Despite Donna Anna's revelations, he retained his doubts about the identity of the guilty party. It was not enough for him to witness the festive tumult at the home of Don Giovanni. He needed still more and better proof, and his judgment only solidifies after the nocturnal exchanges in the second act and the escape of Leporello dressed up as Don Giovanni. The revenge that Ottavio is waiting for and that he believes is fast approaching has the status of a "return" visited on the person "by right." This finely correct attitude and the slightly too smooth arias that Mozart has him sing do not put him in a favorable light. After all, the spectators are in the know from the beginning. Back in act 1 Anna recognized from his voice the true identity of her masked aggressor. Hurt, troubled, and in mourning she does not speak of excess. She suffers.

Ottavio's scruples have a clear dramatic function. They delay human vengeance, whose pathways in this case are slower than that of divine justice. These virtues confine Ottavio to the human order and the role of the consoling fiancé. No sooner is he buried than the commendatore supernaturally takes the upper hand, whereas Leporello, deploring the excess, was speaking from below. The loyal Ottavio has every reason to accuse Don Giovanni in the name of the aristocratic code whose language the libertine disfigures. His serious attachment to the truth and to loyalty allows him to gauge the excess accurately.

The last instance of the word "*eccesso*" comes in the recitative that precedes the aria composed by Mozart for Elvira in preparation for the performances in Vienna in 1788. The words "*misfatto*" and "*eccesso*" uttered by Leporello as he witnesses the death of the commendatore at the end of the opening scene are used again here. The word "*sciagurato*," "the wretched one," used by the murderer to name his victim, applies now to Don Giovanni himself and could be said to announce the end that awaits him. One could of course hold that the vocabulary of libretti is not very rich and that the same words therefore come up again and again. This time the excess was not the murder but the sadistic derision and humiliation undergone by Elvira when she is courted by Leporello disguised in Don Giovanni's clothes:

In quali eccessi, o Numi,
In quali misfatti orribili, tremendi,
E avvolto il sciagurato.

Into such excesses, O Gods!
Into such horrible and terrifying misdeeds
The wretched one sinks!

Elvira guesses that the fatal blow is about to fall on Don Giovanni. The wrath of the heavens will soon erupt. She will then be avenged. But is that her wish? Suddenly the orchestra sighs. It speaks in Elvira's place to avow something that she hesitates to say herself: she wants vengeance, but she is also filled with anxiety. She experiences an inner conflict. "Che contrasto d'affetti!" Caught between extremes of terror and pity, she feels divided. The recitative "Quali eccessi" and the aria that follows, "Mi tradi, quell'alma ingrata"—"This ungrateful soul betrayed me," are situated on the dividing line between feelings, the upshot being that Elvira renounces the illusion of being loved and pure compassion wins out instead. In the key of E flat major and against a persistent battery of violas in thirds and sixths, the aria of Elvira is imitated by the wind instruments, which are followed by the answer of the violins and violas. The aria makes great use of scales distantly related to those that will accompany the words of the commendatore. Elvira tells of an extreme unhappiness and still anxious agitation, but a certain lightness is hinted at, an impatient hope. For her all that counts is the terrible trial (*cimento*) that the guilty one experiences. We see and we hear the resolution take shape that will determine Elvira's last steps. When she bursts in amid the solitary banquet (act 2, scene 16), she demands nothing more for herself. What does she ask of Don Giovanni? "Che vita cangi"—"That you change your life!" As though in echo, the commendatore enjoins, "Cangia vita."

Excess in this last instance is named by one of Don Giovanni's victims who has herself experienced extreme suffering and who discovers freedom through renunciation. The declaration comes no longer from below (Leporello) or from within the human world (Ottavio) but precisely from "on high" when Elvira's voice exclaims "Quali eccessi!" Jouve writes, "Elvira suddenly acquires within a few lines of solo singing an immense grandeur because she entirely leaves herself." In this belatedly composed aria, the music and words, surpassing the moment in the opera in which we hear them, contain already the resolution Elvira will announce so briefly in the *scena ultima*: to seek refuge in a convent and break with the world.

Following this grand solo in which excess is named for the last time, there come the bursts of laughter of Don Giovanni in the cemetery and then the mocking invitation addressed to the statue via the servant. The profanation of the repose of the dead is the ultimate excess. Scaling the cemetery wall is not an invention of the director but an explicit stage direction written in by the creators of the work. A sacred threshold is insulted by laughter, by the pretense of making the dead into a banquet guest, which amounts to the negation of a sanctified limit. Don Giovanni's perfidy in love was certainly a sin, but there was nothing in it to try the patience of the heavens. Don Giovanni had been there a thousand and three times before. The sacrilege committed in the cemetery is the capital outrage that calls for supernatural punishment. The dead man, disturbed in his very home, will enter the home of the libertine to invite him in return. A series of forced border crossings, in other words, until the definitive swallowing up of the guilty one in the infernal abyss.

From the banal sins of lust and lying to the unforgivable sin of contempt for the dead, the excess is gauged in the interval between two circumstances where a hand is offered in response to a call. The attractive peasant girl Zerlina listens to the false promise: "Là ci darem la mano"—"There will we join our hands." The hand caresses while the voice lies. In response to the injunction of the man of stone "Dammi la mano in pegno"—"Give me your hand in promise," Don Giovanni, like the Dom Juan of Molière, answers, "Eccola"—"There it is." The hand is represented as accepting the test of truth. But who guarantees that truth? Only the legend, with the aid of musical genius and all the colors of the orchestra.

Così fan tutte

To Balthus

THE NEAPOLITAN COUNTRYSIDE

"The scene is Naples," announces the libretto. Mozart and Da Ponte's *dramma giocoso* adopts for its setting the homeland of the opera buffa. It asks the audience to turn its imagination to one of the capitals of music and an illustrious countryside.

"Go, run to Naples." In his *Dictionnaire de la musique* (1768) Rousseau delivers this advice to any young musician who believes he has the least spark of genius.[1] Mozart, traveling with his father in 1770, admires Naples but is not transported by the music of Jommelli that Rousseau celebrated as an example of greatness.

The following are among the expected parts of the picture: a few royal festivities, much lively popular activity, the pleasures of blue skies, a shoreline dotted with ships from the East and the West, and a capricious, unpredictable volcano. Theatrical action finds here a stage that is already set for high spectacle. Montesquieu sensed this when he wrote, "Nothing is more beautiful than the situation of Naples within its gulf, it is a seaside amphitheater, but a very deep amphitheater."[2]

Da Ponte knew how to make the most of this site. The *bottega di caffè* in the first scene, with its aromatic atmosphere that favors open speaking, is perfectly suited to this location. In the ladies' room there are a number of mirrors, and luxury will have the scent and savor of chocolate heavily whipped by an agile maidservant. Geographic verisimilitude is respected when a sailboat is said to be carrying two young officers to some unspecified war and when the Albanian lords make their appearance. Naples is so crowded that it makes perfect sense to juxtapose soldiers and ordinary people, then sailors accompanied by singers, and then servants in livery. Along with the little orchestral ensembles that play in a garden in the second act, the three choruses, which are three uses of the same choral singers, are a delegation of the crowd that is always emotionally charged and always in search of riches.

The landscape of the libretto is marked with echoes and symbolic asides. The admirable sets created by Balthus for the Aix-en-Provence performances of 1950 highlight this. *Così fan tutte* (1790) puts onstage the agitations of the heart, and the changing sea constitutes its allusive horizon. Boats dock a little too easily on Dorabella and Fiordiligi's shores. Troubled by the new arrivals, they declare that their lives have become "a sea full of torment" (act 1, scene 14). When she accepts the pendant from her new lover, Dorabella feels the fire of Vesuvius in her heart: "Nel petto un Vusuvio d'avere mi par"—"I feel a Vesuvius inside my breast" (act 2, scene 5). A wisp of smoke arises perhaps on the horizon. With the complicity of Mozart's orchestra, the Neapolitan atmosphere, with its favorable winds that blow over seas and across woods, invites one to yield to the temptation of pleasure. The counselors of infidelity—Despina and Don Alfonso—perfectly incarnate the spirit of the place.

What used to go by the name of philosophy was independence of spirit, casting doubt on prejudices, a strong preoccupation with happiness, and especially a lively interest in experimentation. Despite its severe government, Naples had its philosophers like Ferdinando Galiani who became darlings within Parisian circles where the most heterodox thinking reigned. In this city where Montesquieu saw rampant misery and idleness, a certain freedom with codes and customs was also in evidence and with less hypocrisy than elsewhere. With his rhetorical skill, Latin familiarity, and a taste for poetic quotation (Sannazar, Ariosto, Metastasio), Alfonso is designed to fit the reputation of the intellectuals of his city. Since he does not decline to laugh at the confidence accorded to these outward virtues, he is perfectly qualified to lead the action of an opera buffa. In all his speeches laughter is never far off. "Let me laugh," he exclaims from the very beginning (act 1, scene 1). Throughout the opera the bursts of laughter never stop. In the last couplets, to put an end to the experiment in amorous permutation, the triumphant Alfonso invites the lovers to forget the quickly extorted betrayal. They are called on to join him in laughter: "Laugh all four of you. Me, I've already laughed and I will laugh some more" (act 2, scene 8). As for Despina, right down to her very name, she is the direct descendant of Serpina, the *Serva padrona* of Pergolesi (Naples, 1733), the model of the servant girl in opera buffa who knows how to fool those around her and get her way. Everything, including the lively 6/8 rhythm used here, would seem to attest to the full transmission of realist principles when it comes to the morality of servants. Despina is a champion of female domination. Women must learn to say, like queens, "I can" and "I want." They must make themselves obeyed and "know how to lie." Should they be attacked, they must go on the counterattack and they will win the battle in the end. The Despina doctrine of course wins out over the resistances of her two mistresses, even though the latter believe they are opposed to the principles of unashamed libertinage put forward by their servant. They naively allow themselves to be seduced, whereas they ought to have learned to be indifferent seducers themselves. For lack of boldness, they are destined to suffer.

UNLIKELIHOOD AND FREEDOM

But why insist on the Neapolitan features of the setting called for in the libretto when the music of Mozart transcends any and all national color? I do so because they have a direct bearing on the criticisms of unlikelihood and improbability that were often leveled at the plot. In a legendary setting such as Naples, the use of typical characters excuses the dramaturge from having to construct them ex nihilo in accordance with the laws of psychological verisimilitude. Instead the figures are there in advance. The psychology of each is imposed by the costumes. The theatrical personnel are governed by their location, and no further justification is deemed necessary. What a load off everyone's mind! The myth or fairy tale in its totality, including its gaps and necessary elements, is transported to the stage. A psychological interpretation would go astray if it tried to fill in the disparities of the plot. On the contrary, one must unreservedly welcome the pleasure that results from relaxing the demand for realism. The servant and the philosopher are what they have to be according to convention. They have no individual singularity apart from what will develop in the course of the action. At the beginning the two pairs of lovers resemble any other pair of lovers in theater. Betting on the infidelity of the engaged lovers, the false embarkation of the sailors and the Albanian disguises get the game started. Nothing more (or less) is needed to shape unforeseen events and sentimental reversals and thus hold the interest of the spectator. Every comedy is the story of love blocked, by some impediment, or a misunderstanding, or the opposition of a recalcitrant father. Here, at great cost to themselves, it is the two officers who agree to the game imposed by Alfonso and become each for the other an impediment and rival. In so doing, they risk losing the treasure of love they believed in their possession and instead suffer jealousy and compromise their friendship. The variations in feeling, so extraordinarily represented by the music, can be keenly observed from moment to moment as a relation independent of all other relations.

But who are these very young women? It is superfluous to subject them to the mocking inquisition that Don Alfonso deploys with disguised visitors: "Voi qui? come? perché? Quando? In qual modo?"—"You here? How? Why? When? By what means?" They are from Ferrare, they have a charming house, and they seem to live alone. Their fiancés however have left clothes in the closet. When they see Don Alfonso arrive, they greet him as the friend of their fiancés. After some gratification of Despina, he establishes his power within the house. Gaps and contradictions are everywhere. For example, we are asked to accept that the voices of the disguised fiancés are never recognizable (whereas Anna's fine ear recognizes Don Giovanni's voice and Figaro likewise recognizes Cherubino and Susanna at night). But why demand total verisimilitude if art, and especially music, needs a measure of freedom and blank space within which to appear? Once the frame of the Neapolitan site has been set up, all other accessories can be reduced to a minimum. Let's stay with the event that rides on the crest of the music. The musical evidence is enough in itself and communicates a profound psychic reality. Let's not ask how likely the circumstances that surround it are. The truth engendered by the music will appear all the stronger for having been set against a background of artifice and contrivance. One must let Mozart have the right to give a sincere slant to words considered to be lies and to insert a hint of gravity within a parodic intention. Thus the words and melody of "Smanie implacabili"—"Implacable furor" (act 1, scene 9), sung by Dorabella after the departure of her fiancé, express the sadness building to fury that one finds in the grand arias of opera seria. The effect of exaggeration is of course deliberate, and we are tempted to smile, but the aria is superb and expresses a serious passion.

THE GENERAL LAW OF HUMAN BEINGS

In the eight solemn verses—the octave—that deliver the story's lesson, Don Alfonso proclaims one of the essential tenets of his philosophy. It is a philosophy that affirms the universal and inevitable flux of the emotions. It is therefore a philosophy that takes into account the accusation leveled by all the men (*tutti*) against all the women (*tutte*) but runs to their defense. Of course they are not faithful. But there is no fault in that. It is a necessary effect of the human condition:

> *Tutti accusan le donne, ed io le scuso*
> *Se mille volte al dì cangiano amore;*
> *Altri un vizio lo chiama ed altri un uso:*
> *Ed a me par necessità del core.*

> All accuse the women, but me I excuse them
> If they change their love a thousand times a day,
> It's vice for some and tradition for others:
> For me it is all a necessity of the heart.

One might say, on a first hearing, that excusing the women in this way is a backhanded sign of contempt. The indulgence and the condescension of Alfonso, are they not the height of misogyny? For why, if changefulness is universal, mention only the women, all women, as though they alone were subject to this flux? "Così fan tutte"—"So do all [women]." "Toutes les mêmes," as Michel Orcel's French translation puts it. But how do the others, the men, behave? Are there really within humanity two opposing camps? Despina, in one of the sermons she addresses to her mistresses (act 1, scene 9), proceeds in the same manner and throws opprobrium on all the men: "One is as good as another because none is worth anything." From the opening act she declares, "Di pasta simile son *tutti quanti*." The maxims of Don Alfonso and Despina are exact echoes of each other. Thus the war of the sexes, no sooner started, leads to a draw and armistice. Equality prevails. In the morning altercation with Guglielmo and Ferrando (act 1, scene 1), Don Alfonso puts forward a proposition that shocks them but for which they will themselves more or less unwittingly provide proof: women are all similar and are the same as men. They are creatures of "flesh, bone, and skin," earthly creatures "like us all" ("come tutti noi") and not gods. It is nonsense to accord them any quasi-religious cult status. Despina's feminist lesson is pronounced in precisely similar terms: "Are you of flesh and bone, or what?" (act 2, scene 1) *Tutte* and *tutti* mutually exchange their image of inconstancy.

All is subject to change in the natural world. And if human beings belong to nature, then "a necessity of the heart" is change. The mutability of desire is "the general law of human beings," affirms Diderot, another philosopher and one who shares certain features with Alfonso. What is "more insane," he declares, "than a precept that proscribes the flux that is within us; . . . than an oath of immutability between two mortal creatures under a sky that is never the same for an instant, under shelters that threaten to collapse, at the base of a rock that disintegrates into powder, at the foot of a tree that cracks open, on a rock that splits apart?"[3]

Let's reread the libretto and listen again to *Così fan tutte*. We may notice the fine dexterity with which Da Ponte introduces here and there the verb *"cangiar"* (to change) and the word *"cambio"* (change). In the second scene of act 1, the two sisters utter an imprudent wish: "If ever my heart changes desire, may the god of Love punish me for life!" But no sooner is the first act over (scene 14) than the two women find themselves overtaken by the vertigo of change. "Ah, how in a single moment my whole destiny has suddenly changed." Not much later, in the second act, after the exchange of pendants, Guglielmo and Dorabella can exclaim, "Oh, che cambio felice"—"O, the happy exchange of hearts and feelings! What new pleasures! What sweet pains!" What melancholy, however, in these new pleasures and these new pains! They are sunning themselves on the ruins of the immutable love the ideal of which, or at least the vocabulary, had filled the minds of the young lovers. An absolute—a false absolute, a disincarnate absolute—has melted away.

Don Alfonso, this practically immobile man, has thus been the agent of change. He knows, from experience no doubt, the effects of absence, and he plays on them. A heart cannot remain unoccupied. To know it exists, it must receive the message from the senses. New unknown admirers, be they ridiculous, emphatic, or clumsy, have the advantage of being present. It is impossible not to listen to them when they speak up . . . impossible not to hold their heads when they pretend to poison themselves . . . impossible not to taste the captivating serenade played by the musicians who escort them . . . impossible not to give them your hand for a walk in the garden. So many sensitive messages begin to add up. So what if the first response of the two women is furor—with certain differences, it's true, between the intensity of their refusals and the quickness of their coming around. The way Da Ponte has described it for us, Don Alfonso knows that the energy of an emotion, once awakened, can change into an emotion of a different nature; all displacements are possible. At the end of the first act, Alfonso foresees that the "fire" of indignation will very soon "change" into the fire of love. It is a philosophy whose lessons will not be lost on Stendhal. Someone whose interest we have piqued by an offense is already no longer indifferent . . . and is capable of being taken. The philosopher, aware of these affective modulations and their paradoxical effects, passes easily from theory to practice. He orchestrates his little world provoking experiments in separation, indignation, fawning, jealousy, and weakness. Music is present from the start to develop the various voices of change, to materialize its pathways, and to render it transparent in all its timbres and complex nuances.

The happy denouement and the preferred *lieto fine* do not abolish change but are its last form. We know that change could not stop there. But we do not need to bother ourselves with the fate of these lovers who have undergone this intensive day of lessons. The play ends.

We have witnessed an opera within the opera. With and without the characters' knowledge, they have engaged in a performance of a little spectacle—a *commediola* improvised and staged by a maestro named Don Alfonso. By his will, Guglielmo, Ferrando, and Despina became actors; Fiordiligi and Dorabella unwittingly played their parts despite themselves. Don Alfonso made use of the beach and the gardens for his setting. He stepped in to cue lines and furnished costumes, boats, musicians, and wedding apparel. He was the diabolical scandalmonger and the knowing manipulator, and he passed his laughter on to us. But at the end he assumes a new dignity: he appears as initiator and educator. He taught the lovers what it means to be human beings and not gods. One can even ask if he is not a slightly grimacing prefiguration of Sarastro. All the masks worn on his orders can now fall. They made it possible to destroy the initial deluded overconfidence of the lovers and their illusory possessive presumption. The mask, which is evil, also turns out to be the cure by provoking an unmasking. "My trickery has served to untrick you." What then has Alfonso taught to the untricked Guglielmo and Ferrando? Recognize the universal flux, "the general law of human beings." Accept its authority. Pay it homage. Only then will you find calm: *la bella calma*. One must learn to love without demanding proof. One must simply believe. "Lo credo"—"I believe it." At this final moment, Mozart's music attains a singular gravity beyond all irony. And yet has calm really been won? It is promised, but it reigns only for an instant. It is a tranquilizing word, a step toward the tonic chord to accompany the lowering of the curtain.

CHAPTER 6

The Promise of Idomeneo

The anger of Neptune spans the entire opera of *Idomeneo* and only subsides with the final oracle.[1] For its first performance in Munich in 1781, the set designer, Lorenz Quaglio, probably took great pleasure in constructing the scene. The spectators recognized Greece and a seaport with masts and sails: the Cretan palace (where Minos and Deucalion reigned), the foamy waves, and the artfully drawn temple that of course included dolphins, tridents, and seahorses with flowing manes. These decorative elements might have been used in many earlier operas. An entire memory of the storms in literature and music was awakened when Mozart made the two choruses—*vicino* and *lontano*—call back and forth imploring with high pathos: "Pietà, Numi, pietà!" (act 1, no. 5). It is not unthinkable that the most well read among the spectators in Munich in 1781 might have already encountered Idomeneus in those passages from *The Iliad* that recount the military exploits of the Cretan hero or that they recalled his name appearing in *The Aeneid*. But it is certain that for most of them this name had become insepa-rably linked to Fénelon's *Adventures of Telemachus* (1699), a work that had become a favorite throughout Europe. This book was written for the education of a prince and became a lesson manual for kings. It con-tributed to the formation of the political ideas of all educated classes including those who eventually instigated the first steps toward the French Revolution. In book 5 of Rousseau's *Émile* (1762), the young man goes off to observe the institutions of the European nations. He travels with "a *Télémaque* in his hand" while at the same time receiving from his preceptor a lesson in political science that summarizes the es-sential points of *The Social Contract*. Whereas the normative principles of the contract establish "a measuring stick" for judgment called for by the various existing societies, Fénelon's tale presents models and countermodels of government. An episode from Fénelon's novel offers Rousseau the ideal that Émile and his teacher will nowhere find: "We are looking for the happy Salente and the good Idomeneus made wise from his misfortunes." Fénelon had built there a sort of utopia. More than sixty years later, Rousseau could still seek to turn it into a criterion for evaluating the political reality of the day.

The legend of the return from Troy and the sacrificed child was transmitted in a variety of texts—notably the commentaries of Ser-vius to Virgil—collected by scholars from the Renaissance through to the seventeenth century.[2] No complete story or play treats the subject before Fénelon. The figure called by Rousseau "the good Idomeneus" would not necessarily be the epithet that best applies to the same figure in Fénelon's work. He is, after all, a child-killing king, the murderer of his son, forced into exile by his people. After founding a colony, he begins a second career as an audacious sovereign attracted by the glory of arms and magnificence. He eventually acquires wisdom and accepts the lessons of Mentor. The birth and history of the kingdom of Salente on the Calabrian coast is entirely the product of Fénelon's imagination. It is the moment when the political novel—a "modern" dream—takes over from myth. Unlike Louis XIV, whom he initially resembles in his taste for war, Idomeneus renounces conquest and knows how to make peace with his neighbors. The prosperous countryside and the industri-ous capital are schools of virtue where all live under the rule of law, even the monarch. Everything is brought back to a "noble and frugal simplicity," and within the harmony of a society that carefully distinguishes ranks and functions, everything cooperates toward a common usefulness. Idomeneo becomes a sort of Sarastro.

Fénelon's text constantly imitates classical models and deliberately seeks and attains a high level of beauty in its elocution and rhythm. One feels one is hearing the "passionate declamation" that the archbishop of Cambrai was happy to observe in the music of his day.[3] A story recounting the "misfortunes" of Idomeneus offers a sequence of speeches that seem to be waiting to be treated musically as a set of recitatives and arias.

In the storm, the hero made a foolish promise in the hope of saving his life: " 'O powerful god,' he cried. 'You who rule over the empire of waves, deign to listen to an unhappy man! If you allow me to see again the Isle of Crete despite the fury of the winds, I will sacrifice to you the first head I see.' "[4]

The storm subsides. "But cruel Nemesis, the pitiless goddess, who keeps watch to punish men, especially overly proud kings, pushed Idomeneus with an invisible fatal hand." He is seized with horror when he discovers that "the first head" he must sacrifice is his own son. The latter is surprised and throws his arms around the neck of his father: " 'O father,' he says, 'whence comes this sadness? After such a long absence, are you angry at finding yourself back in your kingdom and giving joy to your son? What have I done? You turn your eyes away from me in fear!' "

Idomeneus does not answer and instead calls again to the divinity: "O Neptune, what have I promised you! At what price did you rescue me from shipwreck? Send me back to the waves and rocks that, in breaking me, ought to have finished my sad life. Let my son live! O cruel god, here, take my blood and spare his."

Idomeneus turns his sword against himself without listening to the advice of a priest who reproaches him his cruelty and invites him to sacrifice "one hundred bulls whiter than snow." The son then comes to offer his life: "Here I am, father. Your son is ready to die to pacify the god. Do not bring down on yourself his anger. I die content because my death will have spared you yours. Strike, father. Have no fear to find in me an unworthy son who would fear to die."

In the opera of Varesco and Mozart this will come in aria 27, "No, la morte io non pavento"—"No, I am not afraid of death." But whereas by generic convention the opera seria multiplies the perils to arrive eventually at a happy denouement, Fénelon's Idomeneus commits the irreparable crime. In a state of supernatural fury, "entirely beside himself and as if torn apart by the infernal Furies, [he] surprises all observers who are near: he drives his sword into the heart of that child." The account of the child's death employs a cut flower image borrowed from Virgil: "The child collapses in a puddle of blood. The shadows of death are covering his eyes, he opens them slightly to the light, but hardly has he found it before it becomes unbearable for him. Like a beautiful lily in the middle of a field cut at its root by the blade of the plow that tips over unable to hold itself upright any longer though it has not yet lost that vivid whiteness and the sparkle that charms the eyes. But the earth no longer nourishes it and its life is extinguished. So the son of Idomeneus, like a young and tender flower, is cruelly cut down in his early youth."

Disoriented, Idomeneus walks toward the city asking for his son. The people, transported by their own madness, force the king to flee toward the sea with his companions.

The scrupulous execution of the promise made to Neptune in order to escape from the storm thus combines human error and divine cruelty. Probably, for a theologian tempted by quietism, Idomeneus's fault lies in having concluded a self-interested bargain and having sought to force the divine decision by an act of his own will. But there is something else beside this interpretation that conforms to a morality that wants man to abandon himself humbly to divine will. One can glimpse on a more archaic level the belief of communities who feel threatened by the staining of their leader, and, according to the ritual of the *pharmakos*, the latter must be expelled.

When some years later Telemachus comes ashore at Salente (book 8), the thriving city looks like a flower to him. One can easily imagine that Fénelon was recalling his earlier comparison of the sacrificed boy to a cut flower, as though a sacred link existed between the votive sacrifice performed in Crete and the new city built on the Italian coast. "Telemachus looked with admiration on this newborn city. It looked like a young plant that, having been nourished by the sweet dew of the night, feels the early morning rays of the sun that come to embellish it further. It grows, it opens its tender buds, it stretches out its green leaves, it spreads open its scented flowers of a thousand new colors, and at every instant one looks on it there is something new and bright. So too did Idomeneus's new city by the sea blossom. Every day and every hour it grew in magnificence, and from far away foreign sailors could see it displaying new ornaments of architecture that rose up to the sky."

It is tempting to interpret the city/plant as the substitute figure for the cut son/flower, that is, as its resurrection. And the son is reborn under another visage, namely, as a living person. When Telemachus appears before Idomeneus, the latter not only recognizes the features of Ulysses in his face but offers to adopt this son who is traveling from shore to shore in search of his father: "Yes, you are the son of Ulysses, but you will also be mine."[5] Telemachus is from that moment placed under the sign of a double family line. During this welcoming scene, a rage, which is always a mark of heroic intensity, intervenes, and one may note its near symmetry with respect to the mad transports of the murderer king and the indignant people. This mark of intensity is expressed by the ecstatic vision of a priest who is suddenly "beside himself" in fury. The prophetic words are uttered during a solemn sacrifice in which Idomeneus offers Jupiter one hundred bulls to favor his victories. And here we discover a second new symmetry. Are not these the same hundred bulls that his friends in Crete suggested he sacrifice to Neptune instead of his son? The outlook would seem to promise success to Idomeneus in his military campaigns with Telemachus at his side. At the end of the story Telemachus receives the promise of a double inheritance. In the end, when the return to Ithaca is accomplished, a moment that ties in with the last verses of *The Odyssey*, we know that Telemachus will marry Antiope, Idomeneus's daughter. Within the succession of Idomeneus's trials, the murder of the anonymous son is therefore only a negative moment. Like Job, Idomeneus will not regain everything he has lost, but he will receive a substitute for the one he lost by his own fault.

There is probably a link between the infanticide that happens in Crete and the founding of Salente. This might be the moment to turn this inquiry back to the legendary foundations of this story and ask about the blood shed by city founders. I am thinking of fratricide: Romulus; of infanticide: Theseus, the first king of Athens provoking the death of Hippolytus; of Brutus, founder of the Roman republic, condemning his son to death, and so on. The myth of William Tell, a story frequently taken up in the eighteenth century, is a significant variation: in place of the execution of the son, one gets the substitute death of the oppressor who had imposed the trial.

But it is also necessary to ask about the myths that concern themselves with the price asked by the divine guardians of these great thresholds. Passing them is not granted without payment. Let us however make the following detour before going there.

NOVELS, OPERAS, AND THEIR DESCENDANTS

Fénelon's book had its imitators, and the reading public welcomed these other educational travel stories. The most well known are Ramsay's *Voyages of Cyrus* (1727) and especially *Séthos* (1731) by the abbé Terrasson. Voltaire's *Candide* (1759) in which Pangloss takes the place of Mentor would be the parody of this genre. *Séthos* is not without importance: it reinscribes the theme of the princely voyage within an Egyptian and Masonic framework. The reader witnesses an initiation into the mysteries of Isis. Similarities have been noticed between it and the *Thamos, King of Egypt* that Mozart worked on in 1778–1779 and especially with the libretto of *The Magic Flute*. There is no doubt an analogy to be drawn between Fénelon's Mentor, the wise Amédès who guides Séthos, and the Sarastro of Schikaneder. The pedagogical tale was thus able to oscillate between pseudomythological narrative and the *Märchen* or fairy tale.

By chance, then—but was it merely chance?—the first and last operas in Mozart's string of masterpieces derive from the same line of fabulous fictions. They set to music a pedagogical fable and the inevitable confrontation between opposed forces. In addition, the princely pedagogy allows for identification by readers and spectators; it passes as the universal prototype for the *Bildung* of the individual, the "men of merit."[6] These fictions invite one to take possession of oneself, while at the same time offering an image of what people are entitled to expect from a good government. The initiation experience is the fundamental theme: what virtues must be acquired and what tests must one pass to earn the right to exercise power? A common source, namely, Fénelon and his grand novel of education, allows one to understand better the lineage of the two operas. The tragic question of succession, the peril of the interruption in dynastic continuity that shapes so many aspects of classical stage tragedy and opera, was able to interest a public infinitely broader than that of just the court. Succeeding the father and acceding to oneself are one and the same event. A message founded on these legendary monarchal images has persisted down to our own democratic era, since it is quite reasonable to assume that within the theatrical peril for the inheritor of the kingdom everyone has the possibility of reading an allegory of what threatens his or her own self. The double requirement is to recognize the law of the father and to liberate Ilia whom the law of the father had enchained. It is also well known that the aesthetic ideas and political morality of Fénelon remained topical throughout the century. Fénelon put sharp questions to warring kings: "Have you not done useless harm to your enemies? These enemies are still men, still your brothers, if you are a true man yourself."[7]

THE APPRENTICESHIP OF A MASTER

Leopold Mozart sought to inculcate in his son an admiration for Fénelon. We know this from a letter sent from Paris in 1766. He was returning from Holland at that time after having passed through Cambrai with Wolfgang. Leopold Mozart insisted on making a pilgrimage to the tomb of the archbishop and tells of his trip in rather pedantic tones: "I contemplated . . . the tomb and the marble bust of the great Fénelon who immortalized himself with his *Telemachus*, with his treatise on the education of young women, with his dialogues of the dead, with his fables, and other writings both sacred and profane."[8] Fénelon's book will pass into Wolfgang's hands during his stay in Bologna in 1770, in other words at the time of the great confirmation of his knowledge of music. Mozart tells his sister that he is reading Fénelon's *Télémaque* and that he is "already on the second part."[9] The remark is somewhat vague. Does he mean book 2 or a second volume? Let us imagine that Wolfgang was paying close attention to the story of the sacrificed child.

In 1778 Mozart may have heard Fénelon talked about in Paris. At the end of his stay in Paris, after the death of his mother, Mozart was living at the home of Mme d'Épinay and Friedrich Melchior Grimm in the Chaussée d'Antin. Grimm was an old acquaintance.[10] Fifteen years earlier, in his *Correspondance littéraire*, he had celebrated the talents of the child genius, and another meeting had taken place in 1766. In 1778, after passing through Mannheim where he met Aloysia Weber, Mozart felt a growing ambition to become a creator of dramas and was fully conscious of the means that he wished to use. But he found no employment for his powers and regretted the difficulty of "finding a good poem": "*la poésie*, which was the only thing the French could be proud of, gets worse every day."[11] He had probably been speaking with Grimm, who for a long time had been wondering if there was any Frenchman capable of writing a poem suitable for music: "Mortal Cold and Bad Taste are the gods that inspire the makers of French opera."[12] In the important entry "Poème lyrique" inserted in the *Encyclopédie*, Grimm had given theoretical formulation to the principles of simplicity and rapidity that agreed already with the formal demands that Mozart never ceased repeating. The librettist then must be "economical with words" but on condition that he remain "energetic, natural, and easygoing." He will know how to make room for music, avoid crowding into its domain, and submit to the composer. Any superfluous text must be resisted as it slows down the dramatic action:

After having . . . named the subject and created the situation, after having prepared it, the poet provides nothing more than certain bodies of material that he abandons to the genius of the composer. The latter infuses them with the requisite expression and develops all the finesse of detail they can harbor. . . . Never should the poet fear giving his musician an overly powerful task. Since speed is a trait inseparable from music, and one of the principal reasons for its prodigious effects, the pace of a lyric poem should always be quick. . . . There is, moreover, this difference between the lyric poet and the poet of tragedy: to the same extent that the latter becomes eloquent and wordy, the former must become precise and economical with words because the eloquence in passionate moments belongs entirely to the musician.

In addition, Grimm became interested in the theatrical treatment of the Idomeneus story. In 1764 the poet Antoine-Martin Lemierre had staged a tragedy of Idoménée. Grimm found it crushingly boring, even worse than the boredom caused by the play of Prosper Jolyot de

Crébillon performed in 1705. Among other flaws, Grimm criticizes the lengthy passages that were the inevitable consequence of the traditional tragic form that relied on the intervention of too many "quibblers." Starting with the Crébillon adaptation, which also invents the name Idamante for the son, the action is complicated by the introduction of a rivalry between father and son, who are both in love with a certain Érixène.

For the Cretan history of Idomeneus to become a tragic play or opera, it would have to add female voices. In 1712 Antoine Danchat composed for Campra a libretto consisting of a prologue and five acts overflowing with mythological pomp. The captive Ilione (a prefiguration of Ilia) is there, and she too is courted by both father and son. Of this rivalry, Giambattista Varesco's libretto keeps only a few very discreet traces. Danchat also introduces an Électre in love with Idamante, and Varesco will keep this character. With Idamante and Ilia being assigned the role of expressing the tenderness and alarms of love and Idomeneo entirely possessed by the torment of the decision of sacrifice, it was necessary to add a role that could register the offense and inscribe the desire for vengeance. From the palette of *affetti*, the wild fits of anger were missing, and it became inevitable to attribute them to a supplementary character similar to Ériphile in Racine's *Iphigénie* or to Oreste in *Andromaque*, that is, rivals whose love has been pushed away and who are thus torn apart with jealousy and invoke infernal powers.

Grimm's judgment of the various Idomeneus plays is precise and fair, and there is every reason to think that he could have repeated all this to Mozart during their Parisian discussions of 1778: "This subject lacks substance. There is not enough material to make a five-act tragedy out of it in the form that it has been given. Our plays are too full of talk, and the subject of Idomeneus does not lend itself to that. Everything in it needs to be passion and movement. The subject of Jephthah, which is essentially the same, has the advantage over Idomeneus of presenting a devoted daughter as victim, and this makes it fundamentally more touching."[13]

Indeed, and I would add that the consequences of the vow made to the sea god elicit enough emotion and thus make it unnecessary, dramatically speaking, to add on the overtly oedipal conflict between father and son.[14]

MYTHS OF RETURN AND MYTHS OF DEPARTURE

Some learned commentators in the seventeenth century had already drawn the analogy between Jephthah and Idomeneus. Fénelon, it would seem, used the story from the book of Judges (11:29–40). It is also not impossible that he was familiar with the beautiful oratorio *Jephte* by Carissimi (1650). As for Grimm, he was most likely aware of Montéclair's *Jephté* (1732), admired by Rousseau, and he may have at least heard of the existence of Handel's superb oratorio (1751).[15]

Other resemblances have been pointed out. If the sacrificial subject of Jephthah and Idomeneus belongs to a category of myths that one might call myths of return, there is another symmetrical category that can be called myths of departure. The passage, in one sense or the other, depends on the favor of a god. One finds this theme in *Iphigeneia at Aulis*. Anyone who had read Euripides and Racine knew the story that Gluck presented as an opera in 1774 with a libretto by Calzabigi. An irritated Diana refuses to grant the Greeks the favorable winds they need to set off on their expedition against Troy. The prophet Calchas informs Agamemnon that the goddess has demanded he sacrifice his daughter. A bloody ceremony is prepared. These preparations are evoked in the sublime first chorus of Aeschylus's *Agamemnon*. In the milder versions, Iphigeneia is saved thanks to the sacrifice of a substitute victim—in Euripides a deer, in Racine a jealous rival with the same family blood and the same name who kills herself in a moment of fury. Another solution, imagined by Du Roulet and Gluck, is to have the goddess arbitrarily set aside her anger for the sake of preserving alliances and concord among the Greeks. Mozart was of course familiar with Gluck's *Iphigénie*, and one can notice more than one point in common between the musical texture of that opera and *Idomeneo*.

In the myths of departure as well as in the myths of return, at a very archaic level of belief, a warrior who would pass a fatal threshold—shore, borderline, bridge, and so on—is obliged to pay to get across. No payment, no passage. Thus a debt gets established that the god in question will not forget. The one who makes a vow cannot have his commitment lifted because these lofty promises constitute unbreakable bonds. The Olympian gods are all familiar with these constraining promises that take the rivers of the underworld as their witness. In their dealings with mortals, they send plagues or monsters into the territory of the perjurer-debtor.

In the case of Idomeneus and Jephthah, the cruel vows make chance intervene to designate the victim promised to the god.[16] Of course it is important to specify the differences between their two vows. Jephthah condemns in advance one of his own (the victim will be the first who "cometh forth of the doors of my house" [Judges 11:31]), whereas Idomeneus vows rather more vaguely to sacrifice "the first head" that he meets once back on the Cretan shore. His vow arguably leaves him exposed to a wider array of chance. It could be a stranger or an animal, for instance. Yet everything transpires as though the divinity had to impose the highest possible price. For victory, for the success of the voyage, and to cross the terrible "green sea" ["*la mer glauque*"] safely, the warrior hero is forced to give up his most precious belonging. His ex-voto will be a part of himself: a child.

"LOVE HAS CONQUERED"

Loving devotion will bring about the denouement. The logic of sacrifice thus resembles the logic of dreams where one figure gets displaced by another. This is a resource that classical tragedy often exploits; however, this commonplace technique of dying in the place of another is nonetheless charged with significance. The man or woman who consents to die in the place of the first designated victim is demanding nothing other than the power to rescue a beloved voluntarily—without any other condition. The vow was an act of bargaining: this for that. Voluntary sacrifice is no longer bargaining, or, at the very, least it profoundly modifies the terms of exchange. The voluntary victim wants only to receive death and in exchange asks only for the survival of the one who should have died. The voluntary victim will never be able to possess what he or she obtains, or even know if it has been obtained. This is the supreme proof, which marks love with the seal of truth, because every self-interest is abolished. The divinity is free to accept the death of this replacement. Or, on the contrary, to grant pardon, because a love that renounces all places itself beyond negotiation. In that case it is the divinity that changes: the terrifying god reveals a compassionate face. Ilia can thus be the redeemer of the condemned son.

True, one could have gotten tired of the conventional ornaments and the predictable rhetoric used in plays and operas of the eighteenth century to adorn the gods and heroes of mythology. And yet it was this mythology that gave access to the unavowable, to the most troubling dreams, and it only took a little sprucing-up of the language to rekindle the fire. If Varesco's poem was devoid of innovation, it did manage, as Grimm's expression that I cited earlier puts it, to "name the subject and create the situation"; he had "provided certain bodies of material" and the rest belonged "to the genius of the composer." Mozart had battled hard to get the words that suited him, and his music breathed life back into the mystery of the mythic theme with a prodigious power of invention. One need only recall the richness of the orchestration, the extraordinary accompaniments in the recitatives, the sublime quartetto in the third act where the sufferings are knotted together. The great enigmatic dream of the child destined for sacrifice—Isaac, Iphigeneia—received there a new life. It is not any literary exegesis of the libretto, worthy though it be, that can shed light on the sources of our emotion. And one should certainly not project on to Mozart's biography and his relations with his father all that to which we gain access via the music.

The final scene of *Idomeneo* takes place under the statue of Neptune that comes alive and speaks at the moment the axe is lifted against Idamante.[17] With Mozart, in the long version of the divine intervention, the oracle, accompanied by the brass, pronounces a more explicit judgment: absolving Idomeneo the father but punishing the king. As a king, Idomeneo is a perjurer and must lose his kingdom. As a father, he is pardoned: Idamante will live and succeed him. The short version that Mozart preferred says all this more peremptorily. The transmission of power is of monumental importance here. One feels one is witnessing the transition from one epoch to another. This opera, which is fundamentally a religious work, delivers the message of the *Aufklärung* insofar as it makes us witness the passage from a time of warriors to a time of charitable, liberating heroes.[18] The final aria of Idomeneo, "Torna in me la pace"—"Peace returns to me," expresses joy reconquered after the abdication of the power to command: the happiness is that all lives are spared, and it is a relief to lay down one's sword and the royal burden. "The old tree blossoms again." Even though the words do not say it explicitly, one is tempted to believe that at the hour of the marriage the final festivities—within the frame of the operatic fiction—celebrate the disappearance of the personal authority of the monarch and that a harmonious anarchy begins. The new prince will not reign by having his personal will prevail but by submitting himself to the superior law of love.

The perfect filial love of Idamante does not prevent him from being above all a liberator, for his heart is generous; we learned this already in the first recitative of Ilia. As the ship transporting the captive Trojans was sinking, it is he who pulls the noble daughter of Priam from the waves. From the very beginning of the opera, his only desire is to take as his wife the woman who served as a war trophy to Idomeneo. At the end of the first act, all the other prisoners are freed, and the occasion is marked by a very beautiful chorus. Then come the decisive tests, which resemble those that will later be reserved for Tamino: face the sadness and silence of the recovered father, obey the order of exile, face the monster (before whom Tamino, being more human, will flee), offer one's life. These resemblances permit some finer differentiations. Mozart had to accept the vocal resources that were available to him. For this reason he modified the accent of love by attributing more virtuosity to Idamante (sung by an unsatisfactory castrato and today by a mezzo-soprano) and also infinitely more tenderness to Tamino. The voices of the oracle and the high priest in the utterances of sovereign authority already have the register of Sarastro's voice. But these sacerdotal voices pronounce orders: they do not converse as Sarastro does.

For the sake of dramatic efficiency, Mozart abridges the words of the oracle. We know of three versions. Two of these begin with the essential words "Ha vinto amore—"Love has conquered." These words had already been heard in a number of operas, notably in a beautiful chorus in Rameau's *Pygmalion*. But here the magic is complete: the decisive victory belongs to Ilia, who offers herself as a surrogate victim. The vow of loving devotion is stronger than the vow of human sacrifice. We are persuaded by the music itself of the profound truth of this love. It is the most beautiful music there is: tormented happiness, suffering become joy. Mozart fashioned the role and arias of Ilia—the captive, the lover—so as to make her love appear as the principal antagonist of Neptune's somber power. It is perhaps the leading antagonism of the entire opera since it must be noted that there is no conflict between the various characters in *Idomeneo*. They are not in battle with each other. There are certainly contrasts among their temperaments, but no interest opposes them. In this opera with a certain oratorio quality, the confrontation with the great Adversary is more important than the interhuman conflicts. The emotions of the characters do not result from their rivalry but from a cosmic hostility. All the action develops the consequences of the vow made to Neptune and flows out of the caprices of an elementary power.

In *Zaide* (1780), *The Abduction from the Seraglio* (1782), and *The Magic Flute* (1791) prisoners are guarded by jailors whose vigilance must be overcome. Their liberation is thus bought with a ruse or piece of magic that undermines the normal precautions of the guardians. We can also remember *Fidelio*, which is the most famous example of a "rescue opera." Rescue and liberation come about very differently in *Idomeneo*. Ilia, liberated and a liberator, a castaway and a voluntary victim, was certainly at first a captive, but she is not held under watch. The different voices—from that of the reckless hero to the collective voices of the chorus—answer from the depths of their being to a faceless necessity that manifests itself in the orchestra starting with the overture. The music, marked by so many energies, is then all the more free to communicate an emotion that goes beyond any individual psychology. One must accept the various fictional roles while at the same time only acknowledging them as instruments transmitting a message from afar. Following an image in Varesco, we can say that the outward sea redoubles the inner heart: "Fuor del mar ho un mar in seno"—"Away from the sea, I have a sea deep in my heart" (act 2, scene 2, no. 12). According to Mozart, the fable tells of the force of love and of a return to life at the very point of death.

CHAPTER 7

Lights and Powers

The Magic Flute

DEGREES OF POWER

There is no shortage of commentaries on *The Magic Flute*. Indeed the author of the text, Emanuel Schikaneder, wanted his fable to be captivating enough to charm the general public while at the same time offering an allegory in which specialists of Masonic thinking could recognize their mysteries. Moreover, with Mozart's music the fable received an even greater abundance of meanings that prevent any interpretation from achieving closure.

The action offers the spectator a pathway that both progresses toward knowledge and leads to conquest of the highest love. In Schikaneder's fiction, Tamino, the young hero, prince of the Orient, is at first a lost traveler who receives from a divine hand the image of a stranger. He falls in love with her, but he only obtains the real presence of his beloved after putting to work the interior force that outer hostility leads him to discover. A series of tests is the price that must be paid for access to knowledge, and they also act as obstacles to be surmounted, thus permitting love to shine with the greatest radiant joy. It is an ancient theme well suited to unexpected renewals. It has been said that *Die Frau Ohne Schatten* (1919) by Hugo von Hofmannstahl and Richard Strauss was a free remodeling of the same myth. The opera offers itself as a continuation of the continuation, left incomplete, that Goethe wanted to add to *The Magic Flute*.[1] Goethe's text pursues the question of the future of Mozart's characters and their desire for children.

Closely related to this first important point is a second that touches on the question of power itself. We are perhaps particularly attentive to this question because of the political concerns of our own day, but it was also present in the minds of Schikaneder and Mozart. Their *Singspiel* is a contemporary of the nascent French Revolution.

Therefore asking about power in *The Magic Flute* is not an arbitrary choice. One could hardly be said to be making a mountain out of a molehill since the libretto is constantly talking about power. The word "*Macht*" (force, might, power) intervenes in crucial moments whether in regard to a power that is exercised or one that is missing.

Scene one: pursued by a snake, the traveling prince Tamino faints ("fällt in Ohnmacht," literally "falls into powerlessness": *ohne Macht* = without power).[2] He is aided by three veiled ladies sent by the Queen of the Night. They kill the monster with their silver lances while crying "Stirb, Ungeheuer, durch unsre Macht—"Die, monster, by our power" (act 1, scene 1). That is the beginning. But this same power at the end of the work admits defeat, and it is again the word "*Macht*" that we hear:

> *Zerschmettert, zernichtet ist unsre Macht,*
> *Wir alle gestürzet in ewig Nacht.*

> Shattered, destroyed is our power,
> We are all thrown into eternal night.
>
> (act 2, scene 30)

By the time the opera arrives at its final destination, we have witnessed a displacement of power. A first power that appears protective is supplanted by a power that is better and stronger.

The major conflict, the only one in fact, opposes the Queen of the Night and Sarastro, high priest of wisdom and the solar principle. Everything else is suspended from this conflict—first the happiness of the couple Tamino-Pamina and secondarily the fate of Papageno, who impatiently awaits a companion. Three couples therefore, each occupying a distinct level of reality, evolve before us—with of course the assistance or resistance of subaltern characters, either supernatural or sacerdotal, subordinate to the Queen or Sarastro: the three ladies, the three boys, the slaves, the priests, the guardians, the armed men, the orator, and, more strikingly, Sarastro's rebellious slave, Pamina's executioner, the somber Monostatos, a figure of the perfidy and obscure desires that rise up in one who holds delegated powers.

How does the question of power pose itself for each of these three couples? The investigation I propose will follow an ascending order, from low to high, inferior to superior, from natural instinct as evinced in children and animals to sovereign wisdom.

Papageno is the role that Schikaneder fashioned for himself. His presence signifies elementary vital energy with its appetites and fears. He represents the part of man that demands natural happiness but will not accede to initiation. He is incapable of keeping quiet. But he knows how to sing with his mouth closed and without articulating. Within the categories of a both intuitive and erudite wisdom, he incarnates the psychological status that Freud will later name the id. Thanks to Papageno, the quest of the traveling prince is redoubled in the mode of farce. Buffoonery counterbalances religious solemnities; scenes of drollery alternate with moments of pathos. These rapid changes in atmosphere pleased Goethe, and he tried to pursue the same effects in the dramatic sketch that he intended as a continuation of *The Magic Flute*. From elementary gaiety to the mysteries of the universe—the distance is considerable, and the oscillation here is brusque. But in passing from anxiety to laughter, from solemn meditation to spontaneous gags, the audience experiences the entire spectrum of human emotions. You entirely discover your whole human being.

A stealer of birds, named after a bird (*Papagei* is German for parrot), and talkative like a bird, Papageno is particularly incapable of suppressing his cowardice, gluttony, and appetite for women. He lets one see immediately what he is, namely, in all things, the man of spontaneous desire, of instinct, of quick simple thoughts. A man who has learned neither repression nor the difference between truth and lies. In the first act, when Tamino regains consciousness, Papageno pretends to be the conqueror of the monster that was actually destroyed by the three ladies. He allows a power to be attributed to him that he does not really possess. The ladies punish him by locking his beak shut. He escapes from this adventure scolded but also with a glockenspiel that has magic powers.

Is it acceptable to speak of power in his case? Yes, provided we recognize that his power is very limited. Papageno, this man of the woods, in fact reigns only over the birdcage he carries on his back. His power is therefore laughable and innocently cruel as he plays the jailer of animals. Nevertheless, there is an irrepressible force within him, the force of elemental life with its simple joys, passing disappointments, and impeccable health. On his deathbed, Mozart asked to hear the songs of Papageno, which are the very warmth of life. This power limited to simple contact and this spontaneous force can be summarized by the notion of immediacy. The latter was viewed with elegiac regret by those who felt themselves separated from it. Immediacy had already been represented in many works during the eighteenth century. One thinks of the noble savage or Harlequin and his innumerable cousins. The child would also soon join the ranks of these figures of immediacy. Papageno, the bird man, is both the noble savage and Kasperl, and we may note as well, following Jacques Chailley's alchemical code, the character's close affinity with one of the four elements: air.

Of the world, Papageno knows only a limited area since he has never left his narrow valley. His home is a straw hut. From day to day, capturing birds is his only occupation. In exchange for this work, the Queen's ladies feed him. It is therefore through an elementary barter economy that he manages to subsist, and this system of transaction links him to the supernatural world. Another particularity is that Papageno cannot experience the satisfaction of desire other than in the moment. He constructs no long-range plans or projects. As a result, when some pleasure presents itself, he can see no reason to postpone enjoying it or looking beyond it. He fails the series of tests because, as he is unable to inhibit or defer his desires, he has no notion of interdiction. Rousseau had described in the same way the "stupidity" and happiness of the man of nature. But if the appetites of Papageno are not subject to education, his elementary erotic power has no heaviness about it. He is a perfect example of a lightweight. The proliferation of little Papagenos and Papagenas that the husband and wife promise each other, and that Mozart's duo expresses with such good humor, is intensified by the repeated syllable "pa" to the point of suggesting the flight of batting wings. Papageno does not achieve the life of spirit, but his is the energy thanks to which the spiritual life could be elaborated. (There is a large gap, however, between him and those who know how to build temples.) Just as one can see in Leporello a kind of double of Don Giovanni, one is free to see in Papageno the vague shadow of Tamino.

In one other respect Papageno conforms to the theater's traditional clown figure. Without being directly implicated in the principal action of the plot, the clown intervenes as either an auxiliary helper or an obstacle. His random erratic interventions sometimes play a providential role. The clown unwittingly is a rescuer. Granted, it is not he who saves Tamino in the opening scene, but in the second act, when he is sent forward as a scout and messenger, the bird catcher appears twice in the right place at the right time to save Pamina from being harmed by the obscure and violent Monostatos. Moreover, it is Papageno who informs Pamina of Tamino's love before the latter has shown itself. For the heroine, Papageno's words play the same role that Pamina's portrait had played for the hero: they announce a beloved object while at the same time making its absence keenly felt. If Papageno is without direct power, his innocence and his gaiety—escorted by his flute and glockenspiel—invest him with an indirect power. Unbeknownst to him, Papageno makes the wheel of fortune turn.

TOWARD AN EGALITARIAN MONARCHY

Let us now raise our sights one degree and turn our attention to Tamino and Pamina. Their adventure will show us the pathways that give access to supreme power.

When the curtain goes up, we find Tamino, a ruler's son, pursued by a monster. He is about to perish and calls for help.

Out of the void into which the fear of the monster made him fall he is reborn in a state of total ignorance. He knows neither where he is nor who saved him. He finds himself in a position of weakness and dependence—in the depths of error, illusion, and credulity. His future power will be found at the end of a path whose point of origin is chaos and darkness.

It is as a man and not as a king's son that Tamino will undergo the initiating tests. The principle of equality is put forward insistently by the libretto. Sarastro, however, tells Tamino that if he emerges victorious from the ritual trials, he will reign as an enlightened prince. After first losing all his titles, this prince by birth will regain his princely status by right of merit. The apprenticeship toward full humanity does not distinguish between the preparations that lead to the best possible exercise of power and that of fully legitimate monarchal authority. I am thinking of Ingmar Bergman's film version that does not hesitate imagining (beyond the libretto) a transfer of power from Sarastro to Tamino at the very end. This choice reproduces the passing of the scepter to the son Idamante from the father Idomeneo who was ready to sacrifice him to Neptune. If Tamino, married to Pamina, became the successor of the unmarried high priest, there would be an extreme contrast between his initial fainting and his final mastery. The accession to power would become one with the couple's wedding march—a dyad more than an individual—toward spiritual maturity and fertility. Victorious over darkness, silence, and misunderstandings, perfect conjugal harmony will reestablish the order of the world. All desirable forms of happiness fuse into a single luminous whole: the accumulation of all the juvenile phantasms at a time when phantasms were still nourished by Fénelon's *Télémaque* and *Le Cabinet des fées*.[3]

The symbolic detail of the walk through the labyrinth and the traversing of the elements is less important than the principle itself of a probationary obstacle course—a passage where the hero discovers an internal force of which he was unaware and of which he now takes possession. This passage, which began in disorientation, leads him to Reason, the ruler of his newfound orient.

The novel of education, or *Bildung*, is the narrative version of what *The Magic Flute* offers us in the mode of solemn and fairylike theatrical action. The novel *Séthos* (1731) by the abbé Terrasson to which the libretto of *The Magic Flute* is highly indebted offers the same thing. Terrasson, who defended the modernist cause, adopts ancient Egypt as the fictional setting of his tale and formulates rationalist convictions amid temples dedicated to Isis and Osiris—a singular fusion of venerable myth and new philosophy. In a similar vein, Rousseau's *Émile* and the two parts of Goethe's *Wilhelm Meister* with its hint of the Masonic vocabulary also feature the stages passed through by young men who attain full freedom.[4] It became tempting to imagine that all mankind was engaged in an education project of the same type. In all the texts I've mentioned, and which are for the most part the same as those discussed in relation to *Idomeneo*, the symbol of the voyage that Christian morality had used so well finds a new use in the context of this philosophical passage toward absolute knowledge. The hopeful desire for the collective progress of humanity that emerges during that time relies on the same images. Tamino's series of tests is readily transposed to the laborious march of history toward the reconciliation of those still separated by ignorance and prejudice.

In *The Magic Flute*, the promise rings out twice in the same terms. The happiness that awaits Tamino and Pamina is the happiness of the whole earth—a new golden age. The priests sing at the end of the first act:

> *Wenn Tugend und Gerechtigkeit*
> *Den grossen Pfad mit Ruhm bestreut,*
> *Dann ist die Erd' ein Himmelreich,*
> *Und Sterbliche den Göttern gleich.*

> When virtue and justice
> Spread glory over this great path,
> Then will earth be a heavenly realm,
> And mortals will be akin to gods.

The three boys will repeat the last two lines when it comes time for the decisive tests (act 2, scene 26), the imminent triumph of light, the fall of superstition, and the return of "sweet serenity." This sentence must be heard as a politico-religious promise, analogous to the myth of the dawn and of solar victory that encircled the beginnings of the French Revolution.

At first Tamino knows only desire, and upon the injunctions of the Queen of the Night he confers on himself the role of liberator. He is ready to brave all obstacles to rejoin the one whose image has fascinated him. He accepts a heroic mission while also obeying the impulses of love. It is worth noting that Schikaneder often uses the word "*Trieb*" (drive), a term heavily employed by Freud, as is well known. It would not be a fanciful interpretation of *The Magic Flute* to say that the Freudian notion lurks around these occurrences of *Trieb* or drive like a shadow. And one might add that Tamino's rites of passage achieve the sublimation of this first awakened desire. In the course of his journey, the hero is led beyond that which he first desired; he accedes to a higher plane, all without renouncing the first object of his desire. "May knowledge of wisdom be my victory, and the sweet Pamina my reward" (act 2, scene 3). Wisdom takes precedence! The loving union becomes a secondary benefit. Tamino consents to delay the marriage so as to better legitimate it. He accepts the intervention of mortal danger and a vow of silence. By consenting to separation as the price to pay, he will obtain a redoubled presence: a marriage and an investiture all in one. Thus renunciation (a faculty unknown to Papageno) gives Tamino access to a future. He will have crossed the worst privations, the most extreme destitution, before conquering a power whose reach will extend throughout the universe. The love of Tamino and Pamina now has a past and a future: he has overcome hopelessness and death, and nothing any longer can threaten him.

From Pamina's perspective, however, the momentary rupture is experienced as an incomprehensible catastrophe. The heroine is represented as a victim on whom all unhappiness falls. She lost a father whom she loved, a mysterious character who returns to her in memories. She was taken away from her mother, the starry queen in whose love she continues to believe. She is at the mercy of a powerful stranger, Sarastro, who appears in no hurry to reveal his good intentions to her. She must put up with the brutality of her guardian, Monostatos. Tamino, after declaring his love, keeps silent and then bids a final farewell. Desperate, she seeks a way to kill herself, and is stopped by the three boys only at the last moment. She is perpetually both terrified and injured. Around Pamina's person there is an atmosphere reminiscent of noir novels or the Sadian imagination, and this is probably meant to justify the pathos-filled emotional character of the arias written for her role. (This aesthetic justification intervenes here as an extra supplement.)

The white daughter of a very dark mother, Pamina is the sister of the martyred sleepers of Füssli and of all the frail creatures atrociously locked away in gothic undergrounds or the prisons of the Inquisition that were favored by late-eighteenth-century novels. The pathos of captivity gave rise to a particular type of lyric work, the "rescue opera"

(*Rettungsoper*). One of the first of these, composed by Henri Berton with a libretto by Joseph Fiévée, was entitled *Les Rigueurs du cloître* (1790, *The Rigors of the Cloister*), and one of the most beautiful will be *Fidelio*. And there is already Constance in *The Abduction from the Seraglio*, a captive whose fate invites one to reflect on tyrants and their repentance. And even though their voice types are not the same, there are resemblances between Osmin and Monostatos.

Pamina, the target of so many offenses, follows her own course of initiating tests. She in effect accomplishes a double voyage. On the one hand, she has left the nocturnal, feminine domain of her mother and entered into the masculine solar domain of Sarastro, and, on the other, she will traverse night and death, first alone and then in Tamino's company, before finally crossing with him the sacred threshold. For Pamina, too, the sufferings endured are compensated by access to a particular power. In the last test (act 2, scene 28), Pamina takes Tamino's hand and guides him. In its sublimated form as music, love is the directing force, a force that can successfully guide over water and through flames. This guidance is not a masculine privilege. Thus Pamina sings:

> *Ich selbsten führe dich*
> *Die Liebe leitet mich*

> I myself lead you,
> Love guides me.

The magic flute protects the couple at this moment and opens the way. In place of the verb "guide" when it is repeated, the flute becomes the subject and takes the place of love, as though it were its synonym. Pamina sings:

> *Nun komm und spiel die Flöte an,*
> *Sie leite uns auf grauser Bahn.*

> Now come and play the flute
> May it guide us over this dark path

United by the flute, Pamina and Tamino have conquered this certitude:

Wir wandeln durch des Tones Macht
Froh durch des Todes düstre Nacht!

The power of music lets us advance
Joyous through the dark night of death!

It is at this moment that we learn from Pamina the origin of the flute given to Tamino by one of the ladies of the Queen of the Night: "My father carved it one enchanted hour out of the deepest heart of a thousand-year-old oak." For one of the first times in opera, we find mention of the cosmic tree from Nordic mythology, Yggdrasil. Wotan's wooden spear comes from the same tree (specified there as ash), though it loses its power when it comes up against the spear of the revolutionary Siegfried. For Mozart's librettists, the flute is not only the source of melodious song, it is also the symbol of the harmony of the world. For harmony is an ordering principle and therefore the most excellent power; it is a gentle, peaceful power and one that the young prince possesses as a custodian only and allows to guide him.

In his theoretical writings, Jean-Philippe Rameau never ceases repeating that the "law of the generation of harmony" produced by the vibration of a sonorous body is the fundamental secret of the cosmos from which follow the geometric proportions that regulate all the laws of nature. Masonic writings spread the same idea. It is thanks to harmony that chaos was able to become order. The specialist of magnetism, Mesmer, extended these principles to medicine without dissociating them from music. Animal magnetism, according to him, is a universal fluid acting rhythmically throughout the universe and our bodies. The magnetic treatment purported to restore the proper concordance of rhythms between our bodies and the world and often included a musical accompaniment. For certain followers of Mesmer, the health of the individual is inconceivable without a harmony that would extend to the entire social body. It is perhaps worth recalling that Mozart was acquainted with Mesmer, that *Bastien und Bastienne*, composed at the age of twelve, was commissioned by Mesmer for a party at his private residence, and that a mesmeric magnet serves as a comic accessory in *Così fan tutte* when Despina pretends to cure the fake Albanians from their simulated poisoning. The bewitching effect of Tamino's flute over the animals in the first act is an echo of the Orpheus myth and further demonstrates how much, when it comes to these motives, the tendency toward syncretism was active at the time.

SARASTRO

The magic of the flute is an impersonal, universal power. That power can only be exercised by a person, however, and living breath must pass through the instrument. As we've seen, power, according to the lesson of *The Magic Flute*, is conditional on the force of spirit that accepts and interiorizes interdictions, beginning with the interdiction of violence and contempt on account of the equal rights to which all humans are entitled. In this case, power calls for the intervention of a person and has as its primary motor an individual conscience and the courageous generosity that goes by the name of virtue. One must recognize that the utopian dream of the Enlightenment thinkers was precisely the reconciliation of two principles: the reign of a universal law and the perfection of the individual.

But is this reconciliation so easily achieved? As his figure for universal law, Schikaneder, like so many of his contemporaries, invokes willy-nilly various ancient myths, Isis and Osiris, light, love, harmony, and so on. Among these principles comes the equal dignity of individuals. But to reign over a society, the cosmic law needs an interpreter.

Sarastro, the master of the temple, assumes this function: he is the supreme officer. He exercises command by virtue of his complete obedience to the law of harmony.

One ought to notice that this justification of power is of the sort used to legitimate modern forms of absolutism. Does Sarastro's power escape from the suspicions that the Enlightenment thinkers continuously expressed against the arbitrary power of kings and priests? The usual criticisms formulated by this thinking against the imposture of priests can with all the more reason be turned against Robespierre and his epigones when they grant themselves the status of vicar to the Supreme Being. Tyranny returns when Saint-Just writes, "Our goal is to establish an order of things such that a universal incline towards good establishes itself and factions suddenly find themselves thrown onto the gallows."[5] Who can assure us that the necessarily singular will of Sarastro will not stray and follow the oblique path of exaggerated pride?

He proclaims that every man is a prince, but his own legitimacy is that of a theocrat.

Let's allow this fictive character to be exempted from the impossible verification of titles. According to the text of the libretto, Sarastro (whose name, we know, derives from Zoroaster or Zarathustra) only reigns over priests and above him are only the gods and their laws. In his famous aria "In diesen heiligen Hallen"—"In these sacred Halls" (act 2, scene 12), the dominant affirmation is that precisely there vengeance is unknown ("kennt man die Rache nicht"). For Sarastro, excluding all ideas of vengeance means renouncing all desires that would derive from his own person. His power is so high that he is able to forget himself within his duty. He expresses himself only after the Queen of the Night, her ladies, and Monostatos are thrown into the abyss. They have only jealous passions: spite, murderous desires, vengeance. A superior power, figured by the thunder and waterfalls (the timpani and brass instruments of the orchestra), renders an impersonal justice.

Sarastro possesses a magic talisman, the "Sevenfold Solar Circle," where the number seven makes planetary space concord with the seven notes of the musical scale. He thus possesses the secrets of time. This he inherited from the spouse of the Queen of the Night, the father of Pamina, upon his death.[6] Admitted to the secrets of the divine, he has himself no history. Similarly, at the opposite pole, Papageno has no history because he is the neighbor of animality, having no projects beyond the present moment and being commanded by physical appetite alone. No danger can threaten the high priest; he has conquered in advance. The Queen of the Night is from the start "under his power"—"steht in meiner Macht" (act 1, scene 18). He knew that Tamino and Pamina were destined for one another; he was not unaware of the felonies of Monostatos; he knew the hearts' secrets; in the marvelous trio where he commands the lovers to separate, he announces that they will find each other again: "Wir sehn uns wieder"—"We shall see each other again" (act 2, scene 21).

It is difficult not to recall here the scene in Rousseau's *Émile* when the omniscient preceptor separates the young lovers and stages their farewells, knowing full well that preparations for the joys of return are thus being laid for Émile and Sophie. Like Rousseau's preceptor, Sarastro guides all the action with a hidden hand. He has a plan that is only revealed to the others at the moment of its realization, and he skillfully turns all adverse forces to the advantage of this plan. Negative powers unwittingly serve his designs. He is therefore powerful enough to forgo all recourse to violence. The words that Sarastro repeats, the mantra of his power, are "to lead" and "to direct" (*führen, leiten*). His orders are carried out to the letter by an assortment of priests, guards, and messengers who, while all addressing their prayers to the gods, never omit their acclamation of Sarastro. Their personal homage becomes so strong as to resemble a personality cult. The naïveté of Schikaneder is at its height in these verses of the chorus:

> *Er ist es dem wir uns mit Freude ergeben*
> *Er ist unser Abgott, dem alle sich weihen*

> He is the one to whom we submit ourselves with joy
> He is our idol to whom all devote themselves
>
> (act 1, scene 18)

Sarastro belongs to that category of characters stretching back to Mentor in Fénelon's *Télémaque* on whom the Enlightenment thinkers pinned their hopes for an efficacious wisdom capable of leading mankind toward knowledge and happiness. Mentor was the human and male disguise of the goddess Minerva—and so he had to be listened to. Today skepticism prevails. A reversal has taken place. Too many idolized "guides" have turned out to be manipulators, and finally monsters.

It is on the symbolic level, however, that the figure of Sarastro culminates. His conflict with the Queen of the Night is one of light versus darkness, and as a by-play it is also the conflict between the masculine and the feminine. The Queen of the Night is the most difficult character to interpret. What does she represent? She has been seen as the representation of political and religious powers hostile to Freemasonry. She has also been believed to incarnate the female lodge in opposition to the rival masculine lodge.[7] I will offer no original interpretation. I accept the literal image of a cosmic force—the starry night with its infinite sparkling riches. I also accept to see in her the bad mother, the mother with the bitter breast, who, to reclaim her power, is ready to sacrifice her daughter and hand her over to the abominable Monostatos. Whereas the gift of the father is the flute that opens the path to salvation, the mother's gift to her daughter is a dagger with which she comes close to committing suicide. One of the symbolic attributes of the night is the veil. Not only are the ladies who serve her veiled, but the way in which the Queen of the Night attempts to reclaim her power is a veiled activity. She attacks Sarastro and the initiated with calumny: she leads others to believe they are hypocritical imposters. The first of the tests that Tamino and Pamina successfully pass consists precisely of lifting the veil of this lie that involves at first mistaking the true face—human and friendly—of Wisdom's followers. Once this veil as been seen through, there remains still the entire series of obstacles that stand in the way of a truth that eludes all direct approaches. The figure of the Queen, at first considered a helper before being recognized as hostile, determines the dramatic tension. She helps then hinders, thus multiplying illusions, errors, and obstacles that serve to draw out the rites of passage and increase the value of the ultimate triumph.

The victory is only glorious if it comes against an adversary who is sufficiently powerful. It was therefore important not to reveal too soon the inferiority of the Queen, and the best way to prevent her from appearing conquered in advance was to make her into a temporarily generous and charitable force during the first part of the opera.

Sarastro is wisdom personified. He has no spouse. Or one can say that he has a female aspect, namely, the Queen of the Night, but one that stands with respect to him as evil stands with respect to good.

The Magic Flute is not a gynophobic opera, but it does reserve for the feminine principle a subaltern role. The feminine, blackened in the character of the Queen, receives a sort of compensation in the figure of her daughter, Pamina, but only so long as there is submission to the viral law of initiation. Woman will be welcomed in the person of Pamina and thrown into the abyss in the person of the Queen and her auxiliaries. The young couple is reconciled, but the black widow, the witch with the sublime voice, loses her power, it would seem, forever. The Queen and Monostatos and the veiled ladies finally only serve to accentuate the triumph of Sarastro. One can follow, against a dark background, the advent of the day, but when the sun shines forth, the night is gone. We can translate this into moral and political terms this way: it is necessary to recognize the existence of a negative delaying principle strong enough to explain why the light of justice is not enshrined in all hearts from the very beginning. If the human world is not yet radiant, it must be because a Prince of Darkness is standing in the way. Here we

Drawings by
KARL-ERNST
HERRMANN

The Magic Flute

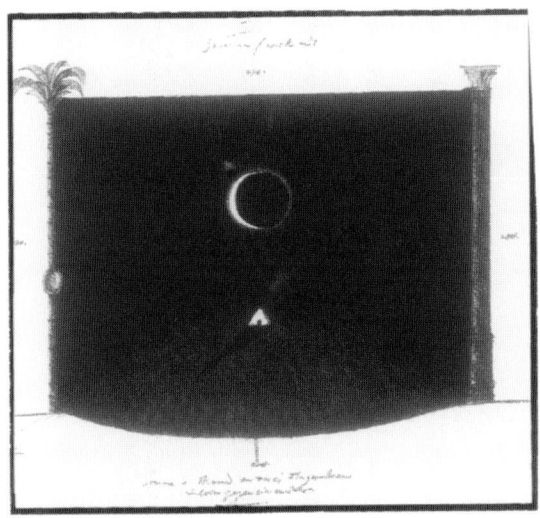

The Magic Flute, overture

For the *staging* of Karl-Ernst Hermann, see page 125

The Three Ladies, act I

Papageno, act I

The house of
Papageno (sketch)

The Queen of the Night, act I

Monostatos, act I

Papagena as an old woman, act I

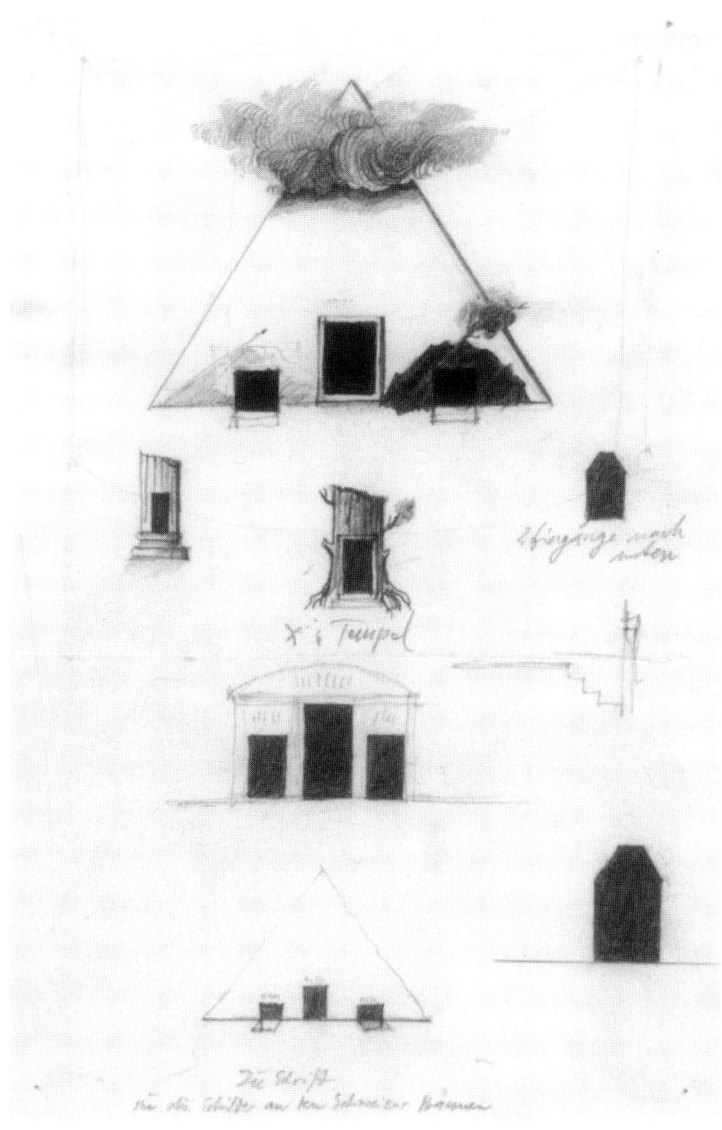

Temple of Wisdom, Temple of Nature, Temple of Reason, act I, scene 15 (sketch)

The Queen of the Night, act II

have a princess of darkness, but that's close enough. Every eschatology and every utopia must cast some figure as the adversary and blame him (or her) for the delay in universal happiness. Every utopia is therefore Manichaean. And Manichaean thinking derives from Zoroaster. And therefore Sarastro's name was the perfect choice for this opera.

THE RETURN OF SHADOWS

The glorious chords in B flat minor, the favorite key of Masons, fill the musical space at the end of *The Magic Flute*. Is it parousia, the end of time? Is it possible to imagine an extension or sequel to *The Magic Flute*? Goethe, for one, had such a dream when he set out to compose for other musicians an analogous work. How did he go about it?

A survey of the very large number of works composed around 1789, works that all attempt to impose an image of light triumphant and clarity victorious in their battle against all obscurities, reveals that among the most perceptive artists shadows are never willing to concede defeat entirely but on the contrary mount counterattacks under various guises.[8] On the political stage, the French Revolution first considers itself to be the great dawn of the human species; then it allows itself to be invaded by doubt, by the obsession with the enemy within, by the Terror.

It is definitely the return of darkness that inspires Goethe in the fragment that he composes as a follow-up to Mozart's *Singspiel*. We first witness a massive triumph of the night. On the Queen's order, Monostatos has entered the royal palace of Tamino. He has seized Pamina's newborn infant and, not being able to make off with it, encloses the child within a golden sarcophagus locked shut with the seal of the Queen of the Night. The infant meets the same fate as Osiris. The king and Pamina are desperate, and each mourns separately. In order for the infant to remain alive inside the coffin, he must be carried night and day. Sarastro meanwhile must surrender his power. The oracle enjoins him to leave the overprotective temple grounds and undertake a yearlong pilgrimage among men. He is welcomed into the hut of Papageno and Papagena, who have remained childless and resent the sterility of their union. Sarastro produces infants inside ostrich eggs—the triumph of a rather unnerving science. The last scene written, which does not constitute a conclusion, transports us to a sanctuary where we witness the opening of the coffin. The infant has stayed alive. Goethe names him Genius. But this genius takes flight and disappears into the sky. Many themes of *Faust Part Two*—the homunculus and the flight of Euphorion—are here prefigured. It is not known for certain how Goethe would have finished his play. The images that we are left with are of centrifugal movements: Sarastro goes away from the temple, the infant delivered from his nocturnal prison flies away and disappears from view. *The Magic Flute* concludes with a marvelously convergent movement, toward a radiant center, as though the world were finally going to attain its immutable truth. Goethe's fragment calls everything into question; it takes up the same mythical characters, the same conflict of light and darkness, and makes of them an enigmatic fragment that expresses the problematic, erring, nocturnal aspect of the modern world that was beginning. The questions raised remain unanswered. Is it possible for genius or Genius to inhabit this world? Can the wise man remain in power? When the "master of wisdom" accepts the erring life of the pilgrim, we are faced with a complete reversal of the certitude uttered in Sarastro's famous aria. The chorus sings after the master's departure:

> *Es soll die Wahrheit*
> *Nicht mehr auf Erden*
> *In voller Klarheit*
> *Verbreitet werden.*
> *Dein hoher Gang*
> *Ist nun vollbracht;*
> *Doch uns umgibt*
> *Die tiefe Nacht.*

> Truth will no longer
> Extend over the earth
> In full clarity.
> Your high passage
> Is now complete,
> And all 'round us
> Is deepest night.[9]

Goethe announces an age of truth in exile, and we sense that our voice could join this disconsolate chorus. This is why our eyes fill with tears when Mozart sings the imminence of the dawn—a "Soon" (*Bald*) that did not take place in our time. He announces:

> *Die düstre Nacht verscheucht der Glanz der Sonne,*
> *Bald fühlt der edle Jüngling neues Leben.*

> The sun's splendor drives away the obscure night,
> Soon the noble youth will feel new life.
>
> (act 2, scene 20)

This was indeed a grand promise. But was it in fact addressed to us? Is it speaking about us? I think instead of a voice that is informing us that this good news and this imminent new day are simply renewing a very ancient fable of the love quest and the cycle of hours. And merely having listened to it is a great pleasure.

EARTH AND STARS

A staging centered on the work, a use of the visual that attracts the spectator toward the musical event become nearly palpable—this is what is rare today and what causes such intense happiness when it is achieved. This is the happiness that I felt when I attended a performance of *The Magic Flute* with the sets and costumes designed by Ursel and Karl-Ernst Herrmann.[10] Thanks to them, I entered into this fable of initiation. They guided me to the antechamber of enigmas and wonders. I found myself welcomed into a fictive universe where everything was deliciously readable and yet also charged with a persistent mystery. I was able to forget, like a bad dream, countless recent productions, now already dated, that all claimed to be centered on the public and that thought more of the effect produced on the spectator than of the work itself. Here finally, I said to myself, is a production where no one is insisting on holding up a mirror to the ladies and gentlemen in their plush seats with the aim of having them encounter a representation of their supposed phantasms. Here, at last, was a concept that had been patiently meditated. It was able to innovate without recourse to current lazy practices such as shocking the naive with some contemporary police uniforms or a few naked bodies. I finally discovered the truth of my dreams fully realized, whereas in so many other "new" versions that promised to be so wonderful, it has seemed to me that the music, obscured and as though swamped with brutal images, sounded like nothing more than a whimpering echo. At no point did I feel any such uneasiness during the superb performance in Brussels. On the contrary, everything that appeared to my eyes seemed spontaneously called forth by the music. This does not imply, I hasten to add, that there was any enslavement to archaeological preoccupations with a resurrection of the past; rather, this was an entirely fresh vision responding to this timeless music.

A staging that is faithful to the law of the work accords with the spirit of *The Magic Flute*. It repeats, in its cheerful obedience to Mozart, the joyous devotional movement of the music toward the mythic figures of the fraternal and conjugal link, of death, and of resurrection, namely Isis and Osiris. The "great opera," when it comes to Tamino, is the story of a voyage toward wisdom, first unrecognized and then progressively discovered. It is the story, when it comes to Pamina, of captivity that evolves into liberation. It is the story of Orpheus, but in reverse: Eurydice is conducted toward the light, life, and sovereignty. The music guides this progression; it marks the stages, the thresholds crossed, and the approach of unity. This is clear from the very beginning when the musical instruments are presented to the prince and the bird catcher, and it becomes even more evident during the last trials that become, to the sound of the flute, a wedding march amid the elements. The only adequate stagings of this opera are those that make the spectators participate in this progress and this liberation. They must be invitations to this journey toward wisdom and the celebration of a grand marriage. This is the preeminent quality that distinguishes the work of Ursel and Karl-Ernst Herrmann. Our gaze is directed toward the stars and our steps are led to the temple.

To be so successful, there needed to be complete fusion between the two components of the opera: it is in all of its pieces a *Märchen* as well as being from beginning to end an imaginary ritual. One must therefore combine the lightness of fairy tale with the solemnity of a religious service. To achieve this in the images and stage movements, the directors had to pay close attention to every single note of the music, every exchange, and every one of the librettist's stage directions. Schikaneder is not a great writer, but it is very likely that he was equal to the demands set out by Mozart, who was a dramatic genius. No detail explicitly required by the score could be neglected. Therefore, Ursel and Karl-Ernst Herrmann had to school themselves with the text using all the resources of their imagination. In respecting the high meanings contained in this text, they nevertheless managed to retain all their creative freedom. Their originality was only more vigorously affirmed with their free use of color, a singularity in the costumes, and an animation of the stage acting that never departed from the space created jointly by the words and the music. Being faithful to Mozart means adding no false weight, no superfluous ornament, no useless extras, and no gesture that does not correspond to a precise textual element. When these conditions are satisfied, the path is open to infinite fantasy. All the visual correspondences chosen by Ursel and Karl-Ernst Herrmann strike one as correct and consonant with the music—with the staccato of the bells, with the melodious legato of the flute, with the *maestoso* of the wind instruments, with an array of voices no less varied than the full compass of the spatial axes. The pyramid, a fundamental element of the set, points to the stars and gives access through its base to the depths of the earth. It links the night of the upper reaches with the night of the lower realm. It shelters the community of wise men who observe, experiment, and with a certain disturbing audacity seek out the light hidden intimately within nature. But surrounding this pyramid are palm trees, animals, birds—an entire unthinking freedom. And in the air there circles the flying machine of the protecting genies. Between earth and stars, the direction is not indicated solely by the will of man who calculatedly erects the triangular volume of stone and brick; there is also the pure song of children without whom the travelers would have despaired. Never had my understanding of it all come together so well.

Usurpations and Revolts

CHAPTER 8

Poppea Victorious

SUPREME POWER

The prologue of *The Coronation of Poppea*, often dropped from stage productions, opposes Fortune and Virtue. The god Love solves the dispute, for it is he who is the absolute conqueror. His power surpasses that of time itself. "Eternity and I are twins." Fortune and Virtue surrender: neither man nor god can resist Love. As an illustration, Love offers us the spectacle of a given day: defeating Fortune and Virtue, he marches alone to victory. The production that begins is to be an effect of his generosity, and it serves to prove that when it comes to the mutability of the world, change is produced at his command. Monteverdi's music can be heard as the expansive movement of love, from secret dawn to glorious night. The opera celebrates the beauty of Poppea, but this beauty is the radiation of a more universal power of which Poppea is the officer: the different voices, the instruments, and lighting are this power diffracted among a multiplicity of appearances. Operating through all the variations in musical material and all the tribulations of the characters is the force of Eros.

G. F. Busenello, the librettist of the *Incoronazione*, made ingenious use of Tacitus's *Annals*. One also finds the tragic plot of a Latin theatrical work, *Octavia*, that has been perhaps mistakenly attributed to Seneca. The heroine in this play is a repudiated empress whom a ship carries to distant shores, where she will be put to death. Poppea makes only a brief appearance to voice dark presages. Her coronation is narrated by her nurse:

> This day's bright dawn has answered all our prayers,
> Our vows to the good gods; by marriage rites
> You are united with your Emperor;
> Whose heart your beauty captured; whose great Venus,
> Goddess supreme, by holy rites, adored,
> Mother of Love, has made your prisoner.
> Ah, what a picture! When you took your seat
> Upon the cushioned divan in the palace!
> How the assembled senators were rapt
> With wonder at your beauty, as you offered
> Incense to the high gods, and poured thank-offering
> Of consecrated wine upon their altars!
> The golden veil that delicately floated
> About your head! And when the Emperor,
> Close by your side, his body pressed to yours,
> So proudly walked, his happiness proclaimed
> In every feature of his face and bearing![1]

Busenello and Monteverdi will later make this into the final scene of their *Coronation*, but their adaptation includes inverting the order of importance of the characters and giving Poppea the lead role. The sad Octavia belongs to the cortege of victims. An opera that glorifies the omnipotence of love has to distribute the roles differently from a Roman tragedy in which traditional conjugal piety constitutes, insults notwithstanding, the absolute value.

TWO OR THREE THINGS THAT WE KNOW ABOUT HER

Poppea made seduction into a supreme art. Montaigne remembered her. Our desire "increases with our discomfort": "Why did Poppea invent this masking of the beauties of her face, only to heighten them in the eyes of her lovers?" And he continues, "Why were these beauties veiled from head to foot that everyone wants to show and that everyone desires to see?"[2] The answer, we know, is in books 13 and 14 of Tacitus's *Annals*. We learn there of the high birth of Poppea, whose maternal ancestor received the honors of the consulate and of triumph: "There was at Rome a woman called Poppaea. . . . Poppaea had every asset except goodness. Her public appearances were few; she would half-veil her face at them, to stimulate curiosity (or because it suited her). To her, married or bachelor bedfellows were alike. She was indifferent to her reputation—yet insensible to men's love, and herself unloving."[3]

Other details about this decidedly free woman who put her liberty to such calculated uses were known by the educated public that attended the performances of the *Incoronazione* in the fall of 1643 at the Teatro dei Santi Giovanni e Paolo in Venice. Notably, that her entourage included many astronomers and that she was a superb redhead and an expert on the subject of beauty treatments: facial masks, lotions, milk baths, and so on. And also that she broke her mirror and wished to die when she discovered marks on her face. So, under the veil was magnificent skin. The anonymous master artist of the School of Fontainebleau who painted the delicious Sabina Poppaea that can be seen today in Geneva's Musée d'Art et d'Histoire knew well the secrets of her youthfulness, for he gave the Roman aristocrat the sweetest complexion. He traced the sharp gaze under the very fine eyebrows, colored the humid half-smile, and revealed the studied shivers of the back of the neck. The whole thing is brought to the highest level of resemblance that a fictional image can attain—an anachronistic disguise. The only betrayal of the masked seductress is the veil that the painter did not omit, but it hides nothing. From then on there can be no doubt: she is indeed a royal mistress, a beauty to conquer princes and impose her will on armored heroes who strut among the trumpets and banners. Why do so many commentators stubbornly insist on labeling her a courtesan?

She is a grand woman who wishes to stand on the top rung and stops at nothing to get there.

A SOLAR MYTH

Nero and Othon, reports Tacitus, were linked by a suspect camaraderie of debauchery. If Othon seized Poppea away from her first husband, it was perhaps to have power over Nero through sharing this prey with him. Then Othon planned to keep her for himself alone. Nero got rid of his rival by sending him off to govern Lusitania. Busenello leaves these inglorious antecedents in the shadows. The opera begins with the return of Othon, who believes he has legitimate rights over Poppea's love. The words he sings before the residence that is now closed to him compare love to the force that animates the world and attracts the elements toward their natural place. Among the exalted images of adoration, Poppea is the law of the world, the center toward which everything moves. At the end of the night, behind the walls that protect her, she is a hidden sun: "Ahi, so io ben, che sta il mio sol qui dentro"—"Ah! I know well that my sun is there inside."[4] One must take literally the metaphors of this soaring mannerist poetry that the generation of the *précieux* in France imitated from a distance. Poppea is a solar woman. And Nero, whom she calls her "incarnated sun" (*l'incarnato mio sole*), is her counterpart. Thus one sees from the very beginning of the first act a solar myth of love joined to a solar myth of power.

INTERLACING AND INTERTWINING

When the opera opens Nero and Poppea are making love at night. When the opera finishes they make love in full view of Rome and the world. At the beginning the double sun is still hidden. At the end nothing more can cast a shadow over it. This is the action's obvious advance. The customary psychological bent that requires opera characters to be analyzed as though they were living creatures matters little. Is Poppea first a figure of love or one of ambition? One must listen to what the words and music say as they are deployed.

From the beginning, the veil has fallen. Poppea belongs to Nero. Love is master. There remains the task of having this recognized by the universe. It is only a question of breaking down obstacles or sweeping them aside. On the chessboard the knight Othon must be made to retreat, the castle Seneca must be defeated, and the queen Octavia overthrown. But first Poppea makes sure of the imperial lover. She embraces him, holds him captive, and calls herself captive. Do the first words of Poppea speak of love or a will to capture? Both at once: "Signor, deh, non partire, sostien che queste braccia ti circondino il collo"—"Ah, don't go, my lord, and allow my arms to encircle your neck just as your graces surround my heart." One is irresistibly reminded of the classic image of love as net. Love's interlacing and intertwining is the primary element, and it will manifest itself in a thousand different ways—in the interweaving of the verbal exchanges, in the suave or exalted repetitions, in the sinuosity of the melodic line, in everything that outlines a tender return—such that the ritornello, on more than one occasion, carries an enhanced meaning. Asking with insistence the caressing question "Tornerai?"—"Will you return?" the voice traces the very movement of return. This is the *stile rappresentativo* carried to perfection. At the same time, this interlacing signifies the exclusion of Octavia. The day will not end before the decision is made. The sky and stars will also have turned to confirm the supreme power of love. Busenello has Love, Venus's son, repeat in an entirely profane manner the theological verse of Dante: "L'amor che move il sole et l'altre stelle"—"Love that moves the sun and the other stars."[5]

The only arias sung by Poppea in Nero's absence are very short, and they tell not of her love but of her ambition. It is the abandoned and the desperate who express in monologues their distress over a lost love. Away from Nero's arms, Poppea does not think of him but of the supreme power that she desires to obtain. She speaks of herself while talking to herself. "Hope, you caress my heart, and flattering my spirit, you cover me with a royal but imaginary robe. No, no, I fear no obstacle: Love and Fortune war for me." For Poppea, enormous pride and self-love—today termed "narcissism"—go together with captivating sensuality. It is surely the feminine type out of which our century's imagination will fashion the vamp and Lulu. How revealing, the beginning of the dialogue where Poppea will finally obtain the condemnation of Seneca! Poppea begins by inviting Nero to expound on the "wild" kisses she has given him and the beauty of her breasts. She seeks in the lover's gaze the mirror of her own carnal perfections. And having made him entirely dependent on the voluptuous deeds that she knows how to perform, she makes the idea of dependence intolerable to him when he is made to see himself dependent on Seneca. At the very moment that he surrenders completely to an absolute mistress, he proclaims his wish to obey no master whatsoever. He orders the death of the teacher who professes to champion reason. Put metaphorically, when the burning sun of pleasure mounts into the firmament, the cold wisdom of an old man and the cold virtue of the spouse are destined to disappear. "Faced with your sun," Nero will sing, "my words are but weak flames." "The day is luminous," the nurse will remark, even when the eyelids of the sun woman are closed, even when Poppea is sleeping.

CELEBRATION OF THE MOUTH

It is Poppea's face but above all her mouth and lips that inspire the exultant effusions of Nero and Lucan after the death of Seneca. Beyond good and evil, beyond the serious and the clownish, the music seems at that moment to celebrate its own power. In a way entirely fitting, it praises the mouth that speaks or laughs, pours forth intoxication, shines like a ruby, and offers itself up like a veritable pomegranate. In the sensorial realm opened up by Monteverdi, tactile, visual, and auditory values intermingle. The mouth that is able to give "biting" kisses is the same that in speaking and laughing "wounds the heart with invisible arms." The exquisite touch and the upsetting aria are closely associated. Poppea admirably expresses the way the voice becomes kiss and then transforms into profound script. Responding to the loving praise of Nero, she says, "Come parole le odo, come baci io le godo"—"Your beloved words, I hear them like words, I enjoy them like kisses. Their meaning is so smooth and lively that unsatisfied with caressing my hearing, they come to imprint kisses on my heart." Hearing (*odo*) and enjoyment (*godo*) are superimposed by virtue of an opulent rhyme.

In the admirable musical and poetic development of the last scene, all the elements of pleasure are united: the ecstasy of the gaze ("pur ti miro"), the interlacing ("pur ti godo, pur ti stringo"), the returns required by the passacaglia form, the intertwining of words ("io son tua, tuo son io"), the insistent call of a word that is never exhausted or spent ("dillo, di"—"say it, say it to me"). The gold of possessive joy is glittering, and in the instant that crowns the day, the couple attains the divine state. In the mode of illusion, but so gloriously, a love song has conquered the heavens.

CHAPTER 9

The Magic of Alcina

THE FIGURE OF PLEASURE

During the 1734–1735 season, Handel's *Ariodante* and *Alcina* were produced at Covent Garden. The librettos of these operas featured two
episodes from Ariosto's *Orlando Furioso*.[1] This marvelous epic poem,
freely inspired by images of chivalric tradition, stood for many centuries as the model of the heroic-comedic narrative passed on by Voltaire
and Wieland and whose final remnants can still be found in Byron,
Musset, and Pushkin.

So, by a singular coincidence, the texts of these two operas are both
borrowed from Ariosto; however, they bring to the stage heroines
whose fates provoke strong emotions for radically opposed reasons.
The heroine of *Ariodante*, Ginevra, libeled and defamed, barely escapes execution. Alcina, an enchantress and usurper, reigns over an
island where everything yields to the magic powers that she employs to

carry out her whims—until the day when she must admit defeat when faced with a countermagic that makes triumph the Good, the Loyal, and the True. On one hand, we have the suspect figure, the victim that masculine power—that of fathers and jealous lovers—treats as guilty. This is the fate of Shakespeare's Desdemona and of Armenaide in Rossini's *Tancredi* (1813), an adaptation of a dramatic tale by Voltaire from 1759. On the other hand, we have the female fairy, *fata*—the femme fatale whose spells enslave men—who fascinates by her gaze, her voice, and the marvels with which she surrounds herself. Nevertheless, a common characteristic unites these sharply distinct female figures: the play of appearance. Just the clothes of Ginevra when worn by her maid are enough to make Ginevra appear unfaithful. Alcina's magical powers give her mastery over all images, beginning with her own. She can paint deserts with the colors of paradise. At every moment in Ariosto's poem the attention of various characters is lost, mistaken, becomes captivated, or pursues the unattainable (prey). The blinding shield and the ring that makes one invisible have their sources in other legends and will be transmitted by Angélique, Renaud, and Bradamante to heroes of other poems just like the magic wand that also becomes an operatic prop in the hands of Circe, Armide, or the Queen of the Night.

So what if the shine is false? Alcina is the mistress of all that can be offered in an instant: palaces, gardens, amusements. And if art chooses as its goal the pursuit of pleasure, it must enter the enchanted circle where the sorceress reigns. Music necessarily plays a part in all this, as does poetry. Pleasure likes to admire its own reflection. In Ariosto, the paladin Roger, newly deposited on the island by the hippogriff (which is boundless imagination) is sumptuously received at Alcina's table after she has rid herself of her previous lover, Astolphe, by changing him into a myrtle. We find the following description in a graceful and unfaithful translation from the nineteenth century: "At Alcina's table lutes, harps, lyres, and other melodious instruments play with sweet harmony and the most touching concord; young poets praise the joys and the follies of love, and their graceful fables excite pleasure. . . . With the tables cleared away, the guests, joined in a circle, begin a game where each in a low voice reveals to the others some tender secrets. The two lovers speak freely of their love, the last part of their discussion is a promise to see each other again during the night."

The following stanzas tell of Roger's impatience and the preparations of Alcina, especially the subtle and rare veil "that no more hid her from others' eyes than a transparent crystal would hide lilies and roses." After the night of love, the day is spent in various amusements: "Two or three times a day they change clothes; parties and games follow one after another; after a dance and the pleasures of the bath, there is wrestling, jousting, and other spectacles. Beside fountains and in the shade of the hillside, they read old love stories."

These pastimes are those of the Golden Age, of the island of Cythera (according to the poet Claudius Claudianus), of the garden of Déduit, the earthly double of Paradise (according to the *Romance of the Rose*). All the pleasant locations of the poetic tradition are here united, and these activities are the infinitely varied pleasures of life at court and not the wild idleness of the beginning of time. Everything is luxury and fulfilled whim.

Many princes of the baroque period found in the Alcina episode the model for their own festivities. Without doubt the most sumptuous was "The Pleasures of the Enchanted Island," a festival hosted by Louis XIV at Versailles in early May 1664 and considered to be the most beautiful of his entire reign.[2] The theme chosen was "the palace of Alcina." On the first day, the king and his courtesans paraded on horseback in costumes representing heroes of chivalric novels. The king was dressed as Roger. "His helmet all covered with feathers the color of fire had an incomparable grace." Different allegorical figures introduced themselves to the queen. There were games such as running at the ring. The ceremonies and dinner were accompanied by a small orchestra and solo violins that played the music of Lully. The second day Molière and his troop presented *La Princesse d'Élide*. The theme of day three was the liberation of Alcina's captive warriors. A ballet represented a combat where demons and Moors were the defenders of Alcina. But Roger receives from the good sorceress Melissa the ring that destroys the enchantments. Lightning. Thunder. The palace of Alcina crumbles, and the entire performance concludes with a superb fireworks show: "It seemed that the heavens, earth, and water were all on fire and that the destruction of the superb palace of Alcina, as well as the liberation of the knights that she held prisoner there, could only be accomplished by prodigal feats and miracles: the height and number of flying rockets, those that flew over the banks and those that having crashed in the water then shot back out, made for such a grand and magnificent spectacle that nothing could have put a better end to the enchantments than this immensely beautiful display of fireworks."

Festivities devoted to other themes continued. Among other entertainments, the king organized a visit of his menagerie. Molière's troupe put on a performance of *Les Fâcheux*. The next day, there was a sumptuous lottery and new contests. "In the evening his majesty called for the performance of a comedy named *Tartufe* that the distinguished Molière had written attacking hypocrites." With *Tartufe* Molière had crossed over from fable to contemporary reality, but the focus on deceptive appearances as well as the interest in disabling the imposture's power to harm remained.

IMMORTALITY AND CHAGRIN

In Handel's *Alcina*, performed seventy years after the Sun King's Versailles festival, thunder will again be heard and Alcina's palace will again crumble: the sea will wash over its ruins, rocks will resume human form, and liberated men emerge out of the waves into which they had been liquefied. Pyrotechnics, if used, were no doubt more modest than in the open-air performance at Versailles. Of course it was necessary that the undoing of spells be once again accompanied by some sort of tumult and by the dawning of a new day produced reliably by the chandeliers and mirrors of the theater. The machinery performed as well as possible to satisfy the necessary conventions of operatic magic. No one ever believed a bit of it. The English public, moreover, was not content to take the pastoral and the opera seria for what they were, namely. sometimes rather boring fictions; instead they took a particular pleasure in the burlesque counterfeiting of these fictions. The success of *The Beggar's Opera* (1728), a work that pushed far in the direction of mockery, is proof of this. The frank laughter at the miseries and truculence of the polloi in the capital was supplanting the still exclusively aristocratic smile at the fantasies that staged traveling knights with changeable feelings and fragile minds.

With the subject of *Alcina*, Handel finds all that he needs to showcase his musical genius. His heroine is not an abstract allegory of pleasure who changes discarded lovers into trees when tired of them. She is also a lover susceptible to anxiety and pain when she loses the one whose love she has captured.

The libretto adds many characters to those that were in the story that inspired the opera. The result is a sentimental plot where disguises and illusions and consequently jealousies and misunderstandings multiply. There is also a proliferation of different versions of love as well as different ways of singing that love—fleeting, bitter, passionate, conjugal, and even filial. On this island of metamorphoses, why wouldn't the styles of love vary infinitely? The fairy Morgane, Alcina's sister, falls in love at first sight with Bradamante when he appears disguised as a warrior. The frivolous principles of Morgane are common to many female figures in the baroque age: inconstancy and changefulness, *amar e disamar*—"From like to love to dislike, such is my will." Abandoned by Morgane, Oronte is reconquered in no time. The fairy's voice in a beautiful aria ("Credete al mio dolore . . .") works the miracle: it is the balm by which love soothes the wounds it has caused.

But the central myth was not debased. In the palace and gardens of Alcina, time stops, beauty shines forth unalterably, spring and youth are in perpetual vigor, and voluptuousness is not exhausted. When the fairy's domain is revealed to our eyes, a beautiful chorus tells us, "Questo è il centro del goder"—"This place is the center of enjoyment." For a warrior hero, to set foot on Alcina's island means to leave behind the glorious adventure and to see both the future and the past fall into oblivion. Clocks have stopped. It thus means the death of reputation and the abolition of all posterity. In the arms of Alcina, Roger is out of commission, on a forced vacation. The metamorphosis of previous lovers into animals, trees, and rocks is for them nothing but a deeper sleep sheltered from time: they have received the immortality of the material.

This atemporal happiness, this immersion into the abyss of elements, changes character instantly when Roger receives from Melissa the ring that destroys the enchantments. In Ariosto, it is Alcina who changes immediately back into her true self: she is now nothing but a decrepit old woman. In Handel's opera, the fantastic is less pronounced, but Alcina's downfall becomes even more poignant: she is stripped of her supernatural powers. She had abused them in full sovereignty, and they are taken away and she is left an abandoned woman. She experiences triumph, then defeat. The situation in which Ariosto places her is the paradox of immortality. She has lost everything and she wishes to die.

But she cannot die because she is a fairy. To live on endlessly in this way is no longer the endless celebration it once was but perpetual melancholy. Alcina shares the destiny of Dido, Medea, and Cleopatra, but without being able to put an end to her suffering: "In the middle of so many disasters, the unhappy Alcina cannot stop sighing and crying. . . . She often accuses Fate for prolonging her distress by opposing her step into death: no fairy can die, so long as the sun continues on its course and the heavens change not their movements! Were that not so, the desperation of Alcina would have been deep enough to soften the Fates and lead them to cut the thread of her days."

Handel devoted his most intense musical expression to Alcina's lament. "Ah! mio cor!" is one of the most admirable arias in the entire history of opera. "Mi restano le lagrime"—"I still have tears." For the listener, it is at the moment when Alcina deplores the loss of her power that she exerts her deepest seductiveness. The disappearance of the dark magic leaves the field open to the pure magic of melodious breath.

"So long as the sun continues on its course." In Handel's music the sun continues on its course. I know of no image more suited to tell of the luminosity, the varied order, the cadenced stability, the anticipated returns, and the miraculous ornaments of this music. In the domain of feeling, Alcina's voice occupies the immense range that goes from sovereignty to desperation, from tenderness to fury. But these metamorphoses of the soul, this pride, and these sad states are comprised within a cosmic frame where the "movements of the heavens" continue according to paths prescribed by a generous nature. Everything, including chagrin, melancholy illusions, and illicit incantations—everything truly comes together and follows with the clarity of an infallible harmony. When the palace of illusion crumbles and the stray wandering ceases, the music reveals that it also possesses the power to open the way toward a higher watchful reason.

CHAPTER 10

Love unto Death

Another *Romeo*

THE SIMPLIFIED LIBRETTO

It is obvious that Felice Romani, the librettist of Vaccai and Bellini, did not turn to Shakespeare's original text for inspiration. His predeces-sor, Giuseppe Maria Foppa, had relied on the French tragedy by Ducis (1772) while also mentioning the *Histories of Verona* by Girolamo Dalla Corte.[1] We may recall that, for Zingarelli, Foppa's treatment involved an extreme simplification of the action, which begins with a party at the Capulets' in a "magnificent space" where the lovers meet for the first time. In the second act, in a garden, the reasonable Gilberto, who seeks to reconcile the two factions, unites the hands of Romeo (played by the male soprano Crescentini) and Juliet (played by the contralto Giuseppina Grassini). The composer had only six singers at his disposal. Choruses and dancers were supposed to compensate for the reduced number of actors. Romani's text in turn will not succeed any better at re-creating the vast and complete world that Shakespeare's lyricism made revolve around the loving couple.[2] One finds neither the hustle and bustle of the street nor Juliet's garden with its nocturnal scents. The talkative nurse, gentle Mercutio, and noble Paris have all disappeared. There are neither servants nor a prince, powerless and disillusioned, trying in vain to restore peace in his divided city. Friar Lawrence, who offers his help to the lovers, has become a mere doctor. And, finally, no maternal figures.

The sole representative of the Capulet family in the opera is the father who stands unbending in his desire for revenge and resolved to have his daughter, Juliet, marry Tebaldo. This choice accords Capulet a disproportionately grand status. On the other side, Romeo is the sole representative of the powerful Montagues. Romani of course depicts him as an adolescent lover but also as a military leader. Grafted onto the family rivalry is the conflict between Guelfs and Ghibellines that divides all of Italy. Felice Romani establishes a military staging: the choruses are composed of knights, soldiers, and special agents with halberds, daggers, and coats of mail. The costume designer is free to exploit the brilliant effects of steel. Along with the reduced number of characters there is a corresponding contraction of the story itself. Everything takes place over a twenty-four hour period in accordance with the classic rule governing unity of time: crisis and catastrophe follow each other quickly. When the curtain rises, the events that take up the first three acts of Shakespeare's play have already happened. Enter Romeo and Juliet, whose love is already irrevocable. We are not witnesses of its genesis. Romeo has shed the most precious blood in killing Juliet's brother and not, as in Shakespeare, the beloved's vain cousin, Tybalt. To list the many other differences would be a lengthy task. Great legendary stories are always retold over and through variations and derivations, and this is what permits, as we shall see, the clearer identification of constants.

With the surrounding world absent, nature erased, characters simplified, and the story contracted, one is not left with a good dramatic poem to read. But who said anything about reading? Pride of place must be given over entirely to the music, and Bellini managed quite well with the text that Romani gave him. The composer had a good libretto in his hands. The garden, the stars, the nightingale, and the lark are not in the text. The music gives them to us. The voices create a new world. The obligatory French horn, the trill of a harp, and two flutes in thirds construct a firmament and a paradisiacal garden for the ears. The syllables of the libretto are only the receptacles of the astral body of the melody. The two high-voiced lovers show their opposition by means of contrast with the other voices, all masculine. The passion of Tebaldo may have flashed heroically, but it will never attain that height. The evidence is all there for the senses for those who are able to hear it.

TROUBLED EXOGAMY

The initial givens are rivalry and violence between clans, which raises the question, how shall this violence be overcome? Fables teach us the answer. When war opposes family against family, faction against faction, city against city, a peaceful resolution of the conflict proffers itself through the marriage of the children of those who were at first enemies. In the most ancient stories, violence still hovers over the unions that put an end to war. The Romans carry off the Sabine women. The men of the tribe of Benjamin ravish the young women of Shiloh. According to anthropologists, seeking out women from within another family is one of the fundamental traits that distinguishes humans from animals. Rousseau linked the very origin of language to the beginnings of exogamy: the first word, which is also the first melody, is pronounced by young people who meet for the first time, motivated by the singular desire to conquer the stranger's heart and the unknown woman's gaze. In the fictitious tales that have fed our imagination, the reconciliation between rival houses is sealed by the vows of marriage. Hostility morphs into the alliance of hosting and husbandry. Adversaries who put down their arms recognize each other as brothers and cousins: they see their differences give way to a common posterity.

By entitling their opera *I Capuleti e i Montecchi*, Romani and Bellini clearly foreground the question of the family feud. The libretto insists on the hatred separating the two clans that have grown into two factions locked in a struggle for power. The time of the production, 1830, coincides with the emergence of public troubles in Europe. In addition, the historical novel is then at the height of its popularity. Despite the vigilance of public censors, the cultural situation allowed storytellers and librettists to talk about the present via the detour of historical fiction. It is a significant fact that when he first appears, an unrecognizable

Romeo has taken on the role of an ambassador carrying a message of peace. Thanks to the faith he has exchanged with Juliet, he is able to ensure the sincerity of his promises. But the union of the lovers remains secret, and therefore it has not put an end to the terrible feud. Were the truth of the reciprocal love to be recognized, it would turn the fighting between clans into absurdity. Thus the civil war continues on as though nothing had happened. Romeo, unmasked, must himself unsheathe his sword and assume the role of enemy. If love had been able or willing to declare itself in the light of day, an entire hateful past would have been erased. On the contrary, as the Capulet chief symbolizes, it is memory of the inexpiable offense that prevails. By preferring vendetta, by considering the alliance proposed by Romeo to be an unworthy degradation, and by forcing Juliet to marry Tebaldo, the tyrannical father is complicit in the ensuing deaths. The final scene of the opera is as sorrowful as the conclusion to Shakespeare's play. The sacrifice of the lovers does permit former enemies to commune in a shared grief, but the new era that begins at the end of the tragedy is "a glooming peace" (act 5, scene 3, line 316). In his concluding remarks that function as a kind of epilogue, the prince confines himself to basic observations:

> All are punished . . .
> For never was a story of more woe
> Than this of Juliet and her Romeo!
> (act 5, scene 3, lines 305, 320–321)

THE FATAL MIX-UP

A tragic knot links the death of the lovers and the missed opportunity for peace between the hostile communities. Although with fewer political implications, the story of the false death and the misunderstanding that truly hastens the lovers' death had already been around for centuries. The fate of the Verona lovers had as its model another pair of lovers from Sienna (known to Masuccio Salernitano, *Il Novellino*, 1483). In a more distant example, one finds the same unhappy adversity in the story of the lovers of Babylon recounted by Ovid in his *Metamorphoses*. Pyramus and Thisbe love each other in secret despite the enmity their fathers. They meet in the country at night in the shade of a tree. Thisbe arrives first. Then a lioness appears with blood around her mouth. Thisbe takes refuge in a cave, but in fleeing she lets fall her veil, which the lion tears apart and stains with blood. Pyramus, discovering this fatal sign, believes Thisbe to be dead and stabs himself in desperation. Thisbe returns only to hear the last sigh of Pyramus and then kills herself, too. As she is dying, she implores the enemy fathers to allow her and her lover to share a common tomb, and she forms the vow that the tree that was splashed with their blood—the mulberry—shall forever bear only dark-colored fruit. Thus we have here both a myth of origins (why is a certain fruit dark red?) and a lesson in semiological caution (a misreading of signs can prove fatal).

The tragic story of "woe" in this form relies too heavily on malicious fate. The lover presumes for certain a death about which he has no absolute proof. Unhappiness occurs because of a truth that has remained hidden, a piece of news that wasn't delivered. Accidental tragedy and misrecognition of the facts is not true tragedy. In the Shakespeare play, a messenger is held up, and Friar Lawrence, a clumsy fellow for sure, arrives a little bit too late. The contingent character of the message's interception makes the tragic outcome look like the effect of a stretch of bad luck. Shakespeare must have noticed this. Soon after writing *Romeo and Juliet* (1597), he inserts within his *Midsummer Night's Dream* a burlesque version of the adventure of Pyramus and Thisbe that takes up the Romeo and Juliet story in the form of caricature (act 5, scene 1, lines 106–363). Is this not the revenge of comedy over tragedy? In the performance put on by Bottom and his amateur companions one is constantly laughing, especially at the drollery of the figures that stand as accidental obstacles: the wall and the lion. With the superior irony of *A Midsummer Night's Dream*, the woeful story of lovers becomes the grotesque, clownish account of a missed rendezvous. In the Bellini opera, Capulet has placed Lorenzo under close watch, thus preventing him from coming to the lovers' assistance. This is an ingenious way of linking the fault and the family disaster to the use of police tactics.

A PASSION THAT SEEKS DEATH

But accidents are not everything. The interception of the message and the apparent death of the beloved are only the indices of what constitutes the heart of Romeo's passion: the wish to die. Along with Tristan, Romeo is one of the exemplary figures of the love passion; that is, of the love that results from an all-powerful potion that inspires the transgression of interdiction and finds its ultimate fulfillment in death.

The love potion-poison. In Bandello's tale (1554) that in various translations and adaptations inspired Shakespeare, the first glance exchanged with Juliet as quick as lightning is compared to a poisoning: the eye of the hero "drinks the sweet poison of love." Shakespeare echoes this: "Now Romeo is beloved and loves again, / Alike bewitched by the charm of looks" (act 2, chorus, lines 5–6). In his commentary on the Shakespeare play, Yves Bonnefoy has wondered if for Romeo the love of love, the exaltation of the condition of being in love, and the cult of the inaccessible image have not taken the place of a truer love that would have remained in the human order and that would have recognized better the real young woman in her simple terrestrial life.[3] With the impulse that leads him to avenge Mercutio's death by killing Tybalt, does not Shakespeare's Romeo take a somber satisfaction in deepening his transgression and thus rendering even more inaccessible his love for Juliet and his clandestine marriage? He hurries readily into an exile that would seem to foreclose all possible futures—except death. Thus the poison of the ideal is no different from the mortal liquid that Romeo acquires stealthily from the "true apothecary" in Mantua (act 5, scene 1, lines 37–91). It is not misfortune but an impatience to die that leads Romeo to the catastrophe. And he is guilty of leading Juliet there. Certainly by taking the powerful sleeping potion that makes her seem dead she evades the marriage arranged by her father. In this way she wrests for herself a last shred of personal freedom and saves herself for the sole partner she has chosen. She accepts the sinister plan to descend into the tomb. She plays with death by playing dead. According to an imperfect calculus, Friar Lawrence's drug was to permit a reawakening, but Juliet emerges from sleep only to observe the victory of death.

In Romani's libretto, Romeo leaps immediately into extreme danger. He risks his life from the first instant. The Juliet character joins him gradually at the end of a fatal delay. Incapable of overcoming the paternal interdiction and feeling the accusing weight of the dead brother, she accepts the role first of captive and then of victim. Obeying the dictates of honor, she refuses to flee as Romeo wishes her to do. The music of the forced marriage must first ring before Juliet will take the drug offered by Lorenzo. When she awakes, she sees Romeo, and now she is ready to flee with him: "Andiam!"—"Let's go!" But it's too late, and the only way to rejoin her lover is to let her life escape when he breathes his last sigh.

THE DUO BEYOND THE GRAVE

In the story by Luigi da Porta (*Giulietta e Romeo*, 1524) and in Bandello's (*Giuletta e Romeo*, 1554), Romeo lifts the coffin lid and believes Juliet to be dead. He swallows the poison, takes his beloved in his arms, and then sees her wake up. In the remaining lapse of time, words unite again the dying man and his wife whose eyes open to witness a fatal agony. One does not find this dialogue in the Shakespeare version: Juliet is welcomed out of her sleep by Friar Lawrence, who tries to get her to leave the tomb. Before her eyes is the lifeless body of Romeo. She chides him, "O churl, drunk all, and left no friendly drop / To help me after!" (act 5, scene 3, lines 168–169). An approaching watchman is heard, and Juliet stabs herself in an instant. The deaths are separate and in succession. Swinburne, an expert on sadomasochism, criticized Shakespeare for "omitting the most beautiful incident in the whole story, . . . the last words exchanged between the dying Romeo and Juliet." We are thus deprived of what would have been "the most tender and noble moment of the most beautiful of tragedies." Foppa's libretto for Zingarelli and Romani's text for Bellini both restore this element of the earlier narrative tradition.[4] The two composers needed a situation that would give them an opportunity to deploy a double song of the imminence of death or the afterlife, a *Liebestod* in duo.

Imagine the sepulchral vault in the way European set designers from generation to generation since the baroque age have sought ingeniously to reconstruct it, with its torches, shadowy areas, statues, arches, and niches. This mournful place lends itself to a canticle for basses. Against this background, two voices (Juliet's soprano and Romeo's mezzo in thirds), rise, float, take wing, and descend, sliding or palpitating. The two voices trace the long smooth melody whose very use transcends pain. It is the moment when Bellini's musical instinct attains its highest power of seduction. It finds its most ample breath precisely there where the music aims to evoke the moment when all breathing stops.

Manon

In the first act of Massenet's *Manon*, in the courtyard of the roadside hotel in Amiens, Des Grieux is waiting for the carriage that will bring him back to his father. He says to himself, "Finally, by tomorrow evening at the latest, I will embrace my father! . . . I feel him, he's drawing me to him, and I take him in my arms!" In this outburst of affection, he turns round and notices Manon sitting alone on a stone bench. This one glance suffices: an instantaneous magic has transformed the world. An almost childlike beauty has replaced the image of the father. Morally speaking, the contemptuous disregard of paternal authority underpins the entire opera. This unknown woman is now the unique love object, the one that has diverted the son's attention. Her apparition—"Is it a dream?"—marks the beginning of a new era of existence: "Where do these feelings come from? It seems as though my life is about to end . . . or begin! . . . It seems to me as though an iron hand were leading me onto another path and irresistibly pushing me forward!" The text of

Meilhac and Gille, though very uneven, transcribes wonderfully the moment of this love shock and the unforeseen direction in which a life feels itself being pushed. In the novel by the abbé Prévost (1731), Des Grieux needs only one long sentence to proclaim this entrance into a new era: "She appeared to me so charming that I, who had neither thought about the difference between the sexes nor looked at any woman with the least particular attention, I, yes, I, whom everyone admired for his wisdom and reserve, I found myself suddenly inflamed and transported."[1]

Manon becomes immediately, before any words are exchanged, the "mistress of my heart." What a moment! This is the first awakening to the life of the senses, when the power to love, in revealing itself, becomes unerringly focused on a single object. The novel does not care a whit for useless details and notes only that Manon remained "alone in the courtyard." She is there as though lost in this last moment of liberty that remains to her before she is sent to a convent. But her solitude is also that of a sovereign who will rule without sharing or concession.

THE GRIP OF LOVE

Thus it comes down to us from Dante and Beatrice, Petrarch and Laura, and all the other poets who have composed love sonnets. The lightning bolt of love at first sight is the initial sign of every noble love. What the poetic tradition used to attribute to Love's arrows and the spells of Venus, this very young schoolboy who knows his theology and who is being groomed for the Order of Malta experiences in the trivial surroundings of a hotel courtyard after having stepped down from a coach when the bustle of the other travelers has barely subsided. The sky has opened up in this place where chance shuffles the cards and mixes together all passersby and passengers. Transposed to our century, this place becomes a bus or train station, as we see in Henze's adaptation in *Boulevard Solitude* (1952): a public place devoted to agitated comings and goings, a place that becomes a sacred spot when a total passion is born there.

What gives rise to this grip of love? How does seduction work? Why, as Des Grieux confesses in the novel, does passion become this "insurmountable" force? Other stories, especially the great myth of Tristan, have a love potion intervene—and we know what music the Celtic potion was destined for. In the Prévost novel, Des Grieux speaks only of Manon's "charm." The word recurs constantly and frees the narrator from giving any more precise description of the process. We are told she is "charming" and has a "store of inexhaustible charms." This word must be taken in its archaic sense. One needs to go back to its etymological origin and hear in it magical incantation, the Latin "*carmen,*" the formula that witches knew how to pronounce to capture hearts and make the moon dance in a wooded clearing. Prévost, who was also the author of a *Manuel lexique* (1750), defines the word "*charme*": "Properly speaking, this word signifies an enchantment or the effect of a power that surpasses that of nature. . . . It is applied to all that is capable of strongly attaching the heart and the spirit."[2] To set Manon to music is to translate her charms into a new language. Prévost's dictionary also contains an entry for the word "*philtre*" (potion), and one is surprised to be referred back to "*charmes*": "The only potions [*les seuls philtres*] that one can recognize are the immediate influences of one sex on another, either by the pure instinct of nature that carries one toward the other, . . . or by the charms of beauty, spirit, and other qualities . . . that all act simultaneously on the senses and the imagination."

THE SENSES AND THE IMAGINATION

The senses. They are all-powerful in the novel. The first readers immediately noticed Des Grieux's indiscretions. Censors meted out their punishment: the hero's disarray and Manon's fluctuations are the result of carnal desire. In this novel where the body is never naked, a diffuse eroticism is constantly present.

The imagination in the novel is inseparable from the senses. Manon knows she has the power to capture the imagination. She is a Circe ingénue. "Too bad for whoever falls into my net," she writes to Des Grieux at the moment she is betraying him. And where does this power she has come from? She wears no mask. She is simply beautiful, changing, and elusive. And what must the imagination do to attach or free itself? "I don't know what" ["Je ne sais quoi"] and "Almost nothing" ["Presque rien"], the classical authors used to say. "Nothing" ["Rien"] is the first word uttered by the first narrator in the novel's prologue. He is

surprised at the gathering in front of the inn at Pacy. He investigates.
A soldier who is accompanying this convoy of deportees replies, "It's
nothing . . . just a dozen prostitutes" ("Ce n'est rien . . . c'est une dou-
zaine de filles de joie"). This brutal "nothing" acts as the point of departure for everything in this novel, leaving the imagination almost un-
bridled freedom. Renoncour—the man of quality who has retired from
the world—observes Manon chained and poorly dressed but sees in her
"an air" and "a figure" that would make one take her for "a princess"
and "a person of the highest rank." Des Grieux is not far off, "shrouded
in reverie." The "*air*" that Prévost constantly associates with charm is
the indefinable light that belongs both to a face and to the imagination of the enthralled spectator. In the visitors' parlor of Saint-Sulpice,
Manon will seduce for a second time the man she has betrayed, one
who deludes himself in appealing for grace, and Des Grieux admits that
he has never ceased to be a slave. It is enough for Manon to appear: "O
Gods! What a surprising apparition! . . . it was she, but more lovable
and more brilliant than I had ever seen her. She was not yet eighteen
years old. Her charms exceeded anything that can be described. It was
an *air* so fine, so soft, so engaging, the *air* of Love itself. Her whole person struck me as an enchantment."

"THEY CALL ME MANON"

There is something else for the senses and the imagination: the very
name of Manon, these two syllables of a familiar, tender diminutive
[of Madeleine or Marie], a hook for the ear and trap for the mind. In
"*Ma-non*" a French ear hears the possessive "*Ma*" and the negation
"*non*"—that which one wants to possess and which refuses possession:
"my not." These two syllables haunt Des Grieux like a leitmotif or an
obsessive image, and it is not by speaking to them in the grandilo-
quent tone of tragic heroes and accusing them of perfidy that he will
manage to deliver himself from their grip: "Perfidious Manon! Ah!
Perfidy! Perfidy!" Perfidy names the broken promise, the inconstancy
that allows no personal identity to be established and endure. But this
breath, this voice, this name—Manon—carries within it a semblance
of permanent identity. Des Grieux repeats it, as though he were thereby
able to hold on to the one who never ceases to escape from him. The

novelist and the musicians all sensed the importance of insisting on the moment when the female stranger, already the "mistress of [his] heart," reveals her name. It is the most precious gift: "My heart opened to a thousand feelings of pleasure about which I never had the least idea," declares Des Grieux when he evokes the late meal of their first evening together. "A sweet warmth pervaded my every waking moment. . . . Mademoiselle Manon Lescaut, *that is how she told me people called her*, appeared very satisfied with this effect of her charms." Massenet (encouraged here by his librettists) knew how to make the most of this effect of the name. The heroine had been listened to when she apostrophized herself: "Come, Manon, no more illusions," Des Grieux will be able to say to her: ". . . And I know your name." And he hears his answer that effects a rhyme that sets up an easy play of mirrors: "On m'appelle Manon"—"They call me Manon." To which the echo immediately replies, "Manon!" Within the magic circle traced by this name alone, Des Grieux makes the grand lyric exclamation:

> *Enchanteresse*
> *Au charme vainqueur!*
> *Manon, vous êtes la maîtresse*
> *De mon cœur!*

> Enchantress
> With your conquering charm!
> Manon, you are the mistress
> Of my heart!

In his *Manon Lescaut* of 1893, Puccini will not hesitate to reuse this discovery: "Mi chiamano Manon." The voice carries off this sentence so well! It gives life to a being who will soon only live on as a memory. Two years later in *La Bohème* the sentence will reappear: "Mi chiamano Mimi." We should be cautious, however, for in this name uttered by an exquisite voice, it is the voice of others that is speaking. Neither Manon nor Mimi possesses her name: each says how *others* name them. In what most resembles a declaration of essential identity, Manon does not own herself: she is the object of others; she exists only as a function of everyone's conventional speech. A proof, let's admit, of the passivity that a long tradition has attributed to women. The seductress, the "enchantress with conquering charms," owes her existence to the caressing nickname she has received. To conclude the opera, the authors wanted Manon herself, as "distanced" from herself, to announce her own death: "And that is the story of Manon Lescaut." The music therefore had the role of rendering audible the way in which a striking and fragile creature allowed itself to be pushed forward by an unmasterable fate.

"IS IT NO LONGER MY VOICE?"

Manon is the ingénue seductress whose charm works with no apparent effort. She employs no strategy for conquest. She has only, it seems, to consent. There are none of the calculations that Laclos attributes to the marquise de Merteuil in his *Dangerous Liaisons* (1782). But this child, who exudes a power that is almost beyond her control, obtains the entire, irrevocable, and obstinate submission of the chevalier Des Grieux. He obeys a fatality, an ascendant star against which no act of opposing will is possible. It is hardly an exaggeration to say that the *Histoire du Chevalier Des Grieux et de Manon Lescaut* is the passionate outcome of an encounter between two types of passivity. Manon's whims win from Des Grieux all manner of abdication: her tears, her games represent absolute orders for him, while whatever society might take for disorder is of no concern. The straight and narrow paths traced beforehand by paternal and religious authority are no longer of any importance. For the chevalier, Manon is the motive for a total renunciation of all the good things that the world could possibly offer. In the novel, Des Grieux rationalizes his behavior: these sacrifices, undertaken to attain a paradise within the pleasures of love, are equal to the sacrifices and demands of religion that are exacted with a view to less certain advantages: "The sight of Manon would make me fall from the heavens. . . . I would let the whole world perish without a care. . . . For me Manon is my glory, happiness, and fortune" Studies, marriage, family inheritance, and ecclesiastic pensions—all these guaranteed comforts are no longer attractive to him. By remaining attached to Manon, Des Grieux opts for a social void that translates into borrowing money, quick fixes, cheating, confidence games, theft, and murder. We may note in passing that in Massenet's treatment of the story the chevalier's delinquency and the punishments he brings down on himself are largely glossed over with only the suggestion of trivial misdemeanors. And in all his shady enterprises, Des Grieux believes that he is going to come out ahead.

But he is continually fooled while setting out to trick others. Though betrayed three times by Manon, he never lacks for arguments to rationalize her behavior and look beyond her insults. He doggedly perseveres in his bad faith and blindness. The nobility of feeling with which he flatters himself along with the unjust fate of which he complains are sufficient excuses for him. In a world where no one earns their money from honest work—except coachmen and servants (who are themselves not above occasional petty larceny)—exploiting the stupidity of the wealthy appears as an opportunity for legitimate compensation. Alas, the wealthy are stronger. They have only to complain to the police lieutenant, and the king's agents act on their orders. For the young lovers, the fall is inevitable. The nineteenth-century librettos discreetly pass over the prison episodes that punctuate the couple's story in the novel. They retain the final moment when Manon, too, sacrifices herself, a convert to true love just as time runs out.

THE DELIGHTFUL ATTRACTION OF DISORDER

Is Manon the sole cause of Des Grieux's disorderly collapse? Is love alone responsible? One can read the book as Walter E. Rex has done and ask a blasphemous question about the sacred character of passion.[3] After all, this madness and these scandalous adventures could be expressing above all else a hatred for the imposed rule, a protest against order, "the attraction of the contrary." For a young nobleman whose life path is all too well traced out, Manon could be a simple pretext, and following this "siren" would then be first of all an overcoming of all obedience to paternal values. Des Grieux's revolt consists in entirely abdicating his own will and allowing himself to be dragged into the most sordid crimes by Manon's brother—a jesting fallen angel, counterfeiter, and pimp who derisively wears the uniform of a guard. With guardians like him, the public order wonderfully reveals all the evil facets that it hides within itself. The immorality of those who profit from this order authorizes every type of disorder. What superiority can a young man who throws himself into a "great refusal" not claim for himself when powerful individuals of the day merely think of their own pleasure (and do so quite openly) without the least regard for the poor creatures they are humiliating!

But whatever role a secret hatred for the father and the social order might be playing, it does nothing to diminish the fact that Manon exists most convincingly. Not a few nineteenth-century readers believe they know her. She is one of the first heroines in whom the sensibility of the rococo age expresses itself; I mean an unstable way of being—discontinuous, capricious, and quick to laugh as well as to shed tears. All the tragic force of the story of these two very young lovers depends on Manon, the figure on whom Des Grieux is so blindly dependent, being herself a profoundly dependent creature—her dependence being a touch more infantile and egocentric. People hardly count for her. What matters are entertainments, pleasures, and surprises that wealth allows to be refined and multiplied. The upshot, when it comes to their love, is an absence of true reciprocity that ceases only on the eve of the tragic epilogue. Des Grieux reopens his wound with his narration: "Manon was passionate about pleasure, and I was passionate about her. . . . She had to have pleasure and pastimes. It was so necessary for her to be occupied in this way by pleasure that without it there was no budging her mood or inclinations."

Manon wants to be taken to the theater and the opera; she loves gambling, social gatherings, and walks in the Bois de Boulogne; she loves costumes and fine meals; she of course has a horror of misery since poverty puts an end to the diverting entertainments that she cannot do without. For Montesquieu, she is quite simply a whore (*catin*).[4] But what a lot of whores there are in this century where feelings impose their law! In her naive need for dissipation, Manon is the perfect example of a consciousness that suffers disquieting feelings as soon as she is idle. The soul only knows it exists, according to the philosophy of the day, at the moment it feels. But sensations are ephemeral; they are quickly exhausted, and the soul returns to its nothingness, that is, into the gaping pit of boredom. New stimulants are necessary for it to rise up from this malaise and feel alive again. Thus, unfaithful to a past that has already been consumed, pursuing emotion in random encounters that will be no less ephemeral, the individual must surrender to the unexpected and seize the intermittent bursts of pleasure that shine out against a perfectly dark background. Moments of frivolous joy alternate with moments of transport. At Saint-Sulpice, Manon exclaims prophetically, "I'm planning to die" ("Je prétends mourir").[5] But shortly afterward we see her bursting with laughter in the company of the old lover who has showered her with jewels when she has the chevalier pass himself off as her brother and play the naive schoolboy.

A SERIES OF ECHOES

In the Prévost novel one can detect deformed, parodied echoes of the rhetoric of religion and tragedy of an earlier age. *The History of Chevalier des Grieux* vulgarizes the myths concerning an irresistible passion as treated by Racine and the Jansenists. The romantic writers take over. Because they greatly empathized with the subject, their reading of *Manon* was not exempt from misunderstandings and distortions. One finds, for example, the image of an old regime romanticized with the passing of time, but in the story of the strong hold exerted by Manon it seems as contemporary as ever. It made Liszt cry. He had probably perceived the dilemma of the nearly heroic challenge: the appetite to live and the insistent call of death. As a future abbot himself, how could Liszt not be moved by the poignant tale of the ex-abbé Des Grieux who recounts his conversation at Saint-Sulpice? "I was shivering, as happens when one finds oneself at night in a distant piece of countryside; one feels transported into a new order of things; one is seized by a secret horror." The realist effect was admired by Musset in the first song (stanza 57) of his *Namouna* (1832):

> *Pourquoi Manon Lescaut, dès la première scène,*
> *Est-elle si vivante et si vraiment humaine,*
> *Qu'il semble qu'on l'a vue et que c'est un portrait?*

> Why is Manon Lescaut from the first scene
> So alive and so truly human that it seems
> One has seen her and is now looking at a portrait?

The younger Dumas echoes this sentiment: "This heroine is so true that I feel I've known her." So true that one has to write again her story, transporting it into the contemporary demimonde. By his own admission, *La Dame aux camélias* (1848) is a modern variation on the theme of

Manon. When *Carmen* was published in 1847, Sainte-Beuve saw Prosper Mérimée's story as a reply to Prévost's novel: "This Carmen is nothing but a more stylish Manon Lescaut who corrupts her chevalier Des Grieux, equally seduced and weak though of an entirely different color."

As Jean Sgard has pointed out, it would take the success of *La Traviata* (1853), itself based on *The Lady of the Camellias* (performed as a play in 1850), for composers to get around to doing operatic versions of *Manon* that would streamline the episodic novel.[6] In 1830 a pantomime ballet version with an accompanying text by Scribe and music by Halévy had been a failure. But in 1856 Auber is tempted to try his hand, and Scribe returns to work on the subject again. The reviews of his *Manon Lescaut* are unfavorable and can only praise "an aria of bursts of laughter." The last act with the death in the deserts of Louisiana is recalled as having, it seems, the gravity of an oratorio. In the absence of further versions, we have to wait for Massenet (*Manon*, 1884), then Puccini (*Manon Lescaut*, 1893), and finally Henze (*Boulevard Solitude*, 1952) to breathe life into the elusive heroine.

There is no question that Massenet was himself taken with her. His music soars to greater heights as soon as Manon enters the stage and especially when Des Grieux declares his love to her. Massenet's deliberate contrast between the love duet at Saint-Sulpice and the infernal environment of the gaming room is very effective dramatically. The flatness of the libretto in many places reveals the speed with which Meilhac and Gille accomplished their task. One has to put up with the duet of Lescaut and Brétigny: "Between the go-getters and the good boys, that's how you do business." For the group and dance numbers, Massenet created adroit compositions that borrowed from the comic opera tradition. He was even able to finesse the contrasting effects of a waltz and an anachronistic gavotte. One has already, but timidly, the superimposition of styles that Richard Strauss toys with in *Capriccio*, but without the irony Strauss wraps around the stiff gallantries that he generally assigns to comic *comprimario* roles. There remains with Massenet's work the feeling of unfamiliarity produced for us by the music of 1884 that itself recalls an earlier century of a supposed "sweet life" such as the Goncourt brothers tried to capture in their little tableaux. This hybrid quality of Massenet's *Manon* can exert a somewhat perverse charm. Stylistically, Manon and the minuet dancers are tied to the blouses, corsets, and hairstyles that can be found modeled in the illustrations of *La Dernière Mode,* published by Mallarmé in 1874. The music requires dressing up the grotesque bon vivants Guillot and Brétigny in frock coats and top hats.

Massenet (or Meilhac) came up with the idea of having Des Grieux sing in the gambling room scene the exalted words from Musset's *Namouna:* "Manon! Fabulous sphinx, veritable siren! A heart of threefold femininity!" It was perhaps only a piece of filler, but the result is rather troubling since it attributes to the hero in the opera the words of a poet recalling the novel. In other words, it introduces a dimension of nostalgic reflection and memory. Thus, by a singular detour, the opera has hit on a fundamental aspect of the novel that was difficult, if not impossible, to transpose on stage at a time when the flashback technique in stage performances was practically unknown. What did Prévost give us? Once back from New Orleans where Manon has died, the chevalier tells Renoncour her (and his) story. By reanimating the past, he brings a dead person back to life; he pursues a shadow, as Jean Sgard puts it, "through the labyrinths of memory."[7] The mourning narrator remembers a Eurydice who led him to the end of the world. She has remained present in his heart, and he makes her exist through the words of his story. In staging this as opera, there would be nothing wrong with having Des Grieux speaking to Renoncour in front of the curtain or somewhere on the side of the stage and having him leave his interlocutor at those moments when he is himself an actor in the story. We may note that Massenet, while not making the entire opera into a retrospective vision, did employ all available means for making the music function as reminiscence. The thematic returns revive the dizzying enthusiasm of the first glance and the love at first sight in the courtyard of the inn. The blindingly powerful initial encounter is inscribed with a melodic line that returns in the Saint-Sulpice scene and during Manon's final agony. Indeed, the composer had a hard time dispelling this memory, since ten years later in 1894 for a one-act *Portrait of Manon,* an elderly Des Grieux appears on stage, but one whose memory has not faltered— and we thus rediscover most of the themes from the opera.

Was this dictated by the taste of the time? Did Massenet ask for it from his librettists? The sentimentality of the most well-known arias certainly derives from effects of memory. The famous aria "Adieu, notre petite table!"—"Farewell our little table"—masks with tender regret the sordid exchange that Manon has accepted. "Ah! fuyez, douce image"—"O, be gone, sweet image"—makes a phantom lover come back to Saint-Sulpice before Manon appears. Prévost had written: "I thought I was at the point of forgetting forever that charming and perfidious creature." In the retelling onstage Des Grieux says simply, "I took her hands in mine." Massenet develops the dimension of memory and has us hear these words spoken by Manon: "Is it no longer my hand that this hand presses? Is it no longer my voice? Is that voice no longer for you a caress, just like before? Am I no longer myself, have I no longer my name? Ah, look at me, is it no longer Manon?" The words invoke the past with melodic effusiveness and recall the first seduction. They will echo later even more powerfully at the instant of death. At the moment of her ecstatic exhaustion, passion circles back to its origin, to the dazzling "nothing" that decided everything. This rings true. It was necessary for the opera to glorify what the music added to the novel: the irresistible attraction of the voice. "Is it no longer my voice?"

CHAPTER 12

Ariane and Bluebeard; or, *The Useless Rescue*

TYRANTS AND SEDUCTRESSES

The dress rehearsal of *Ariane and Bluebeard; or, The Useless Rescue* took place in May 1907 one day after the opening performance in Paris of Richard Strauss's *Salomé*. A singular meeting! The spectator was presented with two legendary figures of the melancholy tyrant: the one, Herod, from a religious fable and the other, Bluebeard, from the fairy tale tradition. As each arrives at the end of his reign, he senses his power slipping away. The dominant role in both works is assigned to a woman, and more precisely to a feminine power that imposes its will before eventually failing. But what differences there are! Salomé is a perverse seductress who, by the magic of her striptease, awakens the desire of the morose tyrant. She asks for the head of the prophet Jochanaan, who has fascinated her, and which, once in her possession, receives her kisses on its cold lips. The intolerable spectacle elicits an order of execution from the mouth of Herod: "Kill this woman!" The sadism in Wilde's imagination mixes with fetishism, thus leading to a desire for murder that ends up turning against the murderer. Ariane, on the other hand, releases an enchantment of light, but without being heard. She traverses the obscure dungeon of Bluebeard without managing to emancipate the captive wives. Subjugated, the latter remain in their alienated condition. Well-intentioned magic, too, meets with failure.

With the play entitled *Ariane and Bluebeard* (1901), an entire first phase of Maeterlinck's theater came to an end. It had been dominated by the forces of death and fatality. The heroines of this theater were misty enchantresses. Uncertain of themselves, inhabited by mystery, they called for loving compassion, and one saw the machinery of misfortune inexorably unfold. When the final curtain fell on this theater of silence and the half-spoken, a fever to live yielded to the soft light of a depopulated dusk. This was the case for the end of *Pelléas and Mélisande,* to which there could be only the resigned comprehension of old Arkel—blind and clairvoyant. With *Ariane* we see a new impulse at work. The heroine is no longer a passive soul. She is a free creature who wants to declare her freedom. The drama in this case is that those whom Ariane wants to win to her hopeful cause refuse her instead. This is why one must not believe Maeterlinck when he says of this work that it is only one of his "little theatrical games," "a short poem intended to provide musicians who ask for such things with a theme suitable for lyrical development." It's true, Paul Dukas found in this dramatic poem, originally meant for Grieg, the material with which he could build a grand musical spectacle. But this demanding musician would not have settled for a trivial subject, and despite Maeterlinck's denegations, it is abundantly clear that the text includes an entire "philosophical and moral undercurrent." For a musician who had such a developed sense of rhythm, extended tonality, and orchestral color, it was necessary to have exceptional raw material capable of inspiring music and of being further enhanced by it.

NEW MORALITIES

This is not the Perrault fairy tale. It is there underneath but reread, reinterpreted, and even, in a certain sense, inverted. In this work written with a freer hand, Maeterlinck's approach resembles that of Laforge in his *Moralités légendaires* (1924). The famous story is taken up at its starting point, but the work proceeds through oblique tangents with new episodes and new characters in an entirely different direction. Bartók will later do the same.[1] If one wants to renew some operatic subject, there is no doubt that one needs to compose a new libretto for music of a new age. The innovations relating to the staging alone confirm the powerlessness of a previous period. Only if it is thought out anew from top to bottom can legendary subject matter take on new life.

In the very earliest versions of the tale, the monster is solitary; he is ugly and fascinating, immensely rich, and without descendants. Further behind him one can make out the profile of ogres and slaughterers such as the Minotaur, Gilles de Rais, or the sinister Count Conomor of the Breton legend, who kills his wives when they are pregnant. In the Perrault tale, the beautiful wife is imprudently "tempted by her curiosity." Her life is saved thanks to her sister Anne and her two cavalrymen brothers: it's the revenge of the large family over the solitary lord confined among his sterile treasures. In terms of peasant wisdom, it could be said that one of the lessons of the tale is that there's strength in numbers, including large families, and that brothers and sisters who stick together can pull each other out of the toughest situations. In *Ariane and Bluebeard* the peasant world is largely triumphant from the very start. As soon as Bluebeard threatens to punish the over-curious wife, he is set upon by the people in revolt. The large family becomes an angry crowd. It is at this point in the opera that the story takes a different path and acquires an allegorical dimension that infuses the fairy tale with something new: the first five wives are not dead, and Bluebeard, on Ariane's order, has been left alive. What's at stake is no longer the punishment of the guilty but something taking place elsewhere, namely, within the conscience of the Master and of those who agreed to belong to him. From the beginning, upon seeing Ariane some "trembling" thing was awakened inside Bluebeard. It was not elementary desire but "conscience" or "some other force"—perhaps true love at last. In the eyes of the peasants who have control over him for the second time, he is nothing but a clownish Pierrot whose "candle is dead." But it is a tragic and mute Pierrot (the orchestra speaks in his place) who pays with his blood for the suffering he has inflicted and who sees his Ariane escape from him—the only woman he has ever truly loved. And what about the five other women? Having opened the forbidden door, Ariane hears their song of captivity rise from underground—"the five daughters of Orlamonde." She brings them her comfort and her compassion. Like Theseus in the labyrinth, she lights the way out. But at the decisive moment the women refuse to leave the darkness and their accustomed woes. Perhaps they are only unreal creatures invented by a poet who has not succeeded in bringing them fully into life. They confirm the law of the tyrant by their voluntary servitude, complicit, as they are, in the violence that has sequestered them. The play and the opera, both written for the actress and singer Georgette Leblanc, defend at face value a feminist cause, but this is only a point of departure.

A LIGHT LISTENED TO

There is a clearly marked opposition between the fearful submission of the spouses and the rebellion of Ariane, who is motivated by the will to know, to overcome obstacles, and to see daylight triumph. "First, one must disobey. This is the primary duty when an order is threatening and does not explain itself. . . . All that is permitted will teach us nothing." The action can be followed in the words and music as a march and the progress of light. For the peasants in revolt, Ariane deserves to be helped simply because she looked at them: "She looked at me.—Me too.—Me too.—She was sad, but she smiled.—She looks as though she loves everyone." That is the initial motive. In the first act, it will reach its zenith when, after the rustling of colored stones through the first five doors opened by the nurse, the blinding fire of diamonds flows from the sixth. In the second act, a supplementary dimension is achieved at the moment when the sea wind, sunlight, and birdsong burst in through the now shattered windows. At the same time, associated with the avalanche of precious stones, the orchestral variations in a succession of different keys inform us of this fact: music and light are consubstantial. In the blinding luminosity that overwhelms sight once the windowpanes are broken, the light can still be perceived because it is also audible. Ariane sings the joy of hearing the eruption of light: "I see nothing and I hear everything! . . . Thousands of rays strike my ears." At the beginning of the last century there was great interest in phenomena referred to as synesthesia. People took pleasure in speculating about the perceptual associations between sounds and colors. Scriabin was among them, as were Kandinsky and Klee. Maeterlinck, for his part, blended the new scientific discoveries of his day with mysticism. He had translated the work of the theologian Jan van Ruusbroek: "When you find yourself amid the blinding rays of the sun and you avoid looking at all colors and avoid all particular attention to distinctions and objects illuminated by the sun, if, then, you simply follow with your eyes the clarity and rays that flow from the sun, you will be guided into the very essence of the sun; and similarly, if you follow the blinding rays that flow from the splendor of God onto your simple vision, they will lead you to the source of your creation and there you will find nothing but God alone."[2]

In a beautiful commentary of the Dukas opera, Olivier Messiaen offers an engaging invitation to read from this religious perspective.[3] For him, the entire work could be summarized with these words from the Gospel of John (1:5): "And the light shineth in darkness; and the darkness comprehended it not." Certainly the text does include expressions that lend themselves to such an evangelical interpretation. In the second act, before opening the shutters and windows, Ariane addresses her frightened companions: "Are you going to go on living in terror? . . . Do you not want to believe in the good news?" But are we really dealing with the light of the beyond here? Is this proclamation or kerygma not primarily about the beauty of the world that the eyes of the captives are unable to behold? Let's listen to the words that explain this "good news": "You don't miss the light of day, the birds in the trees, and the immense green gardens flowering up there? You don't know then that it's springtime? . . . Have you forgotten the sun, the dew on the leaves, the smile of the sea?"

To pass over, yes, that is the movement that Ariane invites the captives to make, but not as an ecstatic flight toward the primary source in the highest heavens. Rather, she points toward terrestrial places and fields of light: winds, harvests, forests. The theology of light in Maeterlinck became detached from all transcendent sources. It animates a pantheistic mystico-materialism in which nature and human beings are sources no less divine. We may leave him with the responsibility for the consequences he arrived at in favor of occultism.

Two extreme points are evoked by the text and magnificently expressed by the music. In its grandest intensity, light invites again toward a transcendence: surrounded by the sparkle of diamonds, Ariane exclaims in the first act: "Immortal dew of light! Moisten my hands, illuminate my arms, overwhelm my flesh! You are pure, tireless, you never die, and what moves in your flames, like a noble people that sows stars, is the passion of clarity that has penetrated all, does not rest, and has nothing more to conquer but itself!"

This light that wants to surpass itself must also be sought at the opposite pole, there where it seems almost nonexistent, born of the night that held it captive. At the end of the work, in the long scene of the third act where Ariane tries to shore up and revitalize her sad companions, there is a fiat lux, an attempt to have light enter bodies darkened by melancholy and resignation. May these extinguished beings find in themselves the power to ignite again! In the third act Ariane makes use of the diamonds and other stones that were scattered in the first act. Most of all she wants the denial of the body to cease: may the arms, shoulders, and hair that allowed themselves to be covered with shadows regain their light. The allusion to theologies of light goes along with the celebration of human radiance. Once awakened to the possibility of affirming themselves in their own light, the spouses choose nonetheless to remain prisoners. Only Ariane will have the courage to leave because she senses something awaiting her: "Over there, where I'm expected still." She leaves behind her those shadows that she was unable to draw forth, those who did not want to follow her into the perils of the open world.

Over there. We must understand this as a world finally acknowledged. Ariane breaks the relationship of pity that bound her to the incurable prisoners who chose to remain blind. It should not be overlooked, moreover, that their names—Mélisande, Aglavaine, Sélysette, Alladine, Ygraine, Bellangère—are those of the heroines of Maeterlinck's first plays. When Ariane leaves them behind, it seems as though Maeterlinck himself is also taking leave of his own Mélisande and the other feminine figures that he had let evolve in the mist of dreams by basing them on Mallarmé's Hérodiade and most notably the sorrowful princesses of Burne-Jones and Khnopff. Though not managing to detach himself from them completely, he bids farewell to the refined naïveté of symbolist imagery and to the faded figures of legend that wore, like art nouveau apparel, such improbable downy names. *Ariane and Bluebeard* is a fairy tale, but one that denounces the illusions of the imagination and casts into oblivion a fallen tyrant and his voluntary captives in that castle engulfed in darkness.

CHAPTER 13

Elektra; or,
The Accomplishment
of Hatred

MYCENAE AND VENICE

In a letter of June 25, 1908, to Richard Strauss, Hugo von Hofmannstahl sketched out a summary of a stage production. For the reader of the
text of *Elektra*, as well as for someone who listens to a recording of the
opera, an imaginary décor rises up. The text and music had the following compelling effect on me.

When the curtain rises, driven up by three violent chords that fall
like strokes of an ax, a specific presence first attracts one's attention:
a facade. This wall with its hostile openings is a first character whose
silent mass accords perfectly with the tumult of the tragic action. It is
the rear facade of the palace and courtyard. We are given a view of a
secret place not intended for the eyes of the prince's subjects. We see
outbuildings and slave quarters. It is a passageway to the stables. This
facade could also serve as a vast watchtower. One senses eyes on the

lookout. And in the courtyard, relaying the gaze of the masters, super-visors with whips in hand are watching servants draw water from a well. Underground rots the corpse of Agamemnon from which the odor and even the blood have not yet disappeared. It is thus the servants' en-trance, where beasts and human rubbish mingle. Electra moves about there furtively.

The facade is a tremendous mask: behind it there is the whole past, the private bedrooms where one sleeps poorly and the ornate rooms where unjust masters put on banquets. These places are inhabited by trickery: every wall, every door, every threshold throws up a new mask. There, we guess, is the spot were the adulterous couple performed the murder: the bathtub where the blood of Agamemnon was shed after he was netted and struck down like a beast. The poet and the musician planned it so that this invisible interior would be felt like the echo chamber of Electra's pain and hatred. Aegisthus and Clytemnestra sow terror about them, but they are themselves subject to terror. In the great dialogue with her daughter, Clytemnestra admits her fears, her nightmares, and the protection that she seeks in vain from the talis-mans with which she is covered and from the numerous sacrifices that she has carried out.

The children of the great deceased have been expelled, thrown out into the exterior space. The two sisters, Electra and Chrysothemis, may have succeeded in not being completely excluded from the paternal residence, but it has become their prison. Chrysothemis—too sweet and too human to revolt openly—would like to flee and begin to live the life of a woman. But even though she ardently wishes to escape from the sinister trap, she remains there as though fascinated. She goes up and down the stairs, "from one landing to another," listening at doors and discovering with fearful alarm an open room that resembles an empty stare. Electra, for her part, "waits in the dark." She is beaten and starved. She does not know day from night. She bursts out laugh-ing when she overhears that the masters threaten to enclose her in a windowless tower where not the least bit of starlight will penetrate. She could not be more alone, more encased in darkness than she already is. As for Orestes—the male heir and the one charged with the task of vengeance—he is absent, far away, and there is no news of him. Is he still living? As in Sophocles, all the tragedy's action revolves around his return from this total absence, and the false announcement of his death keeps him protected and invisible. At the right moment he will allow himself to be recognized—lovingly by his sister so long humiliated and then by Clytemnestra and Aegisthus with horror and screams and the strike of arms. The passage from exile to the reconquering of princely power occurs with the crossing of a threshold. Inside the palace, an ancient crime calls for vengeance. It is erased, but by a new crime that produces an even more serious stain: matricide. Orestes accomplishes that which Hamlet, another expelled figure, will only perform symbolically by presenting a mirror to his mother (act 3, scene 4). In *Hamlet*, Claudius, Gertrude's new husband, occupies the place of Aegisthus, while Hamlet occupies at once the position of both Orestes and Electra. I cannot resist here interpreting the matricide via an evocation of the symbolic value of the space of the body and the space of the palace. Killing the mother, for Orestes, is killing the one whose body first carried and protected him, the one who was the primordial interior that surrounded him with her warmth but who has become the rejecting surface whose pale eyelids signify the refusal of love. The one who must be cherished (because "she nourished him under her belt," as the Furies say in Aeschylus's *Eumenides*) and the one who must become a sacrificial victim are the very same person. The psychic tearing is atrocious, the ambivalence unbearable. That is why in the ancient tragedy Orestes goes mad and must receive at Delphi and Athens the purification that will rescue him from being pursued by the Furies.

For the Greek tragedians the death of Clytemnestra occurs within a chain of other crimes and acts of vengeance. Agamemnon committed infanticide in sacrificing Iphigeneia; by killing Agamemnon, Aegisthus avenges Thyestes; and so on. Hofmannstahl did not want to take up this legendary chain of faults, punishments, and purifications that makes up the grandeur of Aeschylus's trilogy. The basic material that he borrows from Sophocles and on which he sought to confer the greatest poetic intensity was the central figure, the heroine Electra. It is she and not Orestes who goes into a trance after the matricide. And it is in the triumph of her slaked hatred that she is struck dead.

The difficult nights of Clytemnestra, her flood of dreams and impalpable anxieties, do not these owe something to the author of *The Interpretation of Dreams*? Is not Electra a representation of the death instinct that Freud would develop only ten or so years later? These are idle questions that have often been asked. They overlook that the first Clytemnestra in Greek theater, that of Aeschylus, already had a nightmare in which she gives birth to a snake that devours her breasts. The nocturnal warnings are repeated, as we know, in the *Electra* of Sophocles. So let's instead reverse the proposition: it was Greek the- ater—Sophocles' *Oedipus Rex*—that was decisive for one of the leading propositions of Freudian theory. Let's remember that Freud was not all that receptive to the idea of an Electra complex. Hofmannstahl was certainly aware of the signs that were visible in the skies of his time. As a poet, he drew on the same sources as Freud.

ANIMALNESS AND SAINTLINESS

Sunk into mourning and hatred, Electra is compared by one of the servants to a wild cat. She spits, she yells, she casts poisonous looks and cannot stand anyone looking at her. Through an entire side of her being in Hofmannstahl's treatment she has become an animal and sees only animals about her: dogs, flies, vermin. Electra has undergone a physical deterioration, but she has also contributed to it with all of her destructive rage turned against herself. The first stage representa- tion of Electra in Aeschylus's *The Libation Bearers* proclaims, "Thanks to my mother my heart is an untamable cruel wolf" (verses 421–422). Hofmannstahl retained this trait and amplified it within the system of intensified translation that defines his relation to the ancient models. The third servant in the initial scene relates that "she displayed her fin- gers to us like claws and cried, 'I'm nourishing a vulture in my breast.' " And animal figures are certainly present all around her. The servant who carries Clytemnestra's train is "a yellow silhouette with black hair combed back: her smooth face made her look like a snake reared up on its tail."

But the degradation of Electra to a savageness devoid of all modesty does not occur without a counterweight in the opposite direction. We can guess at this counterweight from the words pronounced by the very young fifth servant, "I want to kneel before her and kiss her feet. Is she not the daughter of a king? And she is suffering such torment! I want to anoint her feet and dry them with my hair." The image here comes from the iconography of the Gospels. It is the gesture of Mary Magda- lene at the feet of Christ—a rather surprising image that belongs to a time when poets played freely with the memory of the sacred. One must understand it to mean that in her physical devastation and the violence of her passion for justice, Electra has achieved saintliness. She will say to Orestes, "The father has sent me hateful anger as a fiancé, anger with hollow eyes. And that is how I became a prophetess. From myself and my body I have only received curses and desperation."

Electra is the humiliated figure whose desire for murder is satisfied and who dies from it. The character touches the extremes of the human condition. This woman possesses the highest powers of spirit combined with the worst torments that a captive body can endure. Before recognizing in Electra's frenzy the spirit of a place and time—Vienna 1908—let us consider the figure of the prophetess Cassandra that Aeschylus in his *Agamemnon* made into one of the most striking characters in all classical theater. Cassandra, the daughter of Priam, is the Trojan prisoner that the king of kings brings back to his camp. Clytemnestra hates her: "She is mad, she listens to an evil spirit. . . . She will not have the sense to accept the bit without foaming in bloody fury." It is by Cassandra's voice, and before the event actually takes place, that we see the scene of Agamemnon's murder. It seems, says the coryphaeus, that the outsider has the nose of a dog. She seeks and she will find the murder.

Hofmannstahl thus introduced Cassandra into Electra, and this amalgam of two characters is highly significant. The ties between Cassandra and Agamemnon were ties of love.

In her first great aria ("Allein! Weh, ganz allein . . .") Electra only laments her personal fate in the first four words. All the rest is vision. Her eyes search for the father. She asks him to rise from the depths and show his face. It is the hour when the crime was committed. It is the hour when, the day before, she saw appear the unappeased dead figure. She *sees* once again the scene of the murder; she *foresees* the scene of vengeance and all around her she sees blood pouring; she sings in advance the expiatory celebration where dance music will resound. In the central scene of the opera, facing Clytemnestra, Electra deciphers the contents of her mother's nightmares and spellbinds her by announcing what she will feel at the moment when she becomes the beast offered in sacrifice under the knife of the hunter.

The vision of Electra, whose gaze fixes on faces with such insistence, appears to falter when Orestes returns. The reason is that since the misleading announcement of the death of her brother, her spirit is possessed by one idea only: to disinter, like a dead child, the ax that killed the father and accomplish the act of vengeance with the complicity of Chrysothemis or alone. If Electra does not recognize Orestes, it is because she has substituted herself for him in the mission that has become her unique reason for living. In the duo with Chrysothemis she has changed into a seductress: she sings of the virginal beauty of her sister, the vigor of her arms; she shares in the happiness of the future wedding, but it is with the aim of making her accept complicity in the murder, to play an auxiliary role in the bloody act. Hofmannstahl knew the importance of the scene of recognition in Greek tragedy, and he arranges it so that Electra returns from afar to perceive suddenly, as though a veil were torn apart, Orestes' gaze and to implore that in return she be looked at by him. For the stage representation, the first eight lines of the recognition aria were added by Hofmannstahl upon Strauss's request, the composer wishing to make room here for an intensification (*Steigerung*). In these admirable verses, both poetic and musical necessity become more and more vivid: the brother's face, which had first been only a dream, becomes more and more real, while at the same time Electra prophetically senses that her joy will culminate in death: "So I die happier than I lived." The intensification will culminate in dance and death.

The death of Electra onstage was Hofmannstahl's idea. With the stage tradition, no Electra "dancing like a maenad" ever succumbed "beneath the weight of happiness." This is perhaps the only point, but an important one, where one may glimpse the convergence of the poet's intuitions and the psychodynamic for which Freud was the standard-bearer: the energy of love, intended entirely for the deceased father, also carried hate for the mother. Once the latter was punished, the irrevocable absence of the father is no longer concealed. The world is a desert. The intermingled energies of love and hate find nothing to invest in except the body itself and the excess of dance, at the limits of joy and destruction.

"Ombra adorata"

CHAPTER 14

"Ombra adorata"

UNDER THE EMPEROR'S GAZE

After returning from the Théâtre Italien on February 10, 1825, Étienne-Jean Delécluze opens at midnight a diary that he has been keeping faithfully for some months and writes a long note to himself.[1] "They put on *Romeo e Giulietta*, a work I had not seen performed since 1811 at the Théâtre de la Cour during Napoleon's time. The first measures of the overture took me back to that singular and memorable age when the emperor was at his most powerful."

The memory is so vivid that the earlier performance is recounted immediately. The account of that past experience is much more detailed than his impression of the evening that Delécluze has just spent. He sees again the whole stage where he was in attendance as both the friend of the painter Louis David and as the editor Fiévée's successor at the *Journal des débats*: "I was seated in a private box where I could see without being seen, and I took pleasure in my hideaway that even in the middle of this court allowed me the opportunity to breathe and think freely." From his ideal position, Delécluze had precisely distinguished the different groups of dignitaries. His attention in fact was turned more toward the room and the spectators than to the performance itself:

The galleries of the imperial theater were filled with women of the court and princesses both foreign and French. Generals and chamberlains, dressed in the richest clothes, stood behind the ladies. In the orchestra stalls were all the commanding officers. Foreign ambassadors according to the importance of the nation they represented were seated in boxes either more or less open to view, and the kings of Naples, Holland, Westphalia, Bavaria, Wurtemberg, etc., were there standing when the chamberlains' entrance, the appearance of the pallid-faced emperor, and the opening somber chords of the opera all signaled that the performance was about to begin.

For a disinterested observer, there was nothing more imposing to be seen than the respectful terror that the sight of Napoleon inspired in all these spectators of such different rank, condition, and probably opinions as well. Everyone was surrounded with a luxury and a sparkle that highlighted in such a lively way the serious incertitude of their bodies; they held themselves in such a way as to be able to gaze obliquely toward their master, as much out of fear as from a need to respond immediately to the slightest favorable sign that might be made toward them. During an intermission, Napoleon made a polite gesture to Monsieur de Tolstoï, the Russian ambassador.

Everyone turned to each other zealously—"*The emperor waved to Monsieur de Tolstoï*"—as though everyone were relieved to have some thought that could be expressed openly and without danger.

Later in this note composed from memory, the central figure of this tableau is described with greater precision: "Napoleon—dressed in a green frock coat with his general's epaulettes and showing the forehead of a man tired from work—was attentive to the performance and only looked away now and then to glance at the room. I have never seen a man who so looked to be the master of the people about him as Napoleon did in those circumstances. Even in the attention that he paid to the music there was an appearance of egoism that attracted the looks of other spectators and that isolated him from everyone else's feelings."

This tireless stare of a tired man, what exactly did it see onstage? What spectacle had he come to see?

Grassini played the role of Giulietta and Crescentini that of Romeo. I have never seen or heard anything that can compare to these two singers in the final act of this opera. The appropriateness of their expressions and the beauty of the singing, particularly that of Crescentini, made a prodigious impression on all the spectators. Since proper etiquette forbade applause, when Crescentini (Romeo) fell down dead after kissing his beloved, a movement of curiosity mixed with emotion spread throughout the orchestra stall from which there rose up a stifled sigh, but calm was soon restored and all eyes turned nervously and curiously toward the master, who made a solemn sign of the hand and departed.

Napoleon leaves the performance before the end. But he was intent on seeing the most poignant scene and taking account of the emotion of the audience. He was expecting it. The forceful effect produced by his protégé was for him like an extension of his own power.

The aria that attracted so much attention was known by its opening words: "Ombra adorata." It became famous throughout Europe. It had been composed by the male soprano Girolamo Crescentini for use within the Zingarelli opera (with the latter's agreement). The scene takes place in the mortuary chapel of the Capulets when Romeo discovers Juliet's inanimate body and believes she is dead. Promising to reunite with her, he drinks a fatal poison. Juliet awakes to discover Romeo dying in her arms. The libretto of Giuseppe Maria Foppa departs from Shakespeare and proposes a duet between the two lovers at the end of which Romeo expires ("Ahimè già vengo meno. / —Ah che m'opprime l'anima / Il barbaro tormento"). Then two family servants arrive. Thrown into hopelessness, Juliet tries to seize a dagger, but again contrary to Shakespeare's text she is stopped. It is the intensity of her chagrin that causes her death as she is encircled by the chorus, and the opera finishes. Zingarelli and his librettist wanted to respect the conventional demands of the genre: for the public's taste and the actors' demands there needed to be a balance among the solos, duets, ensembles, and choruses. The opera is thus far from over after Crescentini's moving death when he falls down at the end of his great aria.

In Vienna in November 1805, Napoleon attended for the first time a performance of *Giulietta e Romeo* with the same artists.[2] He was so moved that he had Crescentini brought to Paris and accorded him a generous stipend and an exclusive contract with the Théâtre de la Cour. The singer resided in Paris from 1806 to 1812.[3] During a particularly memorable performance (perhaps the one described by Delécluze) Crescentini "was so moving that the entire audience wept: the next day he was named a chevalier of the Iron Crown of Lombardy." Within the kingdom of Italy the title was the equivalent of the Légion d'honneur. This decision did not please Parisian public opinion. Impolite jokes were made about the castrato. The matter comes up on October 7, 1816, in one of the Sainte-Hélène conversations that Las Cases relates in his *Mémorial*. It was an attempt, explains the emperor, to see if it were possible to give the Légion d'honneur to the great artist Talma without provoking discontent. "I believe my experiment turned out quite badly."[4] Alfred de Vigny, in the seventh chapter of the *La Canne de jonc*, relates another performance in the Tuileries before the same audience of kings and a rather bloated and tired emperor. Crescentini sings in *Les Horaces et les Curiaces* of Cimarosa "with the voice of a seraphim coming out of a dry, wrinkled face."[5]

In his *Journal* Delécluze writes very briefly about the performance that he has just attended. He says plainly that several passages in the opera gave him "true musical pleasure," and he makes careful note that "la Pasta" made him "cry twice." He adds that "a thousand memories, some painful, others sad but sweet" agitated his spirit. Some of these memories concern his personal life. To this is added the macabre impression made by a recent piece of reading that contributes to reviving the image of Napoleon during the performance: "I was thinking of the opening of the corpse of Napoleon (Antommarchi) exhausted by a long illness: I saw this pale thin man stretched out on a little bed in a cabin in the middle of an all but deserted island; that's how I saw him, this man who during a performance of *Roméo* had wanted to have the leading figures of his vast empire think and say 'The Emperor waved to Monsieur de Tolstoï!' "

The vanity of power and glory! Delécluze seems to have let his thoughts float along with the music without caring to make many observations about the work itself that he had just heard. He is a true liberal, and the sad ideas that Antommarchi's book stir up in him are in accord with the lesson he took from the stereotypical, approving, and unthreatening sentence that passed over everyone's lips on that brilliant evening in 1811: *The Emperor waved to Monsieur de Tolstoï.*[6] This murmur perfectly characterizes the self-censorship imposed by the fearful atmosphere that surrounds an absolute master. During that evening under the eye of the emperor, "despite the shimmer of the lights, the fine clothes, and the rare quality of the performance, everyone had an oppressed air about them as though they were all breathing sulfurous vapors."

We may pause and dream here. In 1809, during the intermission of Niccolò Antonio Zingarelli's opera (created at La Scala in Milan for the carnival of 1796), Napoleon makes a polite sign with his hand to the grandfather of the famous writer who will later show him in action in *War and Peace*. Let's remember the page where the wounded Prince André, who has fallen to the ground, catches sight of Napoleon the evening after the battle of Austerlitz. "His head was burning, he felt himself bleeding to death, and he saw above him the remote, lofty, and everlasting sky. He knew it was Napoleon—his hero—but at that moment Napoleon seemed to him such a small, insignificant creature compared with what was passing now between himself and that lofty infinite sky with the clouds flying over him."[7] On the evening of a Napoleonic victory, the emperor is dispossessed of his grandeur and his aura by the gaze of a dying man who has encountered the infinity of the sky. At the end of the work, in his long recapitulation, Tolstoy depicts the emperor as a "wounded beast" in the disarray of retreat, dispossessed of control, as though all his grand fate had only ever depended on chance. What a difference between these looks and spectacles! As seen by Delécluze, the emperor, to complete his domination of Europe, gave open expression to the project of a "Russian alliance" with this display of a particular courtesy toward the Russian ambassador. No matter how scrupulously he recorded this detail, Delécluze could in no way imagine the added significance that it would assume in our belated reading of his diary. For us, reading the name Tolstoy on this page tips Napoleon from his supremely dominant position in the box of the imperial theater into the little man as seen by the wounded soldier at Austerlitz who is simultaneously discovering the immensity of the sky.

On the evening in 1825 at the Théâtre Italien, the role of Romeo was played by Giuditta Pasta. Delécluze will recall this fact two years later when he attends a performance of Shakespeare's play performed by English actors with Richard Kemble playing Romeo.[8] Delécluze finds the way Kemble mimes the "pain caused by the poison" exaggerated. He imitates with too much pathos the "nuances of agony." "I am more completely moved when seeing this same scene played by Madame Pasta." In other words, preference is given to a woman who incarnates with greater softness (and in an Italian far removed from the words of Shakespeare) the role of the lover who drinks the poison. Madame Pasta, a mezzo-soprano, sang within the tessitura of the male soprano Crescentini who created the role. This did not prevent Delécluze, after learning of the singer's success in London in the role of Othello (in the Rossini opera), from raising questions about the nonconcordance between the sex of the singers and that of the characters they are incarnating: "Thirty or fifty years ago it was considered a great improvement in the dramatic arts when in Italy there was instituted the preference for having female roles played by women and not by young men as had been the case earlier. Today there is passion for a manly role, and what a man we get, played by a woman! There is a malady that particularly affects pregnant women called *pica*.[9] When they are afflicted, all natural tastes are inverted. . . . I don't know what Europe will give birth to, but in truth she has contracted *pica*, that is certain."[10]

To confirm the international reputation of *Giulietta e Romeo* by Zingarelli, another piece of evidence is worth mentioning, namely, the triumphant début of Maria Malibran in 1824 at the King's Theater in London. In the role of Juliet, she deploys a talent for ornaments and decorations that eclipses her partner, the contralto Velluti, who was considered the supreme master of this art. Rumor spread that he had expressed his frustration onstage. From that moment Malibran gained the reputation as a "seductress" or "Circe."[11]

A few days after the evening at the Théâtre Italien, Delécluze, in the habit since 1819 of gathering a very free "Sunday society" in his "attic," gives the floor over to one of the regulars, Henri Beyle.[12] This guest reads out loud his pamphlet *Racine et Shakespeare*. Delécluze relates the scene as well as his criticisms. Throughout his *Journal* and in his *Sixty Years of Memories*, the abrupt statements of Stendhal are noted with extreme precision. Delécluze, often upset, finds that his tone is forced. Liberalism in a wide sense nevertheless constituted a point of agreement between this thoughtful man and the inflexible *provocateur* Stendhal. I hazard that the art of Madame Pasta was not a subject of disagreement between the host and his occasionally difficult visitor. But all the genuinely warm admiration was Stendhal's. It hardly seems necessary to recall his regular attendance at the Théâtre Italien, the apartment he takes as close as possible to that of the diva, the evenings in her salon, and so on. It is time, then, to concentrate our attention on him.

"THE SUBLIME PRAISE OF SUICIDE"

Stendhal may have met Crescentini in Paris as early as 1806. Some have thought that they may have met at the Sainte-Caroline lodge where Crescentini was an officer and where Stendhal was received in 1806.[13] Stendhal mentions the singer as being among the guests one evening in Bologna in 1817: "Just when the conversation was about to turn to politics, Crescentini entered." He tells two or three anecdotes that, Stendhal declares, would require thirty pages. Among these: "When the weather's nice at midnight outside the opera . . . everyone sings in low voices as they walk away." Depending on what songs are being hummed, a good observer or spy is able to guess the thoughts of those who are leaving the performance.[14] In Rome, Stendhal is invited to a concert by an amiable marquise: "What eyes I saw at this concert! In this area the rest of Europe is a blank chalkboard. . . . The beautiful aria of Crescentini, *Ombra adorata, aspettami*, filled all those beautiful eyes with tears."[15] In *The Red and The Black* (1830) the name Zingarelli appears accidentally and from rather far off. An unexpected character pays a call one day at Verrières and mopes about in the home of Monsieur de Rênal. It is the singer Geronimo, who becomes animated when telling how he escaped from the tutelage of Zingarelli, the overly severe director of the conservatory in Naples. In the second part of the novel (chapters 6 and 23), we rediscover Geronimo fleetingly at the opera, then on tour during the adventure of the secret note. It is a wink at the happy few.[16] At the beginning of chapter 13 of *The Charterhouse of Parma* (1839) the name Crescentini makes a surprising appearance. When Fabrice, after having killed Giletti, stays in Bologna with "little Marietta," he takes a walk with her almost every evening "to the Reno Falls." "On the way back, he would stop at the home of the friendly Crescentini who considered himself to be something of a father to Marietta." This paternal feeling of a castrato, even if at-tenuated by the restrictive "something of a" ("se croyait un peu"), is puzzling. But the name Crescentini is perhaps only evoked in this pas-sage to prepare for the entrance in the same chapter of the great diva Fausta. "He was surprised at the angelic softness of this voice; he could imagine nothing like it; he owed to it some of the highest sensations of happiness." Between Crescentini and Fausta, there is Giuditta Pasta and the famous aria.

Stendhal, in recounting his evening in Rome, characterizes "Ombra adorata" exclusively in terms of the softening effect on the beautiful women in the audience. In fact he is most sensitive to the personal way in which artists sing a particular aria. At the same time he is attentive to the effect produced among the listeners. His love of music is always directed at vocal works, among which he emphatically notes his prefer-ences. But he always has one eye on the room and an ear tuned to the casual remarks of the spectators that change from year to year and from one country and opera house to another. As an observer of the public's reactions, he discusses them freely and makes comparisons, most often to the disadvantage of the Paris public. The public is thus a sort of third point of triangulation when it comes to the judgments Stendhal forms about composers and singers. With him, the intimate fact of musical listening enters into a relation with the social element of the perfor-mance or the memory of that performance.[17]

It is time now to present the words of the aria "Ombra adorata, as-petta." The purpose is not simply to know better what Crescentini and Giuditta Pasta were singing. In his *Life of Rossini* (1823),[18] Stendhal makes frequent allusions to the aria but sometimes cites only very few of the actual words.

The librettist Giuseppe Maria Foppa knew what was expected of him.[19] The aria he writes for Romeo appropriately uses perfectly con-ventional expressions in a style that had been raised to perfection by

Metastasio and Calzibigi. Success in this type of composition is obtained by achieving an adroit ordering of parts that will be favorable to the musician and using words and phrases that have a long history of idiomatic acceptance. In the Italian words of Gluck's *Orfeo ed Euridice* written by Rainieri de' Calzabigi, one already finds in Orpheus's aria in act 3 expressions such as "ombra bella," "ombra pietosa," "ombra cara," and especially "ombra adorata." These words are addressed to his dead wife whom he tries to bring back to the world of the living. With similar materials, Foppa constructs Romeo's complaint that then evolves into an ardent promise of happy union after death. I give here the text of the libretto published in Milan in 1796.[20]

> [Andante sostenuto, 3/8, F Major]
> *Idolo del mio cor*
> *Deh vedi il pianto mio,*
> *I gemiti, il dolor*
> *Del tuo fedel.*

> Idol of my heart,
> Ah! See my complaint,
> The moans, the pain
> Of your faithful one.

> [Recitativo. 4/4, F Major]
> *Ma che vale il mio duol? Mia bella speme,*
> *Io ti sento; mi chiami*
> *A seguirti fra l'ombra; ebben m'aspetta*
> *Ti seguirò. Se a te compagno in vita*
> *Non mi volle la sorte,*
> *Teco m'unisca almen pietosa morte.*

> But what is my mourning worth? My beautiful hopes
> I hear you, you call me
> To follow you among the shadows. Well, wait for me,
> I will follow you. If to be your companion in life
> Cannot be my fate,
> May compassionate death at least unite me with you.

[Andante sostenuto. 4/4, D Major]
Tranquillo io son: fra poco
Teco sarò mia vita: accogli intanto
Mia speme, anima mia,
Questo ch'io per te verso ultima pianto.

I am calm: soon
I will be with you, my life: Receive only
My hope, my soul
Receive this last lament that I pour out to you.

[Rondo. Andante sostenuto. 4/4, D Major]
Ombra adorata aspetta!
Teco saro indiviso.
Nel fortunato Eliso,
Avrà contento il cor.
Là, fra i fedeli amanti,
Ci appresta amor diletti,
Godremo i dolci istanti
De' piu innocenti affetti,
E l'Eco a noi d'intorno
Risuonerà d'amor.

Beloved shadow, wait!
I will not be separated from you
In the happy Elysium
My heart will be content.
There among the faithful lovers
Love reserves us pleasures,
We will enjoy sweet moments,
The most innocent feelings,
And the Echo around us
Will resound with love.

The aria ends with the repetition of the three first verses of the rondo and with five repetitions of the fourth line "Avrà contento il cor."
One understands how Stendhal was able to declare that the words "can
only ever be a simple outline" and that "the music . . . takes on the task

of covering them with its brilliant colors." The words, he adds, are only "the labels of the feelings," which means that "the *accent* of what is said has much more importance than the words themselves."[21] But the subordinate role of the words—*prima la musica*—does not prevent them from becoming part of an integrated composition with the dramatic situation and the music. As conventional as the verbal expression may be, it is nevertheless an element of meaning. The music certainly transcends the words with which it is associated, but this surpassing assumes its full significance only on condition that the primary verbal layer of the melody not be forgotten. The great masters of this art, beginning with Crescentini, always insisted on the priority that must be reserved for it. A good singer must read the poem before singing it.

Romeo's song is that of an Orpheus who, instead of wanting to rescue the one he believes dead, wants to unite with her in death. There are no more gods to conquer but an eternal happiness to be had in the underground woods. The speech marks a series of moments between a loss and an announced reunion. The resolution to die that the hero makes while singing these words changes into imminent enjoyment. Romeo expresses at first the pain of separation ("il mio duol"). Then he listens: he feels called, expected by Juliet. The enchantress is the dead Juliet in Romeo's thoughts. Finally he promises to join her, and he anticipates the ultimate happiness and desires fulfilled ("avrà contento il cor"). He will form but one being ("indiviso") with his beloved throughout their happy sojourn among the dead ("nel fortunato Eliso"). Eternity will consist of "sweet moments" ("dolci istanti"). Juliet, the beloved, seemingly dead, is at the same time the imaginary enchantress who invites him on a voyage of no return ("mi chiami"). Romeo obeys the call he believes he hears. He celebrates in advance the supreme happiness in the subterranean vault. Note, however, that it's the *voice* of the lover that creates this enchanting call by declaring his complete submission. It is in and through this voice, both imploring and consenting, that the power of seduction of this apparently dead young woman is glorified. The hero's song affirms at once both the seductive power and the happiness in obeying it.

The beautiful voice of the castrato Crescentini was no doubt the most appropriate for expressing both the call of the dead beloved and the response of the lover. But in this role the adorer of a fictive shadow gives himself over in the flux of his musical sound to the adoration of a sensuous reality that transports the audience. The librettist and composer create out of the theatrical character of Romeo a desperate figure preparing for departure and dreaming of a happiness beyond this life. If the music serves this idea and the actor serves the music, the entire house will be ecstatic, and tears are sure to flow. The anticipated effect depends on the interpretation, and it should be noted that this aria, which has been a success for many vocal performers, was composed by a very experienced interpreter. The major key heightens the sadness where the complaint is so intense that it fills with light and becomes voluptuous. It withdraws smoothly into its own beauty and luxuriates in it. The aria describes the idyllic happiness that the couple will enjoy in Elysium, the land of the dead. This happiness, according to the words of the aria, will be surrounded by echoes, and that is precisely what the voice of the singer onstage at the moment of his cadence makes the audience hear. The vocal progression is from middle A in the key of G, rising to high A, and eventually descending stepwise to the B below in regular intervals to a lower B. The higher note is held for two full measures on the second syllable of "*risuonera*" (the echo of the sweet moments of love during the stay among the dead "will resound" around us). This cadence was probably ornamented. The score I have gives no indication. Later, the twice-repeated phrase "avrà contento il cor" ("the heart will have its contentment") concludes on the word "*cor*" with a half note that invites ornamentation. One can easily imagine how specific vocal effects at these various moments could give the impression of a caressing breath encircling the anticipated image of a couple united in the glades of the world beyond. We have, in this Neapolitan music whose expressive language was rapidly surpassed during the nineteenth century, one of the most beautiful examples of seduction exerted by "a voice about to die."[22] A voice that aspires after death to repair a loss, by consummating that loss. A voice that is itself subject to an irresistible enchantment: the beauty of the living dead, Juliet, so beautiful in her sleep. The tragic irony is that Juliet comes out of her sleep at the moment when Romeo knows that the poison must take effect. (It is one of the moments in the story where adaptors have all rivaled each other in their infidelity.)

I return to Stendhal's *Life of Rossini* and in particular to those chapters that focus on the voice and the "revolution in singing brought about by Rossini" (chapters 27–34). Stendhal mentions the castrati Crescentini (1762–1846) and G. B. Velluti (1780–1861) as leading examples of a supreme art of ornament and decoration executed by inspiration. And he criticizes Rossini for wanting to put an end to these liberties taken by the performer. He required them to sing the note as written without adding any embellishment or "vocal frills" of their own invention. That was what was revolutionary about him. A large number of operagoers, however, disapprove of this submission of the singer to the composer, and Stendhal is one of them: "The Rossini revolution has killed the singer's originality."[23] Stendhal's argument is based on the individual and momentary character of slight variations in expression, his leading example of what he has in mind being those performers who excelled at the aria "Ombra adorata." "Crescentini gave to his voice and its inflections a vague and general hint of *contentment* in the song *ombra adorata, aspetta*; it seemed to him *at the precise moment he was singing* that this was the very feeling a passionate lover who is going to reunite with the one he loves should have. Velluti, who understands the situation differently, places some melancholy and sad meditation on the common fate of the two lovers."[24]

The "contentment" expressed by the singer and picked up on by Stendhal corresponded no doubt to the frequently repeated line at the end of the aria: "Avrà contento il cor." Crescentini was thinking of the words! Stendhal's text pursues the idea: "No maestro, no matter how talented you might suppose him to be, could ever manage to note down exactly the infinitely small elements that make for perfection in the singing of this aria by Crescentini—infinitely small elements that change moreover according to the state of the singer's voice at that moment and the amount of enthusiasm and illusion working through him. One day he might feel like executing the ornaments gently and with *morbidezza*; another day it is *gorgheggi* full of force and energy that come to him as he goes onstage. To attain perfection, the singer must yield to the inspiration of the moment."[25]

Stendhal requires the enthusiasm of the singer before he can grant his own. The example of Crescentini mentioned at such length helps to recognize great singers. These reflections on voice precede those pages where Stendhal will speak about the immense admiration he feels for the art of Giuditta Pasta. The long chapter 35 in his *Life of Rossini* is a fervent "musical portrait" of the diva.[26] Stendhal admires her passion, the sovereign manner with which she unites "the head voice and the chest voice," and the way she varies her expressions according to "the situation of the soul." She is too young to have heard Crescentini, but Stendhal sees him (along with three others) as the master and her as someone who could have been his pupil.[27] What's more, there is a work in which she particularly excels, and it happens to be the opera by Zingarelli and the act that contains the famous aria: "Of all the operas in which Madame Pasta has performed since arriving in Paris, I consider only the second and third acts of *Romeo* as being more or less suited to her voice." Stendhal considers the great arias in *Romeo* as the "decisive test of a singer's talent."[28]

It is highly significant that in his *Life of Rossini* the only commentary on "Ombra adorata" that Stendhal proposes comes within a characterization of the style of its interpreters. It is also revealing that Madame Pasta's way of singing it is described as a "creation."

> What I call the creations of this great artist are those means of expression that it is unlikely the maestro who wrote the notes for these roles ever thought of.
>
> I will first cite the importance accorded to the line *Avrò contento il cor* from Romeo's aria *ombra adorata aspetta* and the fast tempo of the cantilena. Another beautiful creation comes with the inflection given to the preceding lines that belong to the same scene:
>
> > *Io ti sento, mi chiami*
> > *A seguirti fra l'ombre*, etc.
>
> All the operagoers of Louvois remember the evening when Madame Pasta used these new singing techniques for the first time and the hushed emotion, much more flattering than applause, that they excited in the audience.

As for the singing itself, Stendhal leaves the commentary to an exiled Neapolitan for whom this music revives the memory of a lost landscape. The intention of this commentary is to convey the effect of the singer's "two voices," an effect that is deployed most advantageously in Romeo's aria. The two words that he will mention ("*ultimo pianto*") are those that immediately precede the beginning of the rondo aria ("Ombra adorata"). It is worth citing the rest of this passage.

That same evening when Madame Pasta employed her technique of the two opposed voices most felicitously, an amiable Neapolitan known for his taste in music and his many successes said to me with an ardor that I would give everything in the world to reproduce here, "These changes in sound of this sublime voice remind me of feelings of tender happiness that I experienced sometimes during the wonderfully pure nights in our unhappy homeland when the twinkling stars shine so well against the dark blue sky and when, from the shore at Mergelina, the moon illuminated the enchanting countryside that I will never see again. The island of Capri could be distinguished far off amid the silvery waves of a sea caressed by a refreshing midnight breeze. Imperceptibly, a light cloud would veil the nighttime sun, and its light would seem for a few seconds even more smooth and tender; nature's aspect would be more touching, the soul more attentive. Soon the sun's partner would appear again purer and more brilliant than ever, flooding our shores with its pure and lively light; and the countryside around would reappear as well with all the sparkle of its lively beauty. Well, for me, Madame Pasta's voice with those changes in register gives the same feeling as that light that becomes veiled for an instant and then just as soon reappears, a thousand times more brilliant.

In the evening, when the sun sets behind Pausilippe, our heart seems to dip naturally into sweet melancholy; I don't know what serious thoughts come over us; our soul seems to enter into harmony with the evening and its tranquil sadness. That feeling is what I just experienced but a little quicker when Madame Pasta said, "*Ultimo pianto!*"

It is also the feeling that comes over me, but in a more enduring way, in those early days of September that are accompanied by a light fog among the trees that announces the approach of winter and the death of nature's beauties.

The variations in light between full clarity and light fog are a visual translation of the artist's "two voices." The musical commentary attributed to the listener is at the same time a reminiscence of a place of beauty—the Bay of Naples—that functions as an emblem of the lost homeland for this character Stendhal is quoting. Crescentini's music and Madame Pasta's voice were experienced with emotion. But the Neapolitan Stendhal stands behind, while sympathizing with Romeo's complaint and his wish to die, does not fix his attention on the tragic outcome of the legendary tale. The mind of this sensitive listener jumps to images from the past that relate to his personal life. The "pain of regret" ["douleur regrettante"] that Stendhal associates closely with musical pleasure is, in this case, nostalgia for a place that the expatriate expects nevermore to see and is also related to images of the evening and of autumn. A patriotic passion blends into tender feelings experienced before a natural spectacle. In a more general perspective, and by means of the same image, Stendhal will see here "the duty of fine arts" ["la tâche des beaux-arts"]. They are "made to console. When the soul has regrets, during the first sad moments of the autumn of one's life, and when doubt rises up like a somber specter behind every country hedge, it's good to be able to turn to music."[29] But here these feelings and images, which are rather far from what Romeo's aria is really talking about, rise up out of the pleasure first stirred by Madame Pasta's voice. An egocentric detour has taken place.

And yet the aria's fundamental theme rings out admirably in the free commentary carried out by Stendhal, namely, the theme of the beloved object lost and the search for that other place where it now lives like a shadow. In Foppa's text, Romeo answers the call of a dead woman: "mi chiami a seguirti fra l'ombre"—"you call me to follow you through the shadows." What the Neapolitan finds in the two voices of Madame Pasta, in their ornaments, is the landscape of the country from which he is now separated. It is another descent into mourning. We notice a series of metaphorical relays between the dramatic fiction and the intimate reverie. From the "beloved shadow" that addresses Romeo to the "veiled and to some extent suffocated sounds" of which the singer possesses the secret, and finally with "the light cloud that comes to veil the nighttime sun," a single theme is taken up and modulated. Coming from afar, operatic music also leads us away. Thanks to the poet and the composer, opera music expresses and even invents the passion of a theatrical hero; thanks to the singers, it provokes a moment of happiness that ends up opening an interior space that the listener can color and furnish with his own emotions and memories. He then takes pleasure in his soul, to use an expression frequently employed by Stendhal. And it then occurs to him to wonder if he likes music for itself or for the personal past of which it is a sign and on which it opens fresh perspectives. In the page that we've just read, the pain diminishes to a "sweet melancholy" in accordance with the welcoming clichés of the end of the day and the end of the beautiful summer season. Listening to music activates listening to oneself. A last question must then be asked. Does the exiled Neapolitan whose long declaration Stendhal has quoted (and who may be the chevalier de Michevaux, who is assigned the role of "preferred friend" of Madame Pasta in the *Souvenirs d'égotisme*) not become a fictional character, a hero whom Stendhal has imagined? At the end of all these metamorphoses and echoes, after the "creation" offered by the vocal invention of the diva, does the reverie of the writer-improviser not engage in novelistic invention? The personal reminiscences and imaginary joys rocked gently by the music ask only to become autonomous. Stendhal engages in this deviation of the music with his eyes wide open.

A charm, a magic power, and a seduction have exerted themselves out from under the surfaces of memory and imagination, and Stendhal constantly evokes these agencies without always openly admitting them. Their highest power showed itself in the succession of sensory moments arising out of the singing. The sky and the Elysium of "Ombra adorata" unfold so long as an unexpected vocal play sketches those fresh perspectives. There is paradise for the listener in a simply agreeable passage [*agrément*] perfectly sung, but there must be the genius and inspiration of the singer. If they are missing, the enchantment ceases and the fall is abrupt: "an agreeable passage that is not so much badly as weakly executed, without *brio*, destroys the charm in the blink of an eye. You were in the heavens and you fall back into your opera seat, and sometimes into a conservatory practice room."[30]

At the end of the book on Rossini, where improvisation has allowed some brilliant threads to wind their way, "Ombra adorata" reappears. Crescentini's composition serves as an example of the curious sociohistorical theory that claims the love song in Italy arose out of church singing (chapter 45). The rigor of ecclesiastical government brought about solitude. In this solitude, the passions had to turn to love, and music is the great means for expressing love. Thus Stendhal can propose the singular idea that the famous *Vatican Miserere*, by Allegri,[31] was the antecedent of a duetto in the first act of Cimarosa's *Il Ma-trimonio segreto* (1792) and of "Romeo's sublime song: *ombra adorata, aspetta*."[32] Beautiful church singing produced beautiful opera singing.[33] The associative bridge is created with the adjective "angelic" that had entered common usage and is employed by Stendhal to describe voices he likes. No matter what one might say about the long-standing dual deployment—sacred and profane—of the same melodies, Stendhal's explanatory system is highly debatable. But he is in his own way a dis-creet symptom of the return of religious vocabulary that started around 1750 in various philosophies of musical art from the most ordinary to the most refined.

Musical language changed rapidly and consigned Zingarelli's work to the past. And then it would be romanticism that would try to show its innovative liberty. That history is well known. I would like only to underline the part played by some new versions of *Romeo and Juliet*. In the English performances recorded in the *Journal* of Delécluze for the year 1827, the Parisian public is invited to attend productions of *Hamlet* and *Romeo and Juliet* (in a version by Garrick). Delécluze teaches us in his ponderous style that Mademoiselle Smithson played Ophelia and distinguished herself in the mad scene (act 4, scene 5) with "equal amounts of grace and truth." As for the role of Juliet, the spectators looked on with certain prejudices in mind. "The audience waited impa-tiently for the fifth act. The Italian opera whose success owed so much to the winning performances of Crescentini and Mme Pasta redoubled their curiosity to see . . . Mlle Smithson play this tragic catastrophe in the English manner. . . . Despite the talent of Mlle Smithson, I am more completely moved seeing the same scene played by Mme Pasta."[34]

The comparison is singular not least because Foppa's text and Shake-speare's are far from being identical. Nevertheless, there was a younger spectator in the audience on that evening of September 15, 1827, who was ignited with a passion for Harriet Smithson, namely, the twenty-four-year-old Hector Berlioz. He will transpose her torment, exaltation, and painful reverie into a *Symphonie fantastique*, performed on Decem-ber 5, 1839. The young Franz Liszt heard it and in his enthusiasm im-mediately transcribed it for piano.[35] French romanticism has several dates of birth, and the premiere of Berlioz's symphony is undeniably one of them. The English actress played both Ophelia and Juliet, the sweet victims of a cruel world. Fascinated, Berlioz wanted to prove his love with a piece of music capable of the same gentleness and the same cruelty. Beyond a marriage entered into in 1833 that would remain unhappy, it is clear that Berlioz was indebted to Shakespeare's Juliet for inspiring a musical interpretation that was more satisfying than all those she had previously received. For him, Shakespeare's play is "a marvelous poem written in letters of fire" compared to which all the librettos it has inspired are mere grotesques. Berlioz does not make it into an opera but instead a "dramatic symphony" with soloists and choruses. Wagner attended the third performance of the piece on December 15, 1839, and would remember it while composing *Tristan and Isolde* (a work that would leave Berlioz perplexed).

The late essay in which Berlioz relates the reproduction of Bellini's opera serves as the occasion to recall the tomb scene as played by the English troupe and also to cast judgment on the works that preceded his symphony.[36] There are "some beautiful aspects" in Steibelt (1793); Dalayrac is worthless; Vaccai (1825) has "neither color nor passion"; the score of "sweet Bellini" (1830) contains "some pretty things and a vigorous finale with a beautiful line sung in unison by the two lovers." As for Zingarelli's opera, "it is tranquil and graceful music; one sees as much trace of the Shakespearean style and intent to express the passions of the characters as one would expect in a composer who had not understood the language to which he was associating his melodies." Berlioz pauses a moment over the famous aria:

People always mention one of Romeo's arias, "Ombra adorata," a celebrated aria that for a long time managed to pack people into the Théâtre Italien in Paris and make them put up with the cold boredom of the rest of the work. The piece is graceful, elegant, and very well executed over all; the flute highlights some pretty little features that enter into happy dialogue with the fragments of the vocal line. But everything is sunny in this song. Romeo who will die expresses his joy at soon seeing Juliet again and enjoying with her the pure delights of love in their happy time together. . . . Juliet sings a mixture of truthful phrases and musical buffoonery. For example, in a grand manner she cries out, "There is not a soul more overburdened with misfortune than his." She then pauses immediately for an instant and then launches con brio into wordless vocalizing of a long series of the most joyous triplets whose lightheartedness is further increased by the joyous figures in the first violins.

As for the final duet that comes during the terrible scene when Juliet, who believed happiness within her grasp, learns instead that Romeo is poisoned, and witnesses his agony, and finally dies on his body—there is nothing calmer than these anxieties, nothing more charming than these convulsions. It's the moment to say with Hamlet, "they do but jest, poison in jest" [act 3, scene 2, line 221]

Berlioz openly mocks the "three Italian maestros" (Zingarelli, Vaccai, and Bellini) who have the role of Romeo sung by a woman: "It is a vestige of the ancient musical ways of the Italian school. It is the result of a constant preoccupation with childish sensualism. They wanted women to sing the roles of lovers because in the duets the two feminine voices could more easily produce the series of thirds so loved by the Italian ear."[37]

Romanticism as understood by Berlioz does not call for a music intended for a "audience of sybarites." Similar remarks can be found in the *Mémoires*: "But, in God's name, where is it written that Juliet's lover must appear without any attributes of virility? . . . His hopelessness at the moment of exile, his somber and terrible resignation upon learning of Juliet's death, his convulsive delirium after drinking the poison, do all these volcanic passions ordinarily erupt from the soul of a eunuch?"[38]

Berlioz does not go along with or any longer understand the fiction of baroque musical theater. The latter, while accepting the rule prohibiting the female voice from religious offices and onstage (in accordance with the Pauline principle "*Mulieres taceant in ecclesiis*"—"Let your women keep silent in the churches," 1 Cor. 14:34), allowed the voices of castrati for both the roles of women and those of heroes and lovers—an artifice within a whole system of artifices.

In truth, in the essays written for the *Journal de Paris* (*Notes d'un dilettante*) and published after his *Life of Rossini*, Stendhal moderated his admiration for Zingarelli's opera. The two first acts do not satisfy him: "The third act of *Roméo et Juliette* is so beautiful that one should set about making the first two more bearable. Opera lovers find them very boring."[39] What he persists in relishing above all is the way Madame Pasta perfected the dramatization of the death of Romeo. She has the great merit of having followed the example of the English actors. Stendhal is deeply moved by the transition from the joy in dying (for as long as Romeo believes Juliet dead) to desperation and horror at undergoing "the cruelest of misfortunes" (as soon as he sees Juliet awaken): "Perhaps Madame Pasta arriving from London was electrified by the way Garrick's arrangement of the fifth act of Shakespeare's *Romeo and Juliet* was played there. There was a cry from the audience at the moment when Romeo, who knows he's fading fast, summons his remaining force to give a last kiss to Juliet and then falls down dead."[40] Giuditta Pasta surpasses herself on October 5, 1826, and in speaking of this performance, the last the actress gave before leaving Paris, Stendhal gives the most complete articulation of what he admires in her and in her accomplished rendition of the aria.

> Never, I think, since her arrival in Paris, has Madame Pasta performed as she did that evening; the emotion of the public could not have been stretched further; there were cries of terror at the moment when Romeo senses the first effects of the poison and presses Juliet against his heart that death will soon turn to ice. Madame Pasta brought back from London the boldness to appear in the third act dressed in black and without makeup. No costume is too tragic for the character who must sing the famous aria *Ombra adorata aspetta*, which is, in effect, nothing but the sublime praise of suicide. And what makes this praise so troubling is that in a way it can appear rational. What's left for an unhappy person agitated by the liveliest and most profound feelings who, like Romeo, has lost forever his life's companion? It is, I think, this reasoning, which we might not be inclined to say out loud but that all hearts born to judge the arts will have formed in secret, that underpins the immense success of the aria *Ombra adorata aspetta*.[41]

Stendhal interprets the suicidal choice of Romeo through the philosophy to which he is himself attached, namely the "ideology" whose program was formulated by Destutt de Tracy and whose task was to retrace clearly the generation of ideas. A reason, he believes, *obscurely* guided the decision to die: What remains? Nothing. Is it a secret deduction that leads Romeo to the fatal act? In moments of desperation, Stendhal had himself experienced the temptation of suicide. For example in 1821 after leaving Milan and Métilde. He puts forward no argument and declares simply, "I had great difficulty resisting the temptation to blow my brains out."[42] Ten years later, in the *Souvenirs d'égotisme*, he tries instead to find the reasons that kept him from "ending it all": "political curiosity" and an unacknowledged "fear" of "harming [oneself]."

What remains? Stendhal turns not to the words of the libretto but to the melody and to what it seemed to reveal to him by its beauty and by its conquest of so many admirers. Nor does he analyze the musical structure that is the only tangible reality. He forms conjectures based on the emotion he experienced. I note here how tempting it is in a given operatic situation to trace a line from an audible perception to a psychological generalization. As though, thanks to the force of music, a fictive dramatic moment changes into an eternal truth of the human soul for one sufficiently sensitive to it. Stendhal's reading may strike us as insufficient, and yet we will return in an entirely different way to the notion of the unavowed, but by alleging "impulses" and not reasoned arguments. Still, it must be said that we are often looking to opera for revelations of the same order and taking the same risks.

E. T. A. HOFFMANN

In one of Hoffmann's tales a young woman sings in public "Ombra adorata." In time, this operatic aria becomes part of the concert repertoire and figures in the programs of soloists who perform it in their recitals. Hoffmann makes it both the subject and title of his tale.[43] Written in the summer of 1812, it is one of the first of his literary texts. The personal drama that he had just endured is expressed elliptically within the tale that sees everything become concentrated and simplified into a unique event without the slightest detour via a fictive plot.[44] What is at stake is represented by allusion in Crescentini's aria. The implication of the writer in these few carefully crafted pages surpasses Stendhal's improvisations glorifying the art of Madame Pasta, no matter if she is the substitute figure for Métilde Dembowski, the lost beloved. Hoffmann's personal tale concerns his impossible love for a very young student, Julia Marc, forced by her mother to marry at sixteen a rich and vulgar character. It is a loss that nothing can compensate and that will provoke a trial of mourning that extends to an entire body of work. Thus the famous aria receives its romantic badge of honor: it carries within it the desperation and the hope of the attentive poet, it unites love and the object of desire under the double aspect of lack and abundance.

Hoffmann (or his double, Kreisler, since the piece is part of the *Kreisleriana*) prefaces his tale with some pages in praise of music. Two voices speak out to get things started. One holds music to be a universe that contains hidden secrets. The other situates its essence within the depths of personal existence. The two discourses become reconciled. Music is at once the far off and the immediate, something supernatural and natural. Like God for Augustine, it is transcendent, but it manifests itself via interiority. Hoffmann clearly writes this hymn to music in an idiom that owes much to religious language. One finds the opposition between the terrestrial and the celestial, the great mystical figures of impetus and abandonment, the aspiration of the soul and the visitation it receives, and the transformation of the old man into a new man. But the religious terminology is transferred to the aesthetic domain. If the reality here below is defined by the requisite suffering, the divine is only invoked in a diffuse and indeterminate way: the divine and the spiritual remain undefined; they are the stuff of epithets. Hoffmann's formulations veer toward a magic naturalism. If there might still be angels for him, there are most certainly "spirits," "apparitions," and "circles." These images have more in common with children's fairy tales and the backdrop of legends than with religion:

What an utterly miraculous thing is music, and how little can men penetrate its deeper mysteries! But does it not reside in the breast of man himself and fill his heart with its enchanting images, so that all his senses respond to them, and a radiant new life transports him from his enslavement here below, from the oppressive torment of his earthly existence? Indeed, he is suffused by a divine power, and by abandoning himself with a childlike and pious mind to whatever influence the spirit arouses within him, he is able to speak the language of that unknown, romantic spirit-realm. Without realising it, like the apprentice who reads aloud from his master's book of spells, he summons all the wonderful images from within his heart, so that they come to life and dance around in brilliant circles, filling all those able to see them with infinite, inexpressible yearning.[45]

That evening the author was to have played the piano, but overcome with chagrin, anxious and tortured, he goes off to sit "in the furthest corner of the hall." A replacement consents to accompany the singer. It is the sign of a separation. After an insignificant overture, a silence intervenes. The narrator experiences a moment of complete absence and forgetfulness that is interrupted by a surprising awakening: "The pause must have lasted rather a long time when finally the ritornello of an aria began. It was very tender in character, and seemed to speak in simple but deeply affecting tones of the yearning that sweeps the pious soul up to heaven and restores every beloved object denied it here below. Then, like a heavenly luminescence, the bell-like voice of a woman radiated upwards from the orchestra: *Tranquillo io sono, fra poco teco sarò mia vita!*"[46]

It is Crescentini's aria sung by an "admirable lady singer." The essence of the events narrated is contained in two statements. We have just heard the first one: "Then, like a heavenly luminescence, the bell-like voice of a woman radiated upwards." The second comes at the end of the tale: "I shall not hear you again." The cantatrice has there become a "you" with neither first nor last name. This magnificent voice and its words have sung of a separation and a promise of reunion in the beyond. Addressing the one whom he has just lost, he says that he keeps inside himself the consoling memory of her voice, the source henceforth of all future creativity. We then understand that we have read a letter of farewell.

This very short text is worth closer examination. Hoffmann speaks of Crescentini's composition as a musician and as a poet. He is very familiar with its words that say soon—"fra poco"—love will be fulfilled in Elysium. But whereas the words chosen by Foppa renewed the mythical landscape of underground woods with conventional images, Hoffmann speaks of "another world" situated in a heaven that is more in keeping with a Christian or Neoplatonic spirituality. In the libretto of 1796, the place of reunion, Elysium, is a fictitious location with the ring of true antiquity. In Hoffmann's text, it is a mysterious beyond, a distant place toward which so many romantics turn their gaze. "Who can describe the feeling that surged through me! How the pain gnawing at my innards was transformed into wistful melancholy that poured the heavenly balm into all my wounds! Everything was forgotten and I simply listened in rapture to the sounds that held me in their consoling embrace as though they were transmitted from another world."[47]

The ornamentation that Stendhal also listens to with such pleasure is, for Hoffmann, the vehicle that leads the spirit to a higher place by means of a moving play of visual correspondences before finally returning to the singer's adorned face:

> How unaffectedly and naturally everything in this simple composition proceeds; the music moves only between tonic and dominant; no jarring changes of key, no contrived detail; the singing flows along like a slivery stream past brightly colored flowers. . . . In his wonderfully bright and clear melismas the soul flies with rapid wing-beat through shining clouds; it is exultant joy of transfigured spirits.
>
> The composition, like any that has been so deeply felt within the composer, demands to be just as deeply understood and performed, and with an awareness, I would say with an explicit recognition, of the sense of spirituality contained within the melody. Also, as the genius of Italian melody dictates, certain embellishments were allowed for, both in the recitative and in the aria. But is it not a blessing that the way in which the composer and singer Crescentini performed and embellished the aria himself has been handed down, as though by tradition? No one would now dare to introduce inappropriate flourishes, at least not without being rebuked. How intelligently Crescentini applied these incidental embellishments, and how they enliven the overall effect; they are the brilliant finery that adorns the beloved's fair countenance, so that her eyes shine more brightly and a deeper purple colours her lip and cheek.[48]

In an emphatic style overloaded with epithets and superlatives, the author apostrophizes the artiste and even translates the message that her singing addresses to him. "Your notes surround me like propitious spirits, and each one said 'Lift up your head, you who are bowed down! Come with us, come with us to that far land where suffering no longer inflicts its bloody wounds, but as if in deepest rapture fills the breast with inexpressible longing!' "[49]

An invitation is addressed to the listener. But what "far land" is being invoked? It is not the place where there would be simple fulfillment of the miracle of rediscovered presence but one where pain changes into ecstasy, where it molts into untiring aspiration as part of a process of re-conquering, and where desire would be endless (Hoffmann employs two words that are very difficult to translate: "*entzücken*" and "*Sehnsucht*"). It is, in any case, as one sees in the next lines, a place where the writer will feel himself safely away from the mean and low and the "rabble's odious mockery." He will hear again the beloved voice resounding in his ears, "a consoling spirit-voice": "Tranquillo io sono. . . ." Finally, at the end of the text, the "far land" is an interior space where a creative fervor will reign, and thanks to it the singing that the narrator has just heard will be resuscitated and glorified. "Inspired as never before, I shall then rise in powerful flight above all earthly degradation. Every sound congealed in the blood from my wounded breast will be revivified, and stir and spring up and throw out flittering sparks like fire-breathing salamanders. And I shall contrive to harness them, and combine them, so that as if merging into a single burst of fire they form a single flaming image, that transfigured and glorifies your singing and yourself."[50]

The discourse of the writer with its verbs in the future tense an-nounces the birth of the vocation of the artist and the blossoming of a higher power. A certitude has gained the upper hand: he will know how to put to work his faculties as a composer, painter, and poet. The sounds radiate light and life in perfect sovereignty. Hoffmann speaks of transfiguration, and his flow of metaphors seems to want to be the im-mediate proof of this. A loss was greeted with a farewell, and here, now, is that loss repaired by a resurrection on another existential plane. It is as though a sacrifice had been consummated, a salvation announced, brought about by the virtues of art. A transfer is thus accomplished be-tween the religious and aesthetic domains. It is in the future work that the apostrophized "you" will become present.

The double citation of the Italian words "Tranquillo io sono" at the beginning and the end of the text is thus the symbol of a redoubling of a different order: the reunion in Elysium announced in the words of the aria are the exact prefiguration of the spiritual fusion that the narrator announces. The words of the melody find their reflection in the tale as though in a mirror. What the tale says is the transposed replica of what the melody says. Crescentini's Romeo was preparing to find Juliet again "nel fortunato Eliso"—in the happy Elysium of mythology. In the account of a final listening to the beloved voice, Hoffmann raises to a superior power the promise of the dying Romeo. The meeting place will be the work of art. It will be the flaming hearth where the souls will unite. The young lady who sings Zingarelli's aria is no longer the interpreter of a fictional Romeo. She is a lost Juliet (is her name not Julia?) that the narrator promises to join by composing a piece of music made with love.

There can be no doubt that this is a romantic variation on the theme of poetic devotion to a lost beloved. Beatrice and Laura were celebrated in this way, and yet there is a major difference between those examples and Hoffmann's tale. In the poetry of Dante and Petrarch, another world exists, and those who have loved each other are welcomed there. In Hoffmann's text, the creation of another world, the elevation, and the spiritual molting fall to the artist. But there is a legitimate question one might ask when it comes to Julia Marc and especially the performer of "Ombra adorata." Does Hoffmann (or his literary double, Kreisler) love a person or a voice? In the written work it is a voice. Out of the energy of his disappointed passion, the listener's own self sets out to invent the music that will be the new existence of the beloved, the place of their loving fusion. What inspired the tale "Ombra adorata" is not a dead woman but the voice that a forced marriage with an undignified merchant takes away from Hoffmann. He lives this loss as a bonus for his art. He exploits the loss to such a degree that one might suspect he arranged it or perhaps even desired it. In Hoffmann's diary for the years 1811 to 1813 there are some peculiar entries that relate in an almost stenographic way the intense fascination caused by the figure of the very young Julia Marc. In these notes Hoffmann glimpses the literary escape route for the dizzying passion that was disorienting him. Age thirty-six (and married), he entered into a hopeless situation by becoming infatuated with a student who was only thirteen when he met her for the first time in 1809. Is he not seeking to live a loss that can then be compensated by something else? For the date March 30, 1812, we read this: "Fate is in my favor and favorable to my life as an artist." On April 27, Hoffmann speaks of an enigma: "When it is resolved, a curtain of fog will descend, and the people behind it will become poetry and behave poetically." Two days later he writes, "Divine irony . . . assist me. It is time, now, to work seriously *in literis*."[51] Hoffmann will repeat this some-what differently in 1815 in the tale "The Court of Arthur": "No, no, Felicity, I never lost you, you remain mine forever, for you are yourself the creating art that lives in me."

The irony to which Hoffmann calls out can be seen at work here very shortly after the disastrous marriage of "Julchen." One notes the prevalence of the fissured self, that is, the very opposite of the amorous fusion on another plane that Hoffmann dreamed of. He gives voice to his various reflections. In one of the first literary projects following Julia's marriage, Hoffmann doubles himself in order to speak through a figure belonging to both the animal world and the literary realm: the dog Berganza who converses with another dog, Scipion, in one of the *Novelas ejemplares* of Cervantes.[52] The self is transported into the fictional body of a being who is all the more aware of the secrets of hu-mans thanks to his lowly vantage point. This type of substitution opens the door to the register of satire: the dog Berganza will not hesitate to utter all the negative opinions he has about Julia's mother, her coquet-ries, and her grotesque intellectual pretensions, and for good measure he also ridicules the regular guests of her salon. But in this liberating writing, the avowal of deeply repressed secrets can also take place. Thus one finds the first name Julia replaced by the that of Cecilia (Cäcilie); however, Cecilia is the name that Hoffmann and his wife, Michaelina, had given to their daughter who died in 1807 at the age of two. And in the first edition of the "News of the Latest Fortunes of the Hound Berganza" one finds a sonnet that Hoffmann wrote in 1811 for Julia's fifteenth birthday: "Spring arrives on the blue wave of clouds. . . ." One could make the conjecture that the mourning for the lost infant bled over onto the figure of Julia who in turn was destined to be lost as well. Interpretation here can run wild. Why was Julia Marc so loved? Was she not the substitute figure on whom was transferred the love destined for the child? This love not only had a new object; it had to have been accompanied by anxiety as well.

The dog Berganza denounces with sarcasm the sessions of "academic mimicry" that the mother of Cecilia (or Julia) enjoys organizing for her guests. The accent is placed on the mimetic relationship to conse-crated masterpieces. A most striking feature in all this is that Cecilia's role is described as something she *plays*, just as the admirable diva in the tale "Ombra adorata" appeared in an aria that she was *singing*. In both cases, the adored person is executing something and excels in the art of representation. If it is legitimate to play the notes inscribed in a musical score, however, there is something absolutely topsy-turvy about wanting to don the clothes and strike the pose of a figure in a picture. Berganza remembers a tableau vivant where Cecilia had to dress and pose like Saint Cecile in the famous painting by the Italian Carlo Dolci. For the time that she was asked to hold this pose, Cecilia had become the image of an image—of the martyr and patron saint of music. For the occasion, the musician in the group (that is, Hoffmann) was given the job of composing an accompanying piece of stage music. "First there resounded far off a long sustained chord that faded into the air. Cecilia softly raised her head, and one heard, as though coming from a distance, a chorus of female voices, the work of our musician. The harmonies of this chorus of cherubim and seraphim, simple and yet strange in their marvelous outpouring and apparently descending from another world, reminded me of some church music that I had already heard two centuries earlier in Spain and Italy; I felt overcome, as before, by a sacred thrill. Cecilia's eyes, looking toward the sky, shone with a saintly ecstasy."[53]

For reasons other than those that led Stendhal to evoke Allegri, there is for Hoffmann an "intimate affinity between sacred music and tragic opera."[54] Hoffmann is thinking of the polyphonic music of the end of the sixteenth century and therefore contemporary to Cervantes's talking dog, Berganza. Here again, he is making use of a configuration that opposes an above and beyond to a down here below, a kingdom of spirits to earthly reality, a superior language and ordinary language. But the transcendental movement remains tied to the world of representation. To reproduce a painting as a living picture is a turn of the screw within the domain of representation, and to relate this attempt, for Hoffmann-Berganza, is to place oneself on an aesthetic plane marked by both sentimentality and irony. The surpassing of speech by music and the opening into spiritual heights remain within an intramondaine performance that borders on parody. After the cherubim and seraphim have made themselves heard, the scene concludes as in the theater: "As the curtain rustled closed, everyone, even the very young girls who were present, remained still, plunged in a silent communion, until a noisy eruption of unanimous admiration intervened to relieve every oppressed heart."[55]

The "saintly ecstasy" of Cecilia, her fusion with a superior world, is perceived at the end of a series of ontological leaps. Cecilia turns herself into an imitator and actress; she has to dress up in a costume in order to be transported by poetry and music and then rise ostensibly into heaven. As though, in Hoffmann's imaginary universe, the passage via unreal substitutes for "myself" were the initiation test prior to the encounter with "you."

Immediately after "Ombra adorata," which dates from August 1812, Hoffmann wrote the admirable tale "Don Juan" and published it in March 1813. The narrator attends a performance where the actress who plays Donna Anna identifies strongly with her character. She has undergone the demonic fascination of Don Juan and loves the one who has violated her. The narrator understands, thanks to her, the entire spiritual dimension of opera. During the intermission, Anna mysteriously joins the narrator in his private box where he sits alone. She knows his work as a composer from having sung it. She has therefore already met him on the most intimate level without his knowledge: "Your soul," she says, "revealed itself to me through those harmonies." The double presence of the performer, onstage and in his box, deeply troubles the author, who feels as though he were in a waking dream. Having stayed in this box that communicates with his hotel room, at two in the morning he breathes the faint perfume of his Italian caller; a trembling runs through the empty room, and the quiet orchestral strings begin to resonate. The narrator believes he hears the distant voice of Donna Anna. The next day in the hotel dining room he learns that Donna Anna died at two in the morning. The reader experiences two tales subsumed into one: Donna Anna cannot live on after the death of Don Juan; an admirable actress dies after a performance. The woman who enters the author's box, was she a double of the "true" Donna Anna? The singer lives the suffering that Hoffmann detected in the character of Donna Anna; she remains fascinated by the seducer to whom she has succumbed and will not be able to survive the punishment that sends him to hell. During the night recounted by Hoffmann, she dies the death that awaits Mozart's character. The events of Mozart's opera thus repeat themselves in the world of the actors who are performing it; moreover, the writer who relates this surprising set of events had the time to converse with the actress who is going to die and learns that she knows his work as a composer to the point of identifying with the melodies he has written: "Yes, I've sung you, I found myself in your melodies." Identities are likely to migrate in Hoffmann's universe from person to person but also from voices to people or from people to voices. In Hoffmann's "Ombra adorata," this permeability of the border between beings, despite the distance that separates them, constitutes its fundamental strangeness. Nothing else occurs except an admission of loss and the promise of reparation through music.

BALZAC

To translate the magic produced by Giuditta Pasta in her interpretations of "Ombra adorata," Stendhal made use of a panorama of the Bay of Naples. For the same aria, Balzac will use a Venetian décor. The night, a legendary location, an expanse of water under moonlight: these are the common elements. Stendhal's approach, let us recall, was indirect: he put words into the mouth of an exiled Neapolitan enthused by the voice of Madame Pasta. Balzac, on the other hand, takes charge of the narration: in an episode from *Massimilla Doni*, four characters on the bank of the lagoon listen to the famous song sung to perfection by the tenor Genovese (a fictional artist trained according to the "wise methods" of the male sopranos Crescentini and Velluti). Earlier in the evening, during a brilliant performance at La Fenice of Rossini's *Moses in Egypt*, the singer had performed badly in his duets with the prima donna Clara Tinti.

This short story, published as part of Balzac's "Philosophical Studies," is constructed out of a double-stranded reflection. First, as a response to a request from the editor of the *Gazette musicale*, Balzac takes music as his principal subject matter, according particular importance to Rossini's *Mosè* and to "Ombra adorata." How can one explain that the tenor who made such a mess of things onstage could recover such poise on the banks of the lagoon? The second strand consists of the singular love adventure of Massimilla and Emilio that is inscribed within a larger philosophical and anthropological development on love. The story presents in narrative form a veritable treatise on the forces that animate a life in love, employing the key term in various senses that today one would convey via the notion of desire or eros. The immediate occasion for this is the obstacle posed by the excessive thinking in the hero's relation with the admirable young woman. Spiritual expenditures (or, we could say, the narcissistic exaggeration of "sublimation") prevent the physical consummation of love. How will this obstacle be overcome? It is worth noting that the two strands of the story both treat (as best they can) two projects that, one after another, confront the problem of failure.

Balzac may have attended a performance of Zingarelli's *Giulietta e Romeo*. When? I have no idea. He considers the final duet of this opera to be "one of the most divine expressions of tenderness" and "one of the most poignant pieces of modern music" that allows one to hear "two swans bid farewell to life."[56] But he has also made use of Hoffmann and his brief tale from the *Kreisleriana*. Balzac tells us that the melody sung in front of the lagoon is "simple and naive." Hoffmann, for his part, had exclaimed, "Oh how everything in this very simple composition comes forth naturally and without artifice!"[57] The beautiful Hoffmannian image of the "singing" that "follows its course like a river of pure silver passing between flowers in full bloom" resurfaces in Balzac's tale when one of his characters, Capraja, speaks of the runs ("the fairy") that "make the shores be seen again as flowering cascades of love."[58]

Balzac, who visited Venice briefly in 1837, sets up the singing scene on the piazzetta as though for a grand performance. The description of the location includes an inventory of every architectural detail as though it were taken from the prose of a guidebook: "At that moment the French doctor, Vendramin, Capraja, Cataneo, and Genovese had walked as far as the piazzetta. It was midnight. The brilliant gulf outlined by the churches of Saint George and Saint Paul at the end of the Giudecca and the Grand Canal, so gloriously opened by the *dogana* and by the church dedicated to Maria della Salute, this magnificent gulf was peaceful. The moon illuminated the boats before the Riva degli Schiavoni. The water of Venice, sheltered from the sea, seemed alive with the shimmer of millions of sequins."[59]

Balzac places on this stage a group of admiring listeners, whereas Hoffmann (or Kreisler) remained painfully alone within his solitary contemplation. Hoffmann wrote, "I listened now only to the sounds that, as though descending from another world, enveloped me with their consolations. The aria . . . expresses the state of the soul, which in the joyous hope of soon seeing fulfilled in a higher better world all the promises that were made concerning it, takes flight above all earthly sufferings. . . . The soul flies with rapid wings across brilliant clouds—it is the exuberant jubilation of transfigured spirits." Balzac takes up the same theme of music as source of consolation but adds no personal message.

No singer ever found himself in a more magnificent theater. Genovese gestured emphatically to the sky and sea as witnesses, then without any accompaniment besides the murmur of the sea he sang the aria *ombra adorata*, the masterpiece of Crescentini. The singing that rose between the famous statues of Saint Theodore and Saint George in the middle of a deserted Venice illuminated by the moon, the words in such perfect harmony with this theater, and the melancholy expression of Genovese—all of this captivated the Italians and the Frenchman. After the first words Vendramin's face was covered with tears, Capraja was as still as one of the statues of the ducal palace. Cataneo appeared to feel an emotion. The Frenchman, surprised, was meditating like a learned professor struck by a phenomenon that overturns one of his fundamental axioms. These four very different temperaments whose hopes were so poor, who believed in nothing, neither for themselves nor after them, who considered themselves lightly as passing, capricious forms, like a blade of grass or some sort of beetle—they glimpsed heaven. Never did music more justly deserve to be called divine. The consoling sounds emanating from this throat enfolded the souls in sweet caressing clouds. These half-visible clouds, like peaks of marble made silvery by the moon surrounding the listeners, seemed to serve as seats for angels whose wings expressed adoration and love with their religious movements. This simple and naive melody, by penetrating the inner senses, carried in light. O, how the passion was saintly![60]

The explicitly religious motifs—angels, churches, statues of saints—are more diverse and concrete than they were in Hoffmann. Stendhal remained discreet, using only the single, clichéd epithet "angelic" to describe the beauty of the sounds. By evoking the religious monuments of Venice, Balzac was careful to fuse the emotion of his imaginary listeners and the picturesque setting that his readers expected.[61]

The four listeners, stereotyped to the point of caricature, have an emblematic function within a plot that Balzac describes with the term "myth."[62] Their fate is not played out within the tale. They are extras whose destiny is known from the beginning. Three of them have undergone a loss or suffer some lack. They illustrate without a doubt the danger that Balzac imputes to excessive amounts of thinking. In addition, their thought [*pensée*] (a word that today would be taken over by the notion of desire) has been oriented in a single direction to the detriment of all others. In psychological terms they are mentally ill. They have only partial or substitute objects of love, and they have forgotten how to live. They bear traits of monomania, even though Balzac does not make use of that term coined during his time. Crescentini's aria, which speaks at once of loss and the hope of reparation, resonates differently to each of them.

Vendramin, the first of the four witnesses named, is the most upset. Descended from an illustrious family, he is an exile in his own city, eaten away by "love for a homeland that no longer exists."[63] He was introduced to opium by "an Englishman." He feels like a survivor in a place conquered by Austria, exhibited to the curiosity of bored tourists, and the only refuge left for him is an alienation aggravated by the phantasms provoked by drug use. According to his whims, either his mind wanders to the city's past, or else he ponders its becoming a modern power. Reality inspires only desperation in him. "I am beginning to see Venice as she is, covered with crepe, naked, bare, deserted." But he "sleeps" with her and wants to die with her. The substitute for what was lost is only a vagabond existence in a "land of chimeras." In the story Balzac gives Vendramin the function of serving as the close friend of the hero. He knows of the latter's sexual hang-up and hopes to save him from desperation and suicide by playing the intermediary between him and Massimilla and later with the "French doctor."

Balzac next identifies a second listener seized with admiration for the voice of the tenor: Capraja, a "famous music lover." He is a "poor old nobleman" who lives in a "hovel" [*bouge*]. But is he really poor? Balzac tells us that he has "two million in public bonds" that he pays no attention to, letting the interest pile up—"thus producing an enormous sum." This neglected fortune is symbolic. It is the sign of a retreat into a solitary intellectual existence without any material goals. Capraja goes every day to the café Florian and lives only for thinking. He is a "passive Diogenes," crazy about music but cut off from all affect. He has "never kissed the hand" of the young pastry chef who will end up taking care of him "like a mother" and inheriting his fortune. His love for melody shuts out everything else. Did he undergo an essential loss, like Vendramin? No, but the character is an incomplete being whose affective energy has been entirely channeled into musical perception and philosophical intelligence. In the story Capraja is nothing but a talker; he intervenes only as a commentator and especially as a theoretician. Gambara, the hero of another one of Balzac's stories about music, initiated him into a doctrine of correspondences between sounds and colors. For his presentation of this doctrine, it is known that Balzac borrowed heavily from the writings of Hoffmann. But the ingenious Gambara encountered certain insurmountable obstacles when it came to constructing the instrument of his dreams; he gave in to alcohol (as did Hoffmann) and finishes his life in misery. Capraja is an idler who has profound views on the unity of the arts but no object or ambition to which to devote his science. It is thus spent entirely in conversation. This caricature of the thinker (a figure who may have been one of the models for Monsieur Teste conjointly with certain characters of Poe that are also of Hoffmannian lineage), having "given himself entirely to ideas" without ever writing anything, can be considered as the spokesman of a secret knowledge. At the end of the tale during the late evening supper where the erotic plot comes to its end, Capraja declares, "Me, I own the whole world."

Balzac fashioned Capraja as a partisan of melody within the outdated debate between defenders of the primacy of melody and defenders of the primacy of harmony.[64] It is one of the last echoes of the controversy between Rousseau and Rameau that Hoffmann in his *Kreisleriana* wanted to consign to history but whose traces are still very noticeable in Stendhal's *Life of Rossini*. Rousseau put forward the thesis that melody alone can reach the soul whereas harmony can produce only physical pleasure. He also used to say that all harmony is contained in unison. Harmony has an ardent defender in the figure of the absent husband of Massimilla, the duke Cataneo, who has exhausted his life in pleasure. The dispute in Balzac's tale takes on greater relief thanks to the contrastive effect of opposed interventions. There is no more distinctly opposed pair than the chaste Capraja who has never known love and the lustful Cataneo exhausted by debauchery and no longer physically capable of love. Capraja takes little interest in the words of an aria, and neither is he at all inclined to be moved by the dramatic situation of

Romeo singing "Ombra adorata"; however, he is extremely attentive to the aria's various runs and ornaments—the melodious sound itself is for him a fairy, an enchantress. His eloquence becomes effusive when it comes to celebrating the art of charming decoration. Because sound, which will search out "the very organizing principles of our sensations," leads to the "ivory door through which one enters into the mysterious land of Reverie." Capraja does not cry on the bank of the lagoon like the mourning Vendramin. He has glimpsed the very zenith of art and remains immobile in ecstasy.

In addition, Balzac lends to this character all the psychological per-spicacity necessary to diagnose the causes of the performer's failure. What provoked Genovese's fiasco was his desire to declare his love in the duets with "la Tinti." He was hissed at because he lost control of his voice and was braying "like a donkey."[65] His voice turned into that of an animal! The reason is that he was experiencing his own passion instead of representing the passion of a fictional hero. He was singing as a lover instead of playing the role of a lover. "When an artist has the misfortune of being full of the same passion that he wants to express, he will not be able to depict it, because he is the thing itself instead of being its image." This is the argument used by Diderot in his essay "Le Paradoxe sur le comédien" ("The Paradox of the Actor") published in 1830. Balzac adopts it whole. The performer must remember that he is responsible for an image. But what does to paint [peindre] or depict mean when it comes to music? The debate begins in Massimilla's box, where she displays the extent of her learning: "In musical language, re-plied the duchess, to paint means to awaken with sounds certain move-ments in our heart or certain images in our minds, and these memories, these images, each have their color, sad or gay. . . . Each instrument has its mission and addresses certain ideas just as each color answers to cer-tain feelings within us." These parallels charm the listener with their synesthesia; they require great knowledge on the part of the composer. Massimilla, in her role as Sybille, proves she is a very attentive student of Capraja.

The third figure named within the group of friends who escort Geno-vese to the piazzetta is Cataneo. He listened to "Ombra adorata," but all that Balzac says of him is that he appeared "to feel an emotion." Indeed, the only source of voluptuousness that remains for him is to perceive the harmony or unison of two voices. But Genovese has sung

alone on the bank of the lagoon. A second voice was missing for Cataneo. As posited by Balzac, it was in order to hear the voice of Genovese
fuse with that of his protégée, Clara Tinti, that the duke had hired him
to join the Fenice company. The lady speaks of this in the course of
the story: "Genovese is the only tenor who can sometimes harmonize
with the timbre of my voice. Either we really approach each other once
or twice each evening, or the duke imagines we do; for this imaginary
pleasure, he hired Genovese; Genovese belongs to him. No theater
director can make this tenor sing without me or make me sing without
him. The duke trained me to satisfy this caprice, I owe him my talent,
my beauty, and no doubt my good fortune."

For Cataneo, the pleasure of hearing voices blended together, especially when he is responsible for producing one of the two instrumen-
tally is a substitute for the pleasure of sexual intercourse, of which he
is physically no longer capable. Balzac has castrated this character just
as he castrated Vendramin and Capraja. "The sense of hearing is the
only one that has survived the shipwreck of his faculties." "Cataneo has
spent one-hundred-and-eighteen years enrolled in the parish of Vice,
though church records show him to be only forty-seven years old."
Once again the voice is a partial substitute object, a fetishized ersatz
that gives access to a displaced pleasure. Cataneo obtains this pleasure
in a perverse way. Balzac has la Tinti ("a simple servant" at a Sicilian
inn before the duke Cataneo chose to train her to sing) relate a rather
extraordinary event but one that has become a routine:

Yes, all his strings are broken, everything is rags and ruin. The
soul, mind, heart, nerves—everything that produces in man an
impetus and makes him reach for the sky through desire or the fire
of pleasure derives not so much from music as from an effect from
among the thousands of effects of music, namely, the perfect harmony of two voices or between a voice and the finest string of his
violin. The old monkey sits on top of me, he takes up his violin,
he plays rather well, he produces some sounds and I try to imitate
them, and when after much searching the moment arrives when
it is impossible to distinguish within the mass of song which is the
sound of the violin and which the note coming out of my throat,
the old man falls into ecstasy, his dead eyes spit out their last fire,
he is content and falls on the ground like a drunken sailor.

Is this surprising encounter between a voice and the note of a violin entirely Balzac's invention? For readers of Balzac familiar with Hoffmann, the image of the violin is likely to awaken a memory of a similar image, namely, the violin of councilor Krespel. It is very likely that Balzac knew this short story published in German under the title "Antonie," then as "Rat Krespel," which was also the title of a French translation, and now commonly known as "The Cremona Violin".[66] The story, which will be taken up in a highly modified form by Offenbach's librettists in *The Tales of Hoffmann*, is as follows.[67] During a trip to Italy, Krespel married a singer by whom he had a daughter. This child, Antonie, has a splendid voice but is afflicted with an "organic problem in her chest." But according to a medical friend, this is precisely "what gives her voice a rare and marvelous force—one, I would even say, above the sphere of human song." Each time she sings she loses a little of the life she has left to live (a theme that is not dissimilar to what one finds in Balzac's *La Peau de chagrin*, 1831). For this reason Krespel is anxious and bullies his daughter by refusing all musical invitations. After acquiring an exceptional Cremona violin, he comes to play it so well that Antonie believes she recognizes her own voice when hearing it and allows herself to be replaced by the instrument. In this way her remaining life lengthens. Possessed with the illusion of singing herself, Antonie ceases to sing.

> No sooner had he produced the first sounds than Antonie cried out with joy, "Ah, but that's me! I'm singing now." Indeed the silvery sounds of the instrument had something very particular about them and did appear to come from a human breast. He played better than ever, and when he ascended and descended with force and a powerful expression in the difficult passages, Antonie, enchanted, said clapping her hands together, "O, I played that so well! I really did play that well!"
>
> From that moment on, a wonderful peace descended on their lives.[68]

Until the final catastrophe! Antonie did not stop loving the fiancé that her father had chased away, a young composer. One night her father is seized with anxiety mixed with inexpressible joy when he hears her singing louder and louder the lied that the fiancé had composed for her. In the morning the father finds her dead; the soundpost and breast of the Cremona violin broke at the same moment. The strange identity of the voice and the violin received a final proof. The violin is to be buried along with the young girl. (We might wonder in passing if the imagination of Hoffmann is not preoccupied by a desire to banish or have killed sublime singers such as with Donna Anna in the story "Don Juan"!)

In truth, there are a number of differences between the two stagings of the association between voice and violin. The transfer of Antonie's voice to that of the violin of the man who is concerned about prolonging her life does not have the same moral hue as the strange ceremonial coupling whereby the young girl's voice becomes indistinguishable from the note played by an impotent "old man." The common element, however, is the relation of identity between voice and violin: the violin as substitute for the voice in Hoffmann, the violin intimately blended with the voice in Balzac. With Hoffmann, one is at the limit of the sentimental and the fantastic. The craftsmanship of the Cremona violin maker combined with Krespel's playing are capable of producing the song that Antonie cannot permit herself without dying and in addition can fool her into believing that its music is coming out of her throat—a double victory of life over death. The young woman who believes she hears herself when the violin is singing is an example of the mobility of self-consciousness that one finds everywhere in Hoffmann's work. In Hoffmann's universe the permeability of me and you, self and other, and the mysterious links between subjects and objects are possibilities that can awaken at any moment. And of course between Krespel and his daughter a reader today is unlikely to overlook an incestuous dimension. Balzac, in accentuating the caricatural aspects, pursues a perverse variation. His Cataneo has us witness the fixation on the partial object and the fetishistic erotization of the voice, a scene that also includes a humiliating relationship of domination over the partner. Everything is there in the short phrase from the account la Tinti gives to Emilio: "The old monkey sits on top of me."

Whereas Cataneo and Capraja are "poets for themselves alone," the last of the four listeners, a figure Balzac drapes in anonymity with the doubly generic reference "the French doctor," has no personal identity, no relation to a self. No physical traits and no gestures are assigned to him. He is an instance of judgment and action. He hovers over the plot but is also the key agent of its denouement. The only pieces of his biography given to us are the names of the masters under whom he studied: Magendie, Cuvier, Dupuytren, Broussais. He is therefore a physiologist. He was sent for by Cataneo, a man wasted by debauchery "who wants to know how long he has to live." He appeared at the performance in Massimilla's box and struck the pose of the unprejudiced observer. He intervenes in a discussion of political principles to defend the liberal ideas held by partisans of an aristocratic conservatism. This intervention permits Balzac to stage an intellectual antithesis, one of many that are encountered in the profusely verbose central section of this short story. "Analyst and materialist," passionately interested in experimentation and equalization, the French doctor has the will to translate his knowledge into power. He puts into practice the monist philosophy that also tempted Balzac. He is quick to diagnose the signs of madness in both Prince Emilio Memmi and Vendramin: "What an opera is the human brain."[69] Sure of himself, he promises immediately to cure both of them. He will disappear before beginning his treatment of Vendramin: the final summary apprises us that the latter did not escape his fate as a nostalgic and drug addict. On this point Balzac's sharp judgment excludes all therapeutic optimism: "Love for a homeland that no longer exists is an incurable passion."

But the French doctor also knows how to exercise his critical faculty on his own projects. As we shall soon see, he is not certain that Emilio will come out ahead in exchanging his spiritual love for a material one.

The function that the narration assigns to the doctor is that of a deus ex machina. He is both a superior judge and a decisive auxiliary within a plot where he is asked to vanquish a strange opponent, namely, a bodily silence that, in this person who becomes his patient, is accompanied by a spiritual love of the highest order. (As in very archaic medical practice, he accepts to act by a secret strategy without the patient's knowledge.)

For anyone looking for figural representations of the unconscious, the prose of organic dysfunction is inscribed against a backdrop laden with symbolic values. The scene of the seduction of Emilio by la Tinti takes place in the bedroom of the palace that the young prince has just inherited. Emilio threw into the sea, without reading completely, the letter from Vendramin informing him that his house was rented. La

Tinti meanwhile did not know she would come upon the young owner
living there: she finds him pleasing and takes hold of him imperiously,
physical love coinciding with the first encounter. He is conquered by a
force that Balzac describes as animal. On the other hand, Emilio's "attempts" in the direction of the very young Massimilla, left intact in her
marriage with Cataneo, have amounted only to "clouds more alert than
his desire." He loves "spiritually." Balzac sensed well that this "hopeless
antithesis" in the eyes of his readers could only be sustained by accompanying it with desperation and a tragic threat. Thus he has his hero
entertain thoughts of suicide. Vendramin informs the French doctor of
this and asks him to "save the life" of his friend.

In reply, the doctor makes the following comment: "The ancients
wanted to depict in their fable of Ixion this force that annuls the body."[70]
Ixion desired Juno, the wife of Jupiter, who disguises herself in the form
of a cloud. The image is fitting if one remembers that near the beginning of the story Balzac had compared the "majesty" of Massimilla's
head to that of Juno! Confident in his medical authority and without
much reliance on physiology, the learned man imagines a stratagem for
transforming the elusive divinity into a mortal. It will consist of adding wine to an "orgy" and organizing an exchange whereby the prince
Emilio Memmi will be delivered from his inhibition that separates "his
sensual love" from "his celestial love." In truth, the method adopted by
the "French doctor" is not at all modern. It involves using the imagination to treat a malady of the imagination. Montaigne was already on to
this in the sixteenth century. The maneuver works. In the confusion of
the end of the late supper in his own palace, Emilio, a bit tipsy, slides
toward the bedroom of the actress; he is received by Massimilla, who,
following the doctor's orders, has accepted to play the role of la Tinti.
The pure idealized figure has descended "to the bed of a courtesan."
What takes place is an exchange of roles that finally makes sexual intercourse between the heroine and the adoring man possible. Is this
a myth out of Ovid? A rustic tale with a refined ending? Both in fact.
It is revealed the next day that in a further accident of crossing paths
Genovese obtained the favors of la Tinti and the latter has "cured" him
according to a prescription that she also received from the doctor. From
that moment, since he's no longer tormented by passion and especially
no longer seeking to "seduce" his partner "with the charms of an angelic method," the tenor regains perfect possession of his great talents

as a performer. He no longer loses his way in "wild gargling" ["gargouil-lades"] and is called back out on stage ("redemandé") by the public.

In the final scenes where the French doctor emerges as the person most in charge, Balzac raises questions about human desire, the heaven of the ideal, artistic invention, and performance. These pages are both laborious and hurried. Balzac discontinuously lays out his whole phi-losophy and recommends it at the very end to "understanding artists." This last apostrophe is extremely important. By addressing himself to artists and making them the addressees of his tale, Balzac reveals the intention that has motivated the whole work.

The scene on the piazzetta is worth returning to one more time. We must ask about the hesitation that seizes the French doctor before the beauty of the singing and the transfiguration of the landscape. Balzac presents him as "surprised" and meditating "like a learned professor struck by a phenomenon that overturns one of his fundamental axi-oms." Which one of the axioms of the doctor is put in danger? Balzac writes that along with his three friends he sees "the sky." This is the phenomenon. But what sky/*ciel* are we talking about?[71] Is it the one of religious faith? Subsequent statements by the doctor do not, in any case, allow one to conclude that he renounces his scientific and mate-rialist convictions. He has just heard a voice and melody that lead one to imagine a sky peopled with angels—a sky and a light that embellish the appearance of the earth and penetrate the "interior senses." This allows one to find it rather less paradoxical than it might otherwise seem when the doctor delivers an eloquent speech to his friend Ven-dramin who has implored him to come to the aid of his friend: yes, by his "ministry" he will reunite the sensual love and the celestial love of Emilio, but he thinks it "folly" to want to "abdicate heaven" ["abdiquer le ciel"] by making of his mistress "a female." In this poignant declara-tion, the doctor seems to defend the most traditional dualism and to place love before the dilemma that requires a choice between terrestrial "mire" and the ideal "that no force can realize here below." No force? Really? The doctor will name Titian and Raphael. He will invoke, as though presiding over a court of love, the cohort of "feminine figures" that were "creations wherein art battled victoriously with nature."[72]

One senses the element that provokes Balzac's hesitation. Uniting celestial love and sensual love in Emilio means replacing art and poetry with something inferior. In the doctor's judgment, the Ideal, the finest choice, from which Emilio turns away by wanting to possess Massimilla physically, is the one where he would be an artist in a relationship of thought [*pensée*] with this "divinity." This "finest choice" is the realm of dream that maintains the distance. If he had wanted, Emilio could have seen "his mistress always sublime and pure, always hear inside himself what we have just heard by the sea." But we see that Emilio Memmi no longer wants that. The doctor accurately noticed that, in his case, the two loves were separated by "a mountain of poetry." But it is for not having given all to poetry that the young man is finally culpable in the eyes of the learned doctor. As a philosopher the French doctor repudiates that which he is in the process of accomplishing as a scientist. As lover or husband of Massimilla, Emilio will only "mess up [*barbouiller*] this poetry" that should have been preserved in all its nobility. The word "*barbouillage*" belongs to the vocabulary of painting and suggests a failed work. In Balzac's world, one never possesses anything except at the price of losing something else or by consenting to some renunciation.[73] In this case, the loss of poetry takes the form of a long list of "angelic immaterial girls," famous figures of art or legend. They were mentioned as the "feminine figures" that the French doctor regretted seeing plunged "into the mire of the earth." Everything concludes with an allegorical cortege: "djinns, water sprites, fairies, sylphs of ancient times, the Greek muses," and so on. I only quote the beginning of the enumeration of imaginary figures that come to cry "around the bed of Massimilla." Interestingly, it is in this same sentence that Balzac apostrophizes the "understanding artists" to tell them that these figures "break their forms to come [to them]." In the aesthetic system defended here by Balzac, the imaginary antecedents, this museum, is considered very important.

One must wait until the very end of the story for the scene where the tenor sings "Ombra adorata" to develop all its consequences. There, the "sky" was glimpsed by the listeners, and that is precisely what the hero will lose as the price paid for the pleasure that he finds in the end with a Massimilla mistaken for la Tinti. In the nocturnal clouds into which the song "Ombra adorata" rises, the friends had seen angels whose wings made "religious agitations." In the denouement orchestrated by the "French doctor," the team of angels loses, the hero is victorious. Emilio's unwitting mistake released him from his inhibition: his Juno accepted to play an entirely different role in falling from her "blue sky" into "the bed of a courtesan." Emilio can no longer be compared, as he was at the beginning of the story, to "those angels to which painters give only a head and wings." He has deserted their company. During the night of his cure, he fathers a child, a denouement that the narrator declares "horribly bourgeois": "the duchess was big." Balzac has great respect for paternity, but there was another antithesis to be underscored here along with the others. In the running commentary with which Balzac escorts this story, he strongly opposes desire and pleasure. Briefly stated, desire, coming from the soul, is a *cause*, whereas pleasure is an *effect* of desire but derives from the body.[74] Balzac's philosophy—always dynamic, mixed with actual experience, and in search of itself—loses its way here in a tangled ball of abstract antitheses. Desire only becomes indestructible when it is directed at ideal figures produced by the imagination or by art. Perhaps out of consideration for the convictions of those men and women (especially Ève Hanska) for whom he is writing, Balzac finds it difficult to acquiesce fully to the "terrestrial."

Massimilla and Emilio reappear for only one brief instant within Balzac's work. Now husband and wife and traveling through France, they cross paths with Gambara and Marianna, who are begging on the Champs-Élysées. They are charitable toward them, and Massimilla, in wonder at the genius of the unhappy musician, comments in melancholy tones: "This man remained faithful to the IDEAL that we killed."[75] This word was already explained in *Massimilla Doni* when the doctor, on Vendramin's request, accepts to intervene to reunite Emilio's "two loves" in order to save his life. It is a cautionary statement about what the impotent one will lose by dint of his cure. His admonishment, as we've seen, is the beginning of the enumeration of the imaginary figures that the narrator will pursue with the final assembly of mythic figures and fictional beauties crying "around the bed of Massimilla." And if one reads the doctor's statement attentively, one sees that the praise of art, which accompanies the wish for the persistence of desire, imposes maintaining a distance. There is a "sky" and luminous rays only for those who keep their distance: the eloquent impetus of the doctor arrives in singular fashion at a comparison borrowed from cosmology. The procedure can appear somewhat twisted and the comparison de-

batable, but one clearly sees the intention to prove concretely, materi-
ally, the danger that accompanies the wish to abolish the distance that
separates us from the "ideal."

> O feminine figures, finely wrought within a pure and luminous
> oval, that recall the creations where art battled victoriously with
> nature! Divine feet that could not walk, narrow hips that an
> earthly breeze would break, long torsos that will never conceive,
> virgins we glimpsed as they emerged from childhood, secretly
> admired, hopelessly adored, enveloped with some tireless desire;
> you, whom we no longer see but whose smile dominates our entire
> existence, what Epicurean swine has never wanted to plunge you
> into the mire of the earth! Eh! Sir, the sun only shines on earth
> and warms it because it is thirty-three million leagues away; go
> closer, science will teach you that it is neither hot nor light.[76]

The cause defended by the French doctor is that of the distance
to be maintained between ourselves and the imaginary perfections to
which we owe fidelity. These statements are immediately approved of
by Capraja, who has enclosed his life within an intellectual relation to
beauty: he cites as an example Dante's Beatrice, "queen of the poet's
fantasies" "made forever younger by unquenched desires." This apology
on behalf of distance and the courtly *amor de longh* is also an allusion
to the distance that at the same time separates Balzac from Ève Hanska—a distance that the author wants to abolish at any price, an effort
that will lead to his own destruction.[77]

The sun is certainly neither hot nor luminous for a human eye
and body that, in getting too close, would be consumed. What is the
knowledge worth that Balzac throws out here rather epigrammatically?
The answer hardly matters. What is certain is that the French doctor
draws on the authority of science and affirms that it "serves a purpose." Balzac wants to make it pronounce a double negation. For one
who wants to "go closer," "the sun is *neither* hot *nor* light." One may
conclude that here, as on other occasions, Balzac is linking science
to the idea of nothingness [*rien*]. It is worth recalling, for example,
the peremptory assertion in the *Théorie de la démarche* (1833): "If you
look closely into all human affairs, you will find the frightening antagonism of two forces that produces life but that leaves to science

only negation when it comes to any formulation. Nothing will be the perpetual epigraph of our scientific investigations."[78] One must also reread the sentence concerning the rapture of the four who listen to "Ombra adorata" on the piazzetta: "These four very different temperaments whose hopes were so poor, who believed in nothing, neither for themselves nor after them, who considered themselves lightly as passing, capricious forms, like a blade of grass or some sort of beetle—they glimpsed heaven ["Ces quatre esprits . . . entrevirent le ciel"]. Music for them therefore merits "its epithet as divine." And yet it is nothing ("ne croire à rien"—"four . . . who believed in nothing") that has the overriding place in their fundamental attitude. Faith has disappeared, replaced by the idea of existing only as the effect of a material necessity. Does Balzac want to tell us that thanks to the perfection of the singing, the thrust of desire and the quest for internal light can be constructed out of nothing, from the absence of any expectation of a beyond? That in melody there is a force that transcends and transfigures the nothing/*le rien*?

I am tempted to believe that this thought of Balzac's receives an extended and radicalized elaboration in the sentences that Mallarmé will write less than thirty years later: "Yes, *I know it*, we are only vain forms of matter—but quite sublime ones to have invented God and our soul. So sublime, my friend, that I want to give myself this spectacle of matter having consciousness of itself, and madly advancing toward the Dream that it knows itself not to be, singing the Soul and all the same divine impressions that have gathered in us from the earliest ages, and proclaiming before the Nothing that is the truth, this glorious illusion [*mensonge*]! This is the plan of my Lyric volume."[79]

"*Rien*" is a word that occurs in both texts. And the reductive affirmation is pronounced in a rather similar way, though with very significant differences as well: "passing, capricious forms," says Balzac, while Mallarmé writes, "vain forms of matter." This is a discovery for us, belated readers, but this resemblance is too indicative of the spirit of the entire period for us to speak of "sources" or "intertextuality" in this case.[80] Other similarities can also be noticed in the function assigned to a certain "music." The vision of the "sky" in Balzac seems to arrive by virtue of song, and, despite the absence of all hope, that vision does not exclude the nothing of "ne croire à rien"—"believing in nothing." The dream in the text of the young Mallarmé effectively originates out of the consciousness of nothing. Its ontological status is that of a lie or illusion [*mensonge*] that claims the only legitimate "glory." Its aesthetic status is that of song, the lyric will whose ambition is to "reclaim from music its wealth." After the utterance of nothing, there is, on the one hand, the rebound of desire, the narrative fertility that consumes Balzac, and, on the other, the enterprise of "digging into verse" ["creuser le vers"] and the impossible Book through which Mallarmé supposedly wished to equal the world.

In *Massimilla Doni*, Genovese is only a performer and not the inventor of the melody he is singing. But for Balzac the job of execution is of capital importance and is part of creative action. He says this in a discussion of sculpture on a famous page from *La Cousine Bette*: conception and execution are "the two hemispheres of Art." Balzac writes, "The hand must advance at every moment and be ready at every moment to obey the head. The head, however, has no more the creative dispositions at its command than is love continuous."[81] Similarly, what is required of the singer is the obedience of the voice. The failure and the success of Genovese—his fiasco onstage and his rediscovered mastery later on the piazzetta—correspond to the loss and recovery of cerebral command. Balzac stated this most clearly in 1837 in a letter to Ève Hanska: "*Massimilla Doni* and *Gambara* in the *Philosophical Studies* feature the appearance of music, under the double form of *execution* and *composition*, submitted to the same test as *thought* in *L[ouis] Lambert*, namely, the work and the execution destroyed by the overabundance of the creating principle, and this dictated to me *The Unknown Masterpiece* for painting."[82] In this story, the elderly Frenhofer, who wants to make a perfect work, exhausts himself excessively in the "poetry" of the conception and especially in the execution. By multiplying the layers of paint, he allows himself to slip into a "slow and progressive destruction" of the painting he has been working on for ten years.[83] Balzac's verdict is clearly marked at the end of the story with the unrelenting repetition of the word "*rien*" that continues until we get the disconcerted exclamation of Frenhofer, "So then, I will have produced nothing." The nothing/*rien*, this time, cannot be transcended. Nicolas Poussin, the young visitor, will have found in this a lesson, at the price of the loss (the sacrifice) of the young woman he loved, as so often happens in Hoffmann. The "nothing" reappears, in another aspect, when the small beggar's bowl of the composer Gambara on the Champs-Élysées comes back "empty" whereas his ambition had been to compose a total work of art, and there remains of it only scraps. The past participle "burned" ["brulé"], which appears in the last sentence of "The Unknown Masterpiece" ("he had burned all his canvases."), is also the last word in "Gambara" ("L'eau est un corps brulé"—"Water is a burned body"). The *"rien"* punctuates the furious exclamations of Sarrasine at the moment when, understanding finally that Zambinella is a castrato, he threatens to kill the enchanting being with whom he'd fallen in love: "You are nothing" . . . "You who can give life to nothing."[84] But we should keep in mind the reappearence of an enchanting voice in the person of Zambinella's great-niece, the return of Antinous-like beauty in the great-nephew, the strange survival of the statue that Sarrasine modeled, that he sought in vain to destroy and that, from copy to copy, became a marble, then an *Adonis* of Vien, then the *Endymion* by Girodet—all this makes one wonder not only about what Roland Barthes called "the aesthetic duplication of bodies" but also about the singular paths of life and the artistic descendants of this *"rien"* that Sarrasine got stuck on in his moment of desperation, just before being stabbed by the agents of Zambinella's protector.[85] Images lead to other images. And this is probably one of the elements of the fantastic in this Balzac story. Sarrasine, at the moment he makes the discovery, cannot stand the fact that Zambinella is already an image, a product of negation-castration, and not a being carrying within himself the origin of self whose image Sarrasine wanted to be the first to have formed. Besides the actress, he would have wished to accede to a real person, but she is already a "creature" in the pejorative sense, a product of artifice.

Let us return to the piazzetta and reread the commentary that Balzac constructs on the enchantment exerted by the perfect execution of "Ombra adorata." It has led us from nothing ("these four spirits who believed in nothing") to the vision of "angels whose wings expressed adoration." There is a big gap between the two. But at the end the gap is no smaller when the narrator reveals the inner thoughts of the singer:

But what a terrible awakening the vanity of the tenor was preparing for these noble emotions.

"Am I a bad singer?" said Genovese after finishing the aria.

All of them regretted that the instrument was not a celestial object. So then this angelic music resulted from a feeling of wounded pride. The singer felt nothing [*rien*], he was no more thinking of the pious feelings or of the divine images that he produced in others' hearts than a violin can know what Paganini is making it say. All had wanted to see Venice lifting up its shroud and singing itself, and it was really only about the fiasco of a tenor.[86]

"He felt *nothing*." Here is what is so dismaying about the singer. His listeners suddenly fall from a great height when they discover the motivation behind the production of this sublime moment. Genovese was not thinking of angels; he just wanted to salvage his reputation as a performer. Solely his personal interest was involved—a disappointing foundation indeed! What he wanted was the recognition of his superiority. As though peeking through a hole in the back of the stage, his listeners get a glimpse of the professional pride of a man of the theater who has worked hard to master his craft and who is fighting for his just recognition. One of the listeners, the fantastical and subtle Capraja, finds a way to explain Genovese's misadventure by way of some Diderot-inspired principles that I cited earlier: the actor must not be "full of the passion he wishes to express," he must "be its image." Art's mission is not to express but to represent. But into every successful performance there slides the nothing that makes it free by discharging it from all obligations of subjective concordance. The successful feint does not require the concerted investment of the self. We see here, then, the emergence of a creative function of the nothing and of negation. (According to Balzac's philosophy, it is the expenditure of spirit that is dangerous.)

"Nothing" is thus at work in different ways at both ends of this page. On the one hand, the effect of art is to surmount the "*rien*" of disbelief by creating an ideal with which the spirits who believe in "nothing" can form a relationship. But, on the other hand, this new relationship is only able to come into being thanks to execution: the artist produces the image by separating it from all passion ("the thing itself") that he harbors within his personal existence. He just has to be a beautiful instrument. The artist has to apply his hand or his voice (or his whole body in the case of an actor) to making a second object exist independent of the feelings that preoccupy him. To engage in this negation is not an act of abolition but of distancing, transmuting, or, as Spinoza said, determining. The nothing (Keats's "negative capability") is the collaborator of the artist that gives form and makes forms move. It is when music takes on words that it becomes clear that the words are not "the thing itself" and neither are they when they are just being whispered. These matters that were already central for the romantics will occupy the aesthetic thinking of modernists for a long time.[87]

At no point does the aria Genovese sings seem to have recalled in the minds of the listeners the dramatic situation of Romeo taking poison that is Zingarelli and Crescentini's point of departure. Genovese's friends are not remembering an opera but levitating toward the divine. The "simple and naive melody" (whose smoothness inspired in Berlioz only a reluctant respect) awakens religious ideas that Balzac illuminates insistently without any fear of redundancy. He speaks of "consoling sounds," "light," "angelic music," "pious feelings," "divine images," and a "saintly passion." As with Hoffmann, one sees the deployment of an all-embracing spirituality whose contours are as imprecise as its center is ineffable. When the divine manifests itself not only by means of music but in the music itself, the theological distinctions become blurred. Is music the messenger of a higher world? Of the depths of the soul? Or of the intimate secret of nature? Is it not all these things at once? Given this expansive exaltation linked for all four listeners to the singing voice, the tenor's return to ordinary speech and his egocentric question, "Am I a bad singer?" produce disenchantment. An abrupt fall interrupts the fervent expansion. It is a return to the prose of the world. This fall is all the more painfully disappointing when one recalls that this quasi-religious ecstasy was overlaid with another sentiment, namely, a patriotic nostalgia for lost glory and liberty, the idea of a funeral dirge for and by Venice itself.

We can easily discern the romantic clichés—religious and patriotic—that command the ecstasies and nostalgias that Balzac attributes to the tenor's audience at the opera and before the lagoon. And yet there are questions one might raise precisely because of the banality of these clichés. How is it that "Ombra adorata," the aria of a lover who hopes to rejoin his beloved beyond the grave, could become a contemplative prayer addressed to heaven or an invocation addressed to the dying homeland? The expected, and in part justified, answer would be that the spirit of the age favored the return of religious themes and that the mythical Elysium of the librettist Foppa lent itself easily to a vertical transposition toward the heavenly skies gazed at by fervid believers. Was not the return of "religious ideas" desired at the time by a number of writers and by a rather large section of the reading public? One also encounters at this time the question of the sacerdotal function of poetry and art. Was this uniquely a wish to recognize a realm of spirit beyond the reality of the world, or was it a reconciliation with a sacredness on which Enlightenment thinking had turned its back, and therefore a type of conversion? I would admit such a reading on condition that one also join to it an inverse reading. Art's return to the religious is just as much an aestheticization of the religious that coincides with art's appropriation of religion's magisterial authority. One could just as well say that, for some, religion found in art its worldly salvation and the proof of its legitimacy.[88] Just as later, with Nietzsche, we will see an aestheticization of philosophical thinking and morality. Going back over the music-related short stories of Balzac, one finds in them no expression of transcendence (or of the divine) except in art, there is no spiritual register other than art. The ideality in *Massimilla Doni* is paired with legendary images and pieces of music—in truth, an entire pantheon—of the kind that Balzac would like to assemble in the rue Fortunée to welcome Ève Hanska.

In the long central section of the story Balzac gives us the representation of Rossini's *Mosè in Egitto* with commentary from beginning to end by Massimilla. There is a great distance between the sacred book of Exodus and its most modern image as represented in Rossini's opera. Massimilla brings them somewhat closer by declaring that she listens to this opera as though it were an oratorio.[89] She thus attributes to it a sacred status. *Mosè in Egitto* is Passover. The event of the evening is a *representation* of this and refers to the founding moments of a faith and a people. But the image is now taking place on the stage of La Fenice. It becomes entirely dependent on the genius of a composer and the talent of a troupe of actors. The religious authority of Scripture is replaced by a spectacle whose aesthetic value receives confirmation through the approval of a "public" according to the rules of a social ceremony.[90] Balzac borrows Stendhal's definition of the opera box in Italy: "a small living room with a window that looks out on the orchestra seats."[91] The fate of an opera is decided by the reactions of those in the orchestra seats and by the conversations in the boxes: a work that isn't able to move and please can flop. In the position of explicator and umpire given to Massimilla by Balzac we see her praise the beauties of a very recent first performance (the action of the story takes place in 1820 and Rossini's *Mosè* dates from 1818). At the same time, we see Massimilla enthusing about the action that takes place onstage. It is the story of a people that comes together and rescues itself from oppression. Its relevance to Italy's political situation is immediate. Balzac's description covers the movements in the room and the exclamations of the audience. The transfer of the sacred has not only taken place from the religious (the book of Exodus) to the aesthetic (the opera) but also from the aesthetic to the political. Balzac joins a profuse tirade by Massimilla to the "prayer of the Hebrews." One sees the music hold in its sway both religious feeling and national hope.

> It seems that in climbing toward heaven, the song of this people freed from slavery meets the singing descending from celestial spheres. The stars answer joyously to the giddiness of the rescued earth. . . . Do you not believe you see the heavens half open, angels armed with their golden sistrums, seraphim prostrate, waving their censers filled with perfume, and archangels leaning on their flaming swords fresh from vanquishing the impious? The secret of this harmony that refreshes the mind belongs, I believe, to a few rare human works; that harmony throws us for a moment into the infinite, we sense it, we glimpse it within those limitless melodies like those sung around the throne of God. . . . From there we perceive a promised land where our eyes, caressed by soft celestial light, immerse themselves unobstructed. . . . Sing, says the duchess, hearing the last stanza executed as it was heard, with a somber enthusiasm; sing, you are free.[92]

Balzac mobilizes all celestial hierarchies. Some hours later, as we've seen, the angels are still present at the piazzetta. So many glances to an opening sky and toward celestial beings prove that romantic literary language possesses a rather limited stock of images to translate music's surpassing of speech. As rich as language may be, it is by definition inadequate when it comes to naming the "beyond language," the signification linked to the melody that transcends the verbal meaning of an aria or lied. Balzac's language deploys, with minor differences, the same strategy of hyperboles both to describe the superb choral prayer of a liberated people and to praise the solo wherein is released the fascination of death transfigured.

In the commentary he attributes to Massimilla, Balzac alludes to the perpetual hosanna of the angels in Dante's *Paradise* (song 28). But one must not think only of "sources." One must also think of what echoes with another text from within the world in which the first was written, because a feeling can be expressed by many voices during the same period. When the inaccessible (then too accessible) Massimilla evokes the "infinite" and the "limitless melodies" of the angels, one might remember that in the year that Balzac's text is published there is someone in Paris who will also have his own idea, but quite a different one, of "infinite melody": Richard Wagner, whom I mentioned was present on December 15, 1839, at one of the performances of Berlioz's "dramatic symphony," *Roméo et Juliette*. On its own, the "*Scène d'amour*" of Berlioz could have awakened or confirmed in the young Wagner the idea of infinite melody. He did not need to have read Balzac's short story, which had just appeared, to think of it. The contiguity is accidental, just as it is accidental, though significant for us at this late hour of our reflections, that Wagner would seem to have chosen Venice and the Palazzo Vendramin as his place to die in 1883. Chance creates superimpositions for those who want to notice them.

To which one may add that great works render visible their precursors. I confess, it took the *Liebestod* [*la mort d'amour*] of Isolde for me to be able to think of reading the song of Romeo as a *Liebestod*. And if in the literary commentaries of Hoffmann and Balzac I was able to discern signs of an aestheticization and then a politicization of the religious, it is because Wagner's *The Art Work of the Future* (1895), *Religion and Art* (1897), and *Parsifal* (1857, 1882) would provide the most explicit proofs. In the future being prepared by the aestheticization and the politicization of the religious, we would see appear in gala performances, notably in 1930s Bayreuth, warlords far more brutal than Napoleon.

This transformation of the status attributed to art and the authority that one sought to give it by making it the inheritor of an earlier theological authority came about along with many other intellectual and social changes that it would be necessary to describe conjointly in a synoptic presentation of their mutual relationships. I took the opposite approach believing that the inclination of a period can be recognized by following the thread of a "simple and naive melody" and by paying attention to the literary invention that echoed it.

NOTES

1. SINGING AND SEDUCING

1. All quotations from the Bible are from the King James Version. Unless otherwise noted, all translations are mine. Whenever possible, in quoted material, I have used English equivalents that are well known and readily available. Also, since cultural literacy today is more heterogeneous than it once was, and since the "*culture générale*" of an educated French person is rather different from that of an educated "common reader" in other cultures, it seemed to me worthwhile to add some documentation that would help situate the artists and works of art discussed or simply mentioned in the present study. Therefore, at the risk of halting somewhat the smooth flow of the French original, I have included some dates between parentheses in the body of text, and in the notes I have added references to English editions of canonical texts and criticism. The titles of many non-French texts are given in English, not French. No note from the original French edition has been dropped, however, and all page references to the sources used by the author have been made available to the English reader who may find them useful. I am very grateful to Miles Clery-Fox, assistant music director at the Théâtre du Capitole in Toulouse, for his bilingual musical knowledge and many helpful comments on an earlier version of this translation.—Trans.

2. *Œuvres diverses de monsieur l'abbé de Chaulieu*, rev. ed. (London, 1740), 2:268.

3. La Bruyère, *Les Caractères*, 1:47.

4. *Dictionnaire de l'Académie française* (1748; Trévoux, 1753).

5. La Bruyère, *Les Caractères*, 1:47. See C. Kintzler, *Théâtre et opéra à l'âge classique: Une familière étrangeté* (Paris: Fayard, 2004).

6. Jean-Jacques Rousseau, *Œuvres completes* (Paris: Gallimard, Bibliothèque de la Pléiade, 1961), 2:1124.

7. Rousseau, "Opéra," in *Dictionnaire de la musique* (1768), in ibid. (1995), 5:948–962.

8. In the eighteenth century, "*substitut*" occurs rather infrequently and usually in a juridical context. Its present-day semantic field was mostly covered, then, by the word "*supplément*." According to dictionaries from that time, the idea of "*supplément*" as meaning "replacement" coexisted with its other meaning as "addition."

9. Rousseau, "Opéra," p. 951.

10. Rousseau, *Confessions*, ed. Patrick Coleman and trans. Angela Scholar (New York: Oxford University Press, 2000), 4:145.

11. Rousseau, *Julie; or, The New Heloise: Letters of Two Lovers Who Live in a Small Town at the Foot of the Alps*, trans. and ed. Philip Stewart and Jean Vache (Hanover, N.H.: University Press of New England, 1997), p. 48.

12. Like English, the French language has the resource of modifying a noun with an adjective built from the present participle of a verb (e.g., "The *Flying* Dutchman"), which in these two instances would give "une gorge enchantante" and "cette musique enchantante." Rousseau's decision to use instead the noun *"enchanteresse"* (enchantress) as an adjective has the effect of personifying the two nouns in question—"throat" and "music"—and in this way makes them into agents of enchantment.—Trans.

13. Rousseau, *Julie*, p. 109.

14. Jean-Jacques Rousseau, *La Nouvelle Heloïse*, in *Œuvres complètes* (Paris: Gallimard, Bibliothèque de la Pléiade, 1961), vol. 2.

15. Maurice Barrès, *Le Bi-centenaire de Jean-Jacques Rousseau* (Paris: Éditions de l'Indépendance, 1912).

16. Arthur Schopenhauer, *The World as Will and Representation*, vol. 3, sec. 52.

17. This is the idea presented by Hoffmann in his *Thoughts on the High Dignity of Music*, which is part of his *Kreisleriana*. Here and later I am quoting from the French translation by Albert Béguin (Paris: Fourcade, 1931), in this instance, p. 30.

18. Interest in Carlo Gozzi in German-speaking countries was already high as early as 1780. Gozzi, for his part, was keenly interested in Spanish literature and theater. Lorenzo Da Ponte became acquainted with Carlo and Gasparo Gozzi in Venice, and he wrote the libretto for *Così* with one of Carlo Gozzi's plays in mind, namely, *Le droghe d'amore*, which was itself partly inspired by the story of the "Curious Indiscreet Man" told by Cervantes in *Don Quixote*. On an analogous subject, Pasquale Anfossi wrote in 1783 a *Curioso indiscreto* for which Mozart composed interpolated arias. Thanks to Hoffmann's commentary, Gozzi, whose work invites an expanded conception of the marvelous, allows one to understand the common denominator that links *Così* and *The Magic Flute*.

19. Hoffmann, op cit., pp. 186 and 182.

20. Ibid., pp. 186 and 188.

21. Ibid., p. 159

22. Ibid., pp. 156–157.

23. Ibid. See Charles Baudelaire, "On Color," sec. 3 of *Salon de 1846*: "I do not know if any analogist has solidly established a complete spectrum of colors and feelings, but I remember a passage in Hoffmann that perfectly expresses my idea, and that will please all who sincerely love nature: 'It is not merely in dreams and in the mild madness that precedes sleep but when still awake and I hear music that I find an analogy and an intimate union among colors, sounds, and scents. It seems to me that all these things have been caused by the same ray of light and that they must come together in a marvelous concert.'"

24. Friedrich Nietzsche, *Fragments from the 1880s*, in *Werke*, 3 vols., ed. Karl Schlechta (Munich: Karl Hanser Verlag, 1956), 3:647.

25. Carl Dahlhaus, *Les Drames musicaux de Richard Wagner*, trans. Madeleine Renier (Liège: Mardaga, 1994), pp. 13–26; Carl Dahlhaus, *Richard Wagner's Music Dramas*, trans. Mary Whittall (Cambridge: Cambridge University Press, 1992). The quotation here is translated from the French.

26. Heinrich Heine, *Aus den Memoiren des Herren von Schnabelewopski* (1831). If one pursues the different versions of the legend, it would seem that Heine was the first, in 1834, to introduce the theme of redemption through love in his *Memoirs of M. de Schnabelewopski*. See Dahlhaus, *Richard Wagner's Music Dramas*, p. 21.

27. *Fragments from the 1880s*, p. 647. The word "*ténébreux*" appears in French in Nietzsche's text.

28. I am thinking here of the beautiful tale of Hoffmann, "*Die Bergwerke zu Falun*" ("The Mines of Falun"), which inspired a dramatic poem by Hugo von Hofmannstahl.

29. See *Der Tannhäuser*, inserted in the chapter "Gods in Exile" in the book on Germany that appeared in 1836 and more completely in 1837 in volume 3 of *Salon* within the ensemble entitled *Elementargeister*.

30. The spectator is called to remember by contiguity the *Ave verum corpus* by Mozart that salutes the body of Christ taken down from the Cross, "cujus latus perforatum / Aqua fluxit et sanguine." This refrain is sung during mass at the moment of Elevation. The myths of the Spear and the Grail go back to the same New Testament source, John 19:34–35.

31. *Parsifal*, act 3, final scene, v. 387. The Greek myth of Telephus (son of Hercules and Auge) tells of a cure obtained according to the same principal. See Jean Starobinski, *Le Remède sans le mal* (Paris: Gallimard, 1989), pp. 165–205.

32. This is the interpretation proposed by Nietzsche in "The Religious Phenomenon," part 3 of *Beyond Good and Evil*, sec. 47. One must remember that speculations about the personality of a fictional character are always the result of a compromise between the text of an author and the projections of a receiver (reader, listener, spectator).

33. Torquato Tasso, *Jerusalem Delivered*, song 16, verses 10 and 11; song 18, verses 17 and 18; and song 16, verses 51 and 53.

34. In the program of the Bayreuth festival for 1975, Claude Lévi-Strauss mentions that Wagner's flower maidens are taken from an episode in *The Alexander Romance* (a text reprinted in Levi-Strauss's *Le Regard éloigné* [Paris: Plon, 1983]). But is that not also the antecedent of the description of Armida's gardens and the episode of the "enchanted forest" in Tasso's *Jerusalem Delivered?* The paths of borrowings and lineage are often multiple.

35. See Georges Liébert, *Nietzsche et la musique* (Paris: PUF, 2000).

36. Nietzsche, *The Gay Science*, book 4, sec. 309. See also *Ecce Homo*, "Why I am so Clever," sec. 5: "I would not for the world erase from my life the days at Tribschen."

37. Nietzsche, *Werke*, 3:1023.

38. See Rüdiger Safranski, *Nietzsche: Biographie d'une pensée*, trans. Nicole Casanova (Paris: Actes Sud, 2000), p. 48. In English, Rüdiger Safranski, *Nietzsche: A Philosophical Biography* (New York: Norton, 2003).

39. Nietzsche, *Werke*, 3:1019.

40. Ibid., 3:1023.

41. Nietzsche, *The Birth of Tragedy*, sec. 19.

42. Quotations from *The Case of Wagner*, passim.

43. Nietzsche, *Werke*, 2:105, 3:785 and 1305.

44. See Safranski, *Nietzsche*, p. 93–94.

45. Nietzsche, *Werke*, 3:295.

46. Nietzsche, *On the Genealogy of Morals*, trans. Walter Kaufman and R. J. Hollingdale (New York: Vintage, 1989), p. 103.

47. "*Lohengrin* is the tragedy of 'the absolute artist.'" (Dahlhaus, *Richard Wagner's Music Dramas*, p. 48).

48. Tomas Tranströmer, "Funeste gondole n. 2," in *Baltiques . . .* , trans. Jacques Outin (Paris: Gallimard, 2004), p. 304. The title of this poem alludes to a piano work by Liszt that is close to atonal and known in French under the title "Gondole funèbre."

49. Nietzsche, *On the Genealogy of Morals*, pp. 107–108. Nietzsche is parodying the expression of Cicero "*Pereat mundus, fiat justitia*"—"May the world perish, let there be justice."

50. Ibid., sec. 7.

51. Ibid., sec. 8.

52. Nietzsche, *Werke*, 3:1351.

53. See Nietzsche, *The Case of Wagner* and *Nietzsche Contra Wagner*, in *Werke*, 2:901–926 and 1037–1061. For the French translation with commentaries, I have used *Œuvres*, 2 vols., ed. Jean Lacoste and Jacques Le Rider, Bouquins (Paris: R. Laffont, 1995), 2:893–930 and 1201–1232; the text cited comes from p. 1214. The afterword by Georges Liébert, "*Nietzsche et la musique*," pp. 1453–1552, is very worthwhile.

54. In italics in the original.

55. *Jerusalem Delivered*, song 16.

2. THE DA PONTE OPERAS

1. Charles Rosen, *Classical Style: Hayden, Mozart, Beethoven* (New York: Norton, 1972).

2. Mozart, *Briefe und Aufzeichnungen*, 7 vols., ed. Wilhelm A. Bauer and Otto Erich Deutsch (New York: Bärenreiter, 1962–) letter 419, 2:265.

3. E. T. A. Hoffmann, *Kreisleriana*, pp. 173–174.

4. Mozart, *Briefe*, letter 633, 3:166–168.

5. Lorenzo Da Ponte, *Memoirs of Lorenzo Da Ponte*, trans. Elisabeth Abbott (New York, 1957; reprint, New York Review Books, 2000), p. 128.

See the bibliographical entries provided by Michel Oncel in volume 3 of his *Trois livrets pour Mozart* (Paris: Flammarion, 1994). Cf. Aleramo Lanapoppi, *Un certain Da Ponte*, trans. D. Autier (Paris: Liana Levi, 1991).

6. E. T. A. Hoffmann, *The Poet and the Composer*, in *E. T. A. Hoffmann's Musical Writings: Kreisleriana; The Poet and the Composer; Musical Criticism*, ed. David Charlton, trans. Martyn Clarke (Cambridge: Cambridge University Press, 1989), p. 205.

7. See Harald Goëtz, "*Da Ponte—era egli un poeta?*" in *Convergo mozartiano* . . . , Atti dei convegni dei Lincei 98 (Rome: Accademia nazionale dei Lincei, 1993), pp. 27–30.

8. Rousseau, *La Nouvelle Héloïse*, part 1, letter 52.

9. Rousseau, *Dictionnaire de la musique*, pp. 837–838.

10. Rousseau, "Opéra," in ibid., p. 955.

11. See Henri de Curzon, *XVIIIe siècle: La vie artistique, La musique* (Paris: Plon, 1914), pp. 164–166.

12. Beaumarchais, "Aux abonnés de l'opéra qui voudraient aimer l'opéra," in *Théâtre complet* (Paris: Magnard, 1952), pp. 164–166.

13. Mozart, *Briefe*, 3:167.

14. Alfred Einstein, *Mozart: L'homme et l'œuvre*, trans. J. Delalande (Paris: Gallimard, 1991), p. 487. In English, Alfred Einstein, *Mozart: His Character, His Work*, trans. Arthur Mendel and Nathan Broder (Oxford: Oxford University Press, 1951). The quotation here is translated from the French.

15. Da Ponte, *Memoirs*, p. 155.

16. Ibid., p. 158 and part 3.

3. THE MARRIAGE OF FIGARO

1. Denis Diderot and Antoine Bemetzrieder, *Leçons de clavecin et principes d'harmonie* (1771).

2. Lorenzo Da Ponte, *Memoirs of Lorenzo Da Ponte*, trans. Elisabeth Abbott (New York, 1957; reprint, New York Review Books, 2000), p. 129.

3. Lorenzo Da Ponte, *Mémoires*, trans. M. C. D. de La Chavanne, ed. Raoul Vèze (Paris: Jonquières, 1931).

4. REGISTERS OF EXCESS

1. Pierre Jean Jouve, *Le Don Juan de Mozart* (Fribourg: LUF, 1942).

2. Michel de Montaigne, "Sur Caton le Jeune," chap. 36 of *Essais*, book 1.

3. Jean Rousset, *Le Mythe de Don Juan* (Paris: Armand Colin, 1978), pp. 130–168 (bibliography). See Enèa Balmas, *Il mito di Don Giovanni nel Seicento francese*, 2 vols. (Milan: Cisalpino Goliardica, 1977–1978).

4. Sören Kierkegaard, *Ou bien . . . ou bien . . .* (Paris: Gallimard, Tel, 1984). In English, Sören Kierkegaard, *Either/Or*, trans. Howard V. Hong and Edna H. Hong (Princeton: Princeton University Press, 1988).

5. Melchior Grimm, "Poème lyrique," in *Encyclopédie* (Paris, 1765), vol. 12.

6. Rousseau, *Julie*, p. 109.

7. Charles Baudelaire, *Richard Wagner et Tannhäuser à Paris*, in *Œuvres complètes*, ed. Claude Pichois (Paris: Gallimard, Bibliothèque de la Pléiade, 1976), 2:796.

8. Jouve, *Le Don Juan de Mozart*, pp. 104–105.

9. The remark is from Jean-Claude Arfouilloux, "*Mille e tre*," *Nouvelle revue de psychanalyse*, no. 43 (Spring 1991): 300.

10. Jouve, *Le Don Juan de Mozart.*, p. 105.

11. Ibid., p. 106.

12. Ibid., pp. 108–109.

13. Ibid., p. 270.

14. Georges Bataille, *L'Expérience intérieure* (Paris: Gallimard, 1943), p. 121.

5. *Così fan tutte*

1. Rousseau, *"Prima intenzione,"* in *Dictionnaire de la musique*, pp. 994–995.

2. Montesquieu, *Voyages*, vol. 1 of *Œuvres complètes*, 2 vols., ed. R. Caillois (Paris: Gallimard, Bibliothèque de la Pléiade, 1949), p. 724.

3. Denis Diderot, *Supplément au voyage de Bougainville*, chap. 3. These are the words spoken by Orou to l'Aumonier. See D. Diderot, *Contes et romans*, ed. M. Delon (Paris: Gallimard, Bibliothèque de la Pléiade, 2004), p. 556.

6. THE PROMISE OF IDOMENEO

1. This study has benefited from some valuable observations of Wolfgang Rehm.

2. See Eduardo Federico, *Dall'Ida al Salento: L'itinerario mitico di Idomeneo cretese*, Memorie, ser. 9, vol. 11, fasc. 2 (Rome: Atti della Accademia nazionale dei Lincei, 1999), pp. 255–418.

3. Fénelon, *Dialogues sur l'éloquence* 2, in *Œuvres de Fénelon*, 2 vols., ed. Jacques Le Brun (Paris: Gallimard, Bibliothèque de la Pléiade, 1983, 1997), vol. 1.

4. Ibid., 2:60–61. The notes appended to this and other passages signal the borrowings from the Bible, Virgil, and other sources. A complete translation of *Les aventures de Télémaque* by Tobias Smollett can be found under the title *The Adventures of Telemachus, the Son of Ulysses*, ed. O. M. Brack Jr. (Athens: University of Georgia Press, 1997).

5. Ibid., 2:119.

6. Women are not forgotten, but theirs is a subaltern position. They are to stay in their place, something the Queen of the Night does not do.

7. Fénelon, *Examen de conscience sur les devoirs de la royauté*, sec. 31, in *Œuvres*, 2:994. For a psychological analysis of *The Adventures of Telemachus*, see Henk Hillenaar, *Le Secret de Télémaque* (Paris: PUF, 1994), especially pp. 81–90.

8. Letter from Leopold Mozart to Lorenz Hagenauer, May 16, 1766. See Mozart, *Briefe*, 1:220: "Habe . . . in Cambray das Grabmal des grossen Fénelons, und seine marmorne Brustbild-Säule betrachtet, der sich durch seinen Telemach, durch das Buch von der Erziehung der Töchter, durch seine Gespräche der Todten, seine Fabeln und andere geistliche und weltliche Schriften unsterblich gemacht hat."

9. Mozart, *Briefe*, 1:388: "Izt lese ich Just den *telemach*, ich bin schon in zweyten theil" (I'm now reading *Télémaque*, I'm already in the second part). We may imagine that Mozart was reading an Italian translation.

10. A guardian figure in whom Mozart's father places overly high hopes. The *Correspondance littéraire is* prepared by Meister starting in 1775. It makes no mention of Mozart's stay in Paris in 1778. During the summer people are preoccupied with the

deaths of Voltaire and Rousseau. Moreover, Grimm is a cold and calculating man. He does not see Wolfgang and does nothing to advance his career in Paris. See his letter to Leopold Mozart of July 27, 1778, where he describes the fate of musicians who run around giving lessons in terms close to those found in *Rameau's Nephew*.

11. Mozart, letter of July 3, 1778, *Briefe*, 2: 389: "Man findet sehr schwehr ein gutes Poëme." It is in this letter that Wolfgang announces to his father the illness of his mother that would prove fatal.

12. *Correspondance littéraire*, December 1, 1763.

13. Ibid., March 1, 1764.

14. Varesco's act 2, scene 2, where Idomeneo offers his treasures to Ilia after having made the decision to push aside his son, only sketches out this conflict. On Grimm and Mozart, see Martin Fontius, "*Mozart chez Grimm et Mme d'Épinay*," *Recherches sur Diderot et sur l'Encyclopédie*, no. 9 (October 1990) 95–108. See also Daniel Heartz, *Mozart's Operas* (Berkeley: University of California Press, 1989).

15. In a *Lettre sur l'opéra* that probably dates from 1745 but was only discovered in the nineteenth century, Rousseau evokes the public's enthusiastic response to "the famous chorus in *Jephté*"; see Rousseau, *Œuvres* (1995), 5:257. He is referring to a piece with two choruses that quickly became famous. Rousseau also mentions it in the entry "Chœur" in his *Dictionnaire de la musique*, pp. 706–707, and he remembers having some difficulty understanding it in a salon in Chambéry (*Confessions*, book 5).

16. This theme is listed under the heading "First thing you meet" in Stith Thompson, *A Motif-Index of Folk Literature*, 6 vols. (Bloomington: Indiana University Press, 1966).

17. From the first act, the body of the god is an episodic pantomime role, dissociated from the Voice and from the grand priest who communicates his will.

18. This is also Fénelon's lesson, but it concerned only Idomeneus. He did not give up his power but renounced the arrogant satisfactions of glory; he adopted new principles, ones more equitable and respectful of the welfare of his people. In other words, he converted.

7. LIGHTS AND POWERS

1. See Jacques Chailley, "*La Flûte enchantée*": *Opéra maçonnique* (Paris: R. Laffont, 1968), as well as the studies by Alfred Einstein, Rémy Stricker, Jean-Victor Hocquard, and Brigitte Massin. Also of note, H.C. Robbins Landon, *1791: Mozart's Last Year* (New York: Schirmer, 1988). Recent publications include Dieter Borchmeyer, *Goethe, Mozart und "Die Zauberflöte"* (Munich: Karl Hanser Verlag), 1994; Dieter Borchmeyer, *Mozart und die Entdeckung der Liebe* (Frankfurt: Suhrkamp, 2005); and the study of the Egyptologist Jan Assmann, "*Die Zauberflöte*": *Oper und Mysterium* (Munich: Karl Hanser Verlag, 2005).

2. According to Jacques Chailley (ibid., p. 135), the fainting symbolizes the death of the self that must precede the initiation tests.

3. *Le Cabinet des fées* is the name of an enormous collection (forty-one volumes) of tales compiled between 1785 and 1789 by the chevalier Charles-Joseph de Mayer (1751–1789) and published in Amsterdam. It served as a rich treasury for

generations of readers and consolidated the reputation of several authors, notably Perrault.—Trans.

4. In the eighteenth century young women were not advised to learn much.

5. Saint-Just, *Rapport relatif aux personnes incarcérées* (A report on prisoners), March 8, 1794.

6. This gift to Sarastro is the motive for the hatred that the Queen of the Night has for him. It implies the submission of women to the initiated. For more on its importance, see act 2, scene 8.

7. This is the central thesis of Jacques Chailley's study.

8. See Jean Starobinski, *Les Emblèmes de la raison* (1973), forthcoming in a new edition from Gallimard.

9. Goethe, *Singspiele*, in *Sämtliche Werke*, 8 vols., special anniversary edition (Stuttgart: Cotta, 1862), 8:310–311. See the study by Hugo von Hofmannsthal on Goethe's *Singspiele* in *Prosa*, vol. 4 of *Gesammelte Werke* (Frankfurt: S. Fischer Verlag, 1955), pp. 174–181.

10. Théâtre de la Monnaie, Brussels, April 1991.

8. POPPEA VICTORIOUS

1. Seneca, *Four Tragedies and Octavia*, trans. E. F. Watling (New York: Penguin, 2004), pp. 284–285.

2. Michel de Montaigne, "Que notre désir s'accroît par la malaisance," chap. 15 of *Essais*, book 2.

3. Tacitus, *The Annals of Imperial Rome*, trans. Michael Grant (New York: Penguin, 1996), p. 306.

4. The extracts from the libretto are from the translation by Michel Orcel: Monteverdi, *Le Couronnement de Poppée* (Paris: L'Avant-Scène Opéra, 1988). This volume also contains a complete bibliography.

5. Dante, *Paradise*, song 33, v. 145. This is the final verse of *The Divine Comedy*.

9. THE MAGIC OF ALCINA

1. See *Roland furieux* (1516), adapted and retold by Italo Calvino (Paris: Garnier-Flammarion, 1982); and *Roland furieux*, 2 vols., trans. Francisque Reynard, preface Yves Bonnefoy (Paris: Gallimard, 2003). See also Winton Dean, *Haendel and the Opera Seria* (London: Oxford University Press, 1970).

2. The original edition dates from 1664, prepared by Robert Ballard, sole printer of music for the king. A second edition, identical to the first, was printed at the beginning of 1665.

10. LOVE UNTO DEATH: ANOTHER *ROMEO*

1. For more on the different versions of the Romeo and Juliet story, see the final chapter in this volume, "Ombra adorata."

2. Prokofiev will want to recover this world in the opening sections of his ballet (1940).

3. I have used the Yves Bonnefoy translation of *Romeo and Juliet*: *Macbeth*, *Roméo et Juliette* (Paris: Gallimard, Folio, 1985). The citations in English can be found in any standard edition of the work.

4. A famous aria from the Foppa-Zingarelli opera, *Giulietta e Romeo* (1796), will be the principal focus of the final chapter, "Ombra adorata."—Trans.

11. MANON

1. Abbé Prévost, *Manon Lescaut*, ed. F. Deloffre and R. Picard (Paris: Garnier, 1965), p. 19. Subsequent quotations, in order, are from pp. 44, 21–22, 51, 50, 45, 43.

2. Abbé Prévost, *Manuel lexique* (Paris: Didot, 1750).

3. See Walter E. Rex, *The Attraction of the Contrary* (Cambridge: Cambridge University Press, 1987), pp. 1–25.

4. Montesquieu, *Le Spicilège*, no. 578, in *Œuvres complètes*, 3 vols. (Paris: Nagel, 1950–1955), 2:853.

5. The verb *"prétendre"* can mean "to pretend or play at," "to intend or plan," or "to claim."—Trans.

6. Jean Sgard, "Manon avec ou sans camélias," in *Littérature et Opéra*, ed. Philippe Berthier and Kurt Ringger (Grenoble: Presses Universitaires de Grenoble, 1987).

7. Jean Sgard, *L'Abbé Prévost: Labyrinthes de la mémoire* (Paris: PUF, 1986).

12. ARIANE AND BLUEBEARD; OR, THE USELESS RESCUE

1. On Béla Bartók's *Bluebeard's Castle* (1911, 1918), see Lydia Flem, *La Voix des amants* (Paris: Seuil, 2002), pp. 89–115.

2. Ruysbroeck l'Admirable, *L'Ornement des noces spirituelles*.

3. Olivier Messiaen, *"Ariane et Barbe-Bleue de Paul Dukas,"* *Revue musicale*, no. 166 (1936).

14. "OMBRA ADORATA"

1. *Journal de Delécluze, 1824–1828*, ed. Robert Baschet (Paris: Grasset, 1948), pp. 121–123. See Robert Baschet, *E.-J. Delécluze: Témoin de son temps, 1781–1863* (Paris: Ancienne Librairie furne Boivin et Cie, 1942). Étienne-Jean Delécluze (1781–1863) was above all a great journalist. A friend of Stendhal and Mérimée, he kept his distance from the romantic poets. When he died, Sainte-Beuve, disdainful and upset, devoted a long study to him while also keeping his distance (*Nouveaux Lundis* [Paris, 1865], 3:77–124).

2. Following the narrative retellings by Matteo Bandello and Luigi da Porta, the Foppa-Zingarelli opera title inverts the names from the customary order used "mistakenly" by Delécluze.—Trans.

3. Crescentini completed his career as a singing teacher at the conservatory in Naples. In the study "L'importation des solfèges italiens en France à la fin du XVIIIe

siècle," Sylvie Mamy lists six works by Crescentini (or under his name) published in France. See *L'Opera tra Venezia e Parigi*, ed. Maria Teresa Muraro (Florence: Olschki, 1988), pp. 67–89. Also attributed to Crescentini are collections of *canzonette*. See also the entry for Crescentini by V. Gualerzi and T. Seedorf in *Personalteil*, vol. 5 of the dictionary *Musik in Geschichte und Gegenwart* (Kassel: Bärenreiter, 2001). We may also recall that a very young Arthur Schopenhauer heard Crescentini in Venice in 1805 and made an admiring note of the occasion in his journal.

4. Las Cases, *Le Mémorial de Sainte-Hélène*, 2 vols., ed. Marcel Dunan (Paris: Flammarion, 1951), 2:408–409: "And what could have been the title of a Crescentini?" cried a "smooth talker" in a Parisian salon. "To which the beautiful Madame Grassini, rising majestically from her seat, replied with the most theatrical gesture and tone of voice, 'And *his wound*, then, sir, what account do you make of it?' . . . The emperor, hearing this anecdote for the first time, laughed a great deal." See also ibid., 1:742. Cf. Théo Fleischman, *Napoléon et la musique* (Brussels: Brepols, 1965); Jean-Claude Bonnet, ed., *L'Empire des muses* (Paris: Szomogy, 2004); and chap. 2 of Laurence Tibi, *La Lyre désenchantée: L'instrument de musique et la voix humaine dans la littérature française du XIXe siècle* (Paris: Champion, 2003), pp. 51–90

5. *La Canne de jonc* (1835) by the French writer Alfred de Vigny (1797–1863) is available in English as "Lights and Shades of Military Life." The opera by Domenico Cimarosa, *Gli Orazi e i Curiazi* (1797) tells the story of the tragic feud between the Horatii and the Curiatti, two sets of triplets.

6. *Mémoirs du docteur F. Antommarchi; ou, Les Derniers Moments de Napoléon*, 2 vols. (Paris: Barrois l'Aîné, 1825), 2:153–178.

7. Leo Tolstoy, *War and Peace*, trans. Louis Maude and Aylmer Maude (New York: Simon and Schuster, 1942), book 3, p. 312.

8. Delécluze, *Journal*. Delécluze does not classify the Shakespeare play among the finest works. In 1828 he published a "small book" on the history of Romeo and Juliet. In it he compared the Luigi de Porta story and Shakespeare's play and included translated extracts from both texts. The piece performed in Paris by the English troupe was itself an adaptation.

9. "*Pica*" is derived from "*la pie*," the magpie, and with allusion to this bird's voracity, it is defined as a morbid taste for inedible substances.—Trans.

10. Delécluze, *Journal*, p. 494.

11. See Arthur Pougin, *Marie Malibran: Vie d'une cantatrice* (Paris: Plon, 1911), pp. 53, 171.

12. Delécluze appears in the last pages of *Souvenirs d'égotisme* under the name M. de l'Étang.

13. I am referring to a note by Henri Martineau in his edition of Stendhal's *Le Rouge et le Noir*, 2 vols. (Paris: Cluny, 1942), 1:261.

14. Stendhal, *Rome, Naples et Florence en 1817* [1826], in *Voyages*, ed. V. del Litto (Paris: Gallimard, Bibliothèque de la Pléiade, 1973), p. 467. One must be cautious when it comes to the authenticity of the alleged meetings of Stendhal in this work. His meeting with Rossini at Terracina in January 1817, for example, is an invention.

15. Stendhal, *Rome, Naples et Florence en 1817* (1817), ed. H. Martineau (Paris: Le Divan, 1956), p. 32.

16. "Happy few" is in English in the original.—Trans.

17. On this point, see Massimo Colesanti, *Stendhal: Le regole del gioco* (Milan: Garzanti, 1983).

18. Published in English as *The Life of Rossini*, trans. Richard N. Coe (Seattle: University of Washington Press, 1972).—Trans.

19. Foppa was the author of eighty-two librettos including four for Rossini: *La scala di seta, Il signor Bruschino, L'inganno felice*, and *Sigismundo*.

20. I am using the original libretto of 1796 edited by Giovanni Batista in Milan, which is kept in the library of the conservatory of Milan. The indications of the tempi are taken from a version for voice and piano (a French edition with no date or press indications) in the archives of the Geneva conservatory library. My sincere thanks go to Maria Golub Majno and Jacques Tchamkerten for making these documents available to me.

21. Stendhal, *Vie de Rossini* [1824], 2 vols. (Paris: Le Divan, 1929), 2:168–169. Soon after its publication, the book fell into the hands of Eugène Delacroix, who read it attentively but took exception to the tone frequently adopted by Stendhal. On October 27, 1822, the author had noted the end of the previous day: "Madame Pasta in *Roméo*, which I saw again with great pleasure."

22. The expression is from Michel Schneider, who uses it as the title of the fine concluding chapter in his study *Prima Donna: Opéra et inconscient* (Paris: Odile Jacob, 2001), pp. 283–300. He underlines the fundamental importance of the feeling of loss in a great number of operas.

23. Stendhal, *Vie de Rossini*, 2:147.

24. Ibid., 2:148.

25. Ibid., 2:148–149.

26. He will speak of her again in the same terms in the seventh part of the *Souvenirs d'égotisme* (Paris: Le Divan, 1927): She is the only woman in whom "the tragic . . . was pure, perfect, and unblended. . . . Madame Pasta . . . played *Tancrède, Othello, Roméo et Juliette* . . . in a way that was not simply never equaled but that had certainly never been anticipated by the composers of these operas" (pp. 130, 126). Stendhal also says to his closest friends that "the way she had played Roméo in the last performance" was "an eternal subject of discussion" (p. 131). See Philippe Berthier, "Stendhal et la voix de Giuditta," in *Figures du fantasme: Un parcours dix-neuviémiste* (Toulouse: Presses Universitaires du Mirail, 1992); and Ph. Berthier, "Milan à Paris: L'opéra imaginaire," in *Espaces stendhaliens* (Paris: PUF, 1997), pp. 113–130.

27. Stendhal, *Vie de Rossini*, 2:192.

28. Ibid., p. 173. Stendhal published his *Life of Rossini* in the fall of 1823, long before Vaccai and Bellini (himself a student of Zingarelli) take up the subject of Romeo and Juliet. I have noticed that in *The Red and The Black* (vol. 1, chap. 23), the singer Geronimo, inviting himself to the home of the Rênals, charms his hosts by telling of how he managed to get himself thrown out of the Naples conservatory by the severe

"signor Zingarelli." In Balzac's story *Massimilla Doni*, the fictional singer Genovese is said to be a student of Velluti.

29. Stendhal, *Vie de Rossini*, 2:152. On this subject, see Michel Crouzet, *La Poétique de Stendhal* (Paris: Flammarion, 1983), pp. 209–218.

30. Stendhal, *Vie de Rossini*, vol. 2. On this subject, see the fine pages of Massimo Colesanti: *Stendhal*, pp. 53–171.

31. Stendhal affirms that the work was composed "around 1400," when in fact Allegri lived from 1582 to 1652! His *Miserere* for two choruses and nine voices was famous. The Vatican wanted to retain exclusive rights to it. The young Mozart transcribed it from memory in 1770. In Madame de Staël's *Corinne*, it is to hear the *Miserere* that the heroine and Lord Nelvil go to the Sistine Chapel on Good Friday. They are separated by an iron partition: "It seemed to her that it was in a moment of exaltation such as this that one would like to die" (*Corinne*, book 10, chap. 4).

32. Stendhal, *Vie de Rossini*, 2:288.

33. Ibid., p. 113.

34. Delécluze, *Journal*, pp. 464–465.

35. It is through Liszt's transcription that Robert Schumann learned of the Berlioz symphony. When Hugo Wolf did battle against pure music as defended by Brahms and Hanslick, he enlisted in support of his theses not only Wagner but also Liszt and Berlioz.

36. The major Romeo and Juliet adaptations that follow are Gounod's opera (1867), the overture by Tchaikovsky (1870), the Delius opera (1901) inspired by a G. Keller story, *Romeo and Juliet in the Village*, the Prokofiev ballet (1940), the musical and movie *West Side Story* by Leonard Bernstein (1957), and the operas by Riccardo Zandonai (1922), Heinrich Sutermeister (1940), and Pascal Dusapin (1988).

37. Hector Berlioz, "*Romeo and Juliette*, opéra en quatre actes de Bellini. Sa première représentation au théâtre de l'Opéra. Début de Mme Vestvali," *Journal des débats politiques et littéraires*, September 13, 1859, cited in *À travers chants*, 2d ed. (Paris: Michel Lévy, 1862), pp. 331–344; reprint, ed. Léon Guichard (Paris: Gründ, 1971), pp. 349–360. See also Berlioz's *Mémoires*, chaps. 18, 35, and 49. In 1831 during Carnival season in Rome, Berlioz sees on the Piazza Navona a "little man with a round belly and malicious smile who affects a serious air." It is Monsieur Beyle, "a man of spirit" who wrote "under the pseudonym Stendhal . . . the worst stupidities about music" (chap. 36).

38. Hector Berlioz, *Mémoires*, chap. 35. Berlioz nevertheless has great admiration for the final duet in unison in Bellini's opera where the two lovers promise to see each other again "in heaven" ["aux cieux"]: "These two voices, vibrating together like a single voice, a symbol of their perfect union, give the melody an extraordinary driving force; and either because of the framing of the melodic phrase and the way it was executed, or because of the unfamiliar but motivated character of this unison that one is far from expecting, or on account of the melody itself, I admit I was suddenly very moved and applauded with abandon."

39. Stendhal, *Notes d'un dilettante*, in *Vie de Rossini*, 2 vols., ed. Henry Prunières (Paris: Cercle du bibliophile, 1968), 2:300 (performance of September 29, 1824).

40. Ibid.

41. Ibid., p. 405.

42. Stendhal, *Souvenirs d'égotisme*, chap. 2, p. 8.

43. Hoffmann, *Kreisleriana*, pp. 18–23.

44. The only earlier work of importance is the story "Ritter Gluck" written in 1809, probably under the influence of the recent German translation of *Rameau's Nephew*. The story "Ombra adorata" appears for the first time in Hoffmann's *Fantasiestücke, Fantasy Pieces in the Manner of Callot* (1814).

45. E. T. A. Hoffmann, "Ombra adorata," in *Kreisleriana*, in *E. T. A. Hoffmann's Musical Writings: Kreisleriana, The Poet and the Composer, Musical Criticism*, ed. David Charlton, trans. Martyn Clarke (Cambridge: Cambridge University Press, 1989), vol. 1, book 2, p. 88.

46. Ibid., p. 89.

47. Ibid.

48. Ibid., pp. 89–90. This passage suggests that the manner of executing ornaments, including by Crescentini himself, was known about as far away as Bamberg! It should be recalled as well that the text "Höchst zerstreute Gedanken" ("Very Fragmented Thoughts"), which is also part of the *Kreisleriana* of 1814, was one of the sources for Baudelaire's "Correspondances."

49. Ibid., p. 90.

50. Ibid., pp. 90–91.

51. E. T. A. Hoffmann, *Tagebücher*, ed. Hans von Müllers, ann. Friedrich Schnapp (Darmstadt: Wissenschaftliche Buchgesellschaft, 1971), p. 147 ff.

52. Reference is being made to "El coloquio do los perros" (1613). See Miguel de Cervantes, *Novelas ejemplares II*, ed. Harry Sieber (Madrid: Catedra, 1995), pp. 297–359. In German, the story in question is entitled "Nachricht von den neuesten Schicksalen des Hundes Berganza" and is also referred to in English as "News of the Latest Fortunes of the Hound Berganza" (1814).—Trans.

53. E. T. A. Hoffmann, *Fantaisies dans la manière de Callot*, trans. Henri de Curzon, in *Intégrale des contes et récits*, ed. Albert Béguin and Madeleine Laval (Paris: Phébus, Verso, 1979), p. 159.

54. E. T. A. Hoffmann, "Le Poète et le compositeur," in *Kreisleriana* (1931), p. 185.

55. Hoffmann, *Fantaisies*.

56. Honoré de Balzac, *Mémoires de deux jeunes mariés*, part 16, in *La Comédie humaine* (henceforth *CH*), 12 vols., ed. Pierre-Georges Castex (Paris: Gallimard, Bibliothèque de la Pléiade, 1976), 1:267; *Béatrix*, in *CH* (1976) 2:746.

57. Balzac, *Massimilla Doni*, ed. René Guise, in *CH* (1979), 10:612 n. 1. I am greatly indebted to the edition prepared by Max Milner that includes the formerly unpublished original manuscript, an introduction, notes, and musical appendices (Paris: Corti, 1964).

58. E. T. A. Hoffmann, *Kreisleriana* (1931), p. 21; Balzac, *Massimilla Doni*, p. 583. Balzac had read "all of Hoffmann" (letter to Madame Hanska, November 2, 1833). See *Lettres à Mme Hanska*, 2 vols., ed. Roger Pierrot (Paris: R. Laffont, Bouquins, 1990). Two days earlier, he had compared himself to Kreisler in his admiration for Madame Vigano.

In the Balzac story the figure of the waterfall is given an explicitly erotic significance, notably on pages 560–561.

59. Balzac, *Massimilla Doni*, p. 611.

60. Ibid.

61. Balzac was perfectly aware of the fashionableness of these landscapes, which had become widely distributed "clichés" in the illustrated press of the day. During his Italian voyage of 1837, he arrived on a rainy day in Venice and was somewhat disappointed for reasons he explains to Clara Maffei: "The reason is all those miserable English engravings that circulate everywhere in souvenir books, and all those paintings by hundreds of miserable little genre painters that have so often shown me views of the ducal palace, the piazza, and the piazzetta" (*Correspondances*, ed. Roger Pierrot, 5 vols. (Paris: Garnier, 1960–1969), 3:265). See Arlette Michel, *Le Réel et la beauté dans le roman balzacien* (Paris: Champion, 2001), pp. 243–246.

62. Balzac wrote to Madame Hanska, "I have caressed nothing so much as that mythic page, because myth is profoundly lodged underneath reality" (*Lettres à Mme Hanska*, 1:412 n. 130.

63. Balzac, *Massimilla Doni*, p. 619.

64. On the various aspects of this debate at the beginning of the nineteenth century, see Nicolas Perot, *Discours sur la musique à l'époque de Chateaubriand* (Paris: PUF, 2000), pp. 91–146.

65. Starobinski's text quotes Balzac as saying "he brayed"—the French verb is "*bramer*"—"like a deer"—"*comme un cerf*," but in English, donkeys, not deer, bray, hence my modification. The verbs "to bray" and "bramer" derive from the same Old French verb, "*braire*": "to cry out."—Trans.

66. The name "Crespel" [*sic*] appears in a draft of *Entre savants*, in *CH* (1981), 12:523 n. 6.

67. In the Offenbach opera, the hallucinatory relation of Antonia to her mother is the invention of the librettists Barbier and Carré. This innovation is certainly admissible. See Michel Schneider's commentary in *Prima Donna*. In the Hoffmann tale, Antonia is placed between her father and the young composer B., her fiancé. They both end up losing her. Her dead mother had been a caricature of an Italian cantatrice.

68. E. T. A. Hoffmann, *Le Violon de Crémone*, in *Intégrale des contes et récits*.

69. Balzac, *Massimilla Doni*, p. 576.

70. Ibid. In fact, we have here another echo of Hoffmann. In the second series within the *Kreisleriana*, Hoffmann imagines an exchange of letters with Baron Wallborn, the hero of *Ixion*, a tale written by Hoffmann's friend La Motte Fouqué, also the author of *Ondine* and a libretto for an opera of the same name for which Hoffmann composed the music. The pseudo-Wallborn writes to Kreisler as follows: "Do not laugh, my dear Johannes. You must admit there is nothing more painful in life, nor more upsetting, than to find one's Juno change into a cloud! Ah! Cloud, cloud, beautiful cloud!" (*Kreisleriana* [1931], p. 89). As though he were replying to the "Do not laugh" of Hoffmann-Fouqué-Wallborn, Balzac has his "French doctor" behave sarcastically: "The Frenchman did what Frenchmen do at every opportunity: he began to laugh."

71. The potential for ambiguity is great in French since "*le ciel*" can designate either the physical sky or the metaphysical heaven.—Trans.

72. Balzac, *Massimilla Doni*, p. 614.

73. Emilio Memmi becomes the owner of his family palace upon the death of his relative Facino Cane in Paris in 1819. Condemned for murder in Venice, he had lived in exile. After going blind, he subsisted as a clarinetist in a café theater.

74. Balzac, *Massimilla Doni*, p. 566. See Pierre Brunel, "*Mosè* dans *Massimilla Doni*," *Année balzacienne* (1994), pp. 39–54.

75. Balzac, *Gambara*, in *CH* (1979), 10:516.

76. Balzac, *Massimilla Doni*, p. 614.

77. See Gaëton Picon, *Balzac par lui-même* (Paris: Seuil, Écrivains de toujours, 1956).

78. Balzac, *Théorie de la démarche*, in *Œuvres diverses*, 3 vols., ed. M. Bouteron and H. Longnon (Paris: Conrad, 1935–1940), 2:642–643.

79. Stéphane Mallarmé, letter to Cazalis, April 28, 1866.

80. Mallarmé had read Balzac. In a letter to Cazalis (April 25, 1864), he speaks of the phrase and of the fullness that must be given to it by the artist. He mentions *Seraphita* and Balzac's phrase, "digging amid the furthest depths and in the seventh heaven of mysticism."

81. Balzac, *La Cousine Bette*, in *CH* (1977), 7:241–242.

82. Balzac, *Lettres à Mme Hanska*, 1:382.

83. Balzac, *Le Chef-d'œuvre inconnu*, in *CH* (1979), 10:436–438. Hoffmann's "The Baron of B" is the model of failure coming at the moment when execution is supposed to confirm the theoretical reasoning, the conception. Disastrous execution is the principal link that must be made between "The Unknown Masterpiece" and "The Baron of B" ("Der Baron von B," 1819, also known in French as "L'Élève du grand Tartini").

84. Balzac, *Sarrasine*, in *CH* (1977), 6:1074.

85. Roland Barthes, *S/Z* (Paris: Seuil, 1970), p. 207.

86. In a draft version one reads, "All had wanted to see Venice raising her shroud and singing *Tranquillo io sono*." These three Italian words, no doubt borrowed from the Hoffmann text, must have seemed inappropriate to Balzac since they disappear from the definitive version of the story. These words from the aria cannot, it's true, be sung by Venice, which is the lost "object" (especially for Vendramin and Capraja). In the Crescentini-Foppa aria, these are the words of the lover who, at peace with his decision to die, prepares to reunite with his beloved in the afterlife.

87. This is the point of departure for the reflections of Maurice Blanchot. See Georges Poulet, *La Conscience critique* (Paris: José Corti, 1971), pp. 219–232.

88. On the debate that surrounded Chateaubriand's *Le Génie du christianisme*, see Perot, *Discours sur la musique*.

89. Balzac, *Massimilla Doni*, p. 587.

90. At the limit of the aestheticization of the religious, there is the return against the image within an incomplete opera, namely, the *Moses and Aaron* of Arnold Schoenberg. Aaron turns to the beauty of images that Moses refuses. The aesthetic of the second half of the twentieth century is an aesthetic bent on the destruction of the image. But it is still from within "Art" that this negation intervenes.

91. Balzac, *Massimilla Doni*, p. 569.

92. Ibid., p. 607.

KARL-ERNST HERRMANN

After completing his studies at the Berliner Akademie für bildende Kunst, Karl-Ernst Herrmann had his first experiences as a stage designer in 1961 at the Stadttheater in Ulm. From 1971 to 1982 he worked at the Schaubühne in Berlin, where he collaborated with Peter Stein and Luc Bondy, among others. In 1972 he had his first contact with the Salzburg Festival, working with Claus Peymann on a production of Thomas Bernhard's play *Der Ignorant und der Wahnsinnige*. He continued his collaboration with Claus Peymann for several years at the Burgtheater in Vienna. In 1982 he collaborated with his wife, Ursel Herrmann, for the first time in a codirected production of *La Clemenza di Tito* at the Théâtre de la Monnaie in Brussels. Similar collaborative projects followed in the same theater for stagings of *Don Giovanni*, *La Finta Giardiniera*, *The Abduction from the Seraglio*, *The Magic Flute*, *Orpheus and Eurydice*, and *La Traviata*. In 1992 Gerard Mortier invited the Hermanns to Salzburg, where they put on the suite of Mozart scenes *Ombra felice*, Rameau's *Les Boréades*, and *Così fan tutte*, among other works. During this Salzburg period, Karl-Ernst Herrmann also designed the sets for *Das Gleichgewicht* by Botho Strauss, Chekhov's *The Cherry Orchard*, and Schönberg's *Moses and Aaron*.

Karl-Ernst and Ursel Herrmann also directed *Semele* at the Berlin Staatsoper and the Innsbruck Festival and *Giulio Cesare* at the Nederlandse

Opera in Amsterdam. More recently Karl-Ernst Herrmann developed the sets for *Die eine und die andere*, by Botho Strauss, at the Berliner Ensemble (directed by Luc Bondy) and for Jon Fosse's *Death Variations* in Bochum (directed by Matthias Hartmann).

In April 1991, in response to a request by the Herrmanns and Gérard Mortier, Maurice Olender invited Jacqueline and Jean Starobinski to attend a performance of *The Magic Flute* at the Théâtre de la Monnaie in Brussels.

JEAN STAROBINSKI

Jean Starobinski studied humanities and medicine simultaneously at the University of Geneva. He practiced internal medicine and psychiatry for many years in hospitals in Geneva and Lausanne. In 1958 he started teaching the history of ideas and French literature at the University of Geneva. He is an associate member of the Academy of Moral and Political Sciences.

Principal Works

Montesquieu. Paris: Seuil, 1953, 1994.

Jean-Jacques Rousseau: La Transparence et l'obstacle. Paris: Plon, 1958; reprint, Paris: Gallimard, 1971. [*Jean-Jacques Rousseau: Transparency and Obstruction*. Chicago: University of Chicago Press, 1988.]

L'Œil vivant. Paris: Gallimard, 1961, 1999. [*The Living Eye*. Cambridge: Harvard University Press, 1989.]

L'Invention de la liberté. Paris: Skira, 1964. [*The Invention of Liberty, 1700–1789*. Cleveland: World Publishing/Skira, 1964.]

Les Mots sous les mots: Les Anagrammes de Ferdinand de Saussure. Paris: Gallimard, 1964, 1971. [*Words Upon Words: The Anagrams of Ferdinand de Saussure*. New Haven: Yale University Press, 1980.]

Portrait de l'artiste en saltimbanque. Paris: Skira, 1970; reprint, Paris: Gallimard, 2004.

La Relation critique. Paris: Gallimard, 1970.

1789: Les Emblèmes de la raison. Paris: Flammarion, 1973; reprint, Paris: Gallimard, 2006. [*1789: The Emblems of Reason*. Cambridge, Mass.: MIT Press, 1988.]

Trois fureurs. Paris: Gallimard, 1974.

Montaigne en mouvement. Paris: Gallimard, 1982. [*Montaigne in Action*. Chicago: University of Chicago Press, 1986.]

Garache. Paris: Flammarion, 1988.

Table d'orientation. Lausanne: L'Âge d'homme, 1989.

La Mélancolie au miroir: Trois Lectures de Baudelaire. Paris: Julliard, 1989, 2004.

Le Remède dans le mal. Paris: Gallimard, 1989. [*Blessings in Disguise; or, The Morality of Evil*. Cambridge: Harvard University Press, 1993.]

Diderot dans l'espace des peintres. Paris: RMN, 1991.

Largesse. Paris: RMN, 1994. [*Largesse*. Chicago: University of Chicago Press, 1997.]

Action et réaction: Vie et aventures d'un couple. Paris: Seuil, 1999. [*Action and Reaction: The Life and Adventures of a Couple*. Cambridge, Mass.: Zone, 2003.]

EUROPEAN PERSPECTIVES

A Series in Social Thought and Cultural Criticism
Lawrence D. Kritzman, Editor

Julia Kristeva	*Strangers to Ourselves*
Theodor W. Adorno	*Notes to Literature*, vols. 1 and 2
Richard Wolin, editor	*The Heidegger Controversy*
Antonio Gramsci	*Prison Notebooks*, vols. 1, 2, and 3
Jacques LeGoff	*History and Memory*
Alain Finkielkraut	*Remembering in Vain: The Klaus Barbie Trial and Crimes Against Humanity*
Julia Kristeva	*Nations Without Nationalism*
Pierre Bourdieu	*The Field of Cultural Production*
Pierre Vidal-Naquet	*Assassins of Memory: Essays on the Denial of the Holocaust*
Hugo Ball	*Critique of the German Intelligentsia*
Gilles Deleuze and Félix Guattari	*What Is Philosophy?*
Karl Heinz Bohrer	*Suddenness: On the Moment of Aesthetic Appearance*
Julia Kristeva	*Time and Sense: Proust and the Experience of Literature*
Alain Finkielkraut	*The Defeat of the Mind*
Julia Kristeva	*New Maladies of the Soul*
Elisabeth Badinter	*XY: On Masculine Identity*
Karl Löwith	*Martin Heidegger and European Nihilism*
Gilles Deleuze	*Negotiations, 1972–1990*
Pierre Vidal-Naquet	*The Jews: History, Memory, and the Present*
Norbert Elias	*The Germans*
Louis Althusser	*Writings on Psychoanalysis: Freud and Lacan*
Elisabeth Roudinesco	*Jacques Lacan: His Life and Work*
Ross Guberman	*Julia Kristeva Interviews*
Kelly Oliver	*The Portable Kristeva*
Pierre Nora	*Realms of Memory: The Construction of the French Past* vol. 1: *Conflicts and Divisions* vol. 2: *Traditions* vol. 3: *Symbols*
Claudine Fabre-Vassas	*The Singular Beast: Jews, Christians, and the Pig*
Paul Ricoeur	*Critique and Conviction: Conversations with François Azouvi and Marc de Launay*
Theodor W. Adorno	*Critical Models: Interventions and Catchwords*